Index

Windhoek, 25–46, 47–52, 54, 57, 60, 83, 110, 119, 121, 123, 126, 129, 134, 138, 145, 164, 165, 167, 176, 177, 181, 182, 210, 249, 251, 256, 288, 289, 294, 299 (Plates 2 and 12)
Winter, Adulf, 99
Witbooi, Hendrik, 59
Witboois, 30, 173
Witwatersrand, 204, 205

Wood, J. G., 190–1, 226–7, 241
Wordsworth, 41

Yeats, W. B., 22, 234

Zambesi, 242
Zebra, 178–9
Zimbabwe, 113
Zulus, 238–9

Index

Steinkopf, 54
Stel, Simon van der, 108, 243, 252
Stevenson, Adlai, 296
Stow, George, 233
Street Signs, 168–9
Streicher, Hans, 134
Sudan, 114, 224
Sudwes, Lugdiens, 256, 288
Swakop, River, 53
Swakopmund, 29, 31, 88–96, 97, 99–100, 108, 119, 121, 126, 128, 134, 160, 167, 173, 251, 294, 297, 299 (Plates 5 and 6)
SWANLA, 203–5, 206, 221
Sykes, Gerald, 216, 217

Table Bay, 75
Tanganyika, 265
Texas, 51, 53, 82, 105, 115, 174, 284, 291
Thirstland and Thirstland Trek, 51, 123, 125, 253–7
Thomas, Elizabeth Marshall, 221, 229, 233
Thorer, Paul, 288
Threlfall, William, 250
Tidewater Oil Company, 284
Tiger's Eye, 170
Tintenpalast, 47–8
Tjamuaha, Chief, 57–9, 242
Tjimba, 22, 164
Towns in South West Africa, 194
Transvaal, 143, 223, 243, 253, 254, 255, 259, 271
Trekkboers, 147–8
Trek-wagons, 29, 257
Trichardt, Louis, 253
Trotha, General von, 38, 134
Tsama, 107, 155, 229, 230
Tsaobis, 29
Tsumeb, 171–7, 178–84, 185, 186, 190, 198, 205, 216, 221, 294
Tsumeb Corporation, 171–6, 177, 206
Tutankhamun, 116

Ugab, River, 100, 110
United Nations, 11, 48, 292–7
Upington, 156

Uplingtonia, Republic of, 255
Uys, Piet, 253

Vaal, River, 142, 179, 253
Valley of the Kings, 116–17
Vedder, Dr. Heinrich, 236–8
Veldkos, 229–30
Verne, Jules, 137
Vespasian, Emperor, 92
Victoria, Queen, 133
Vigiti Magna, 250
Vioolsdrift, 54 (Plate 3)
Vogelsang, Heinrich, 133
Voortrekkers, 253–7

'Wa-Benz', 217, 219
Wakefield, e.g., 78
Wales and the Welsh, 31, 41, 65–7, 174, 175, 176, 210, 282
Waley, Arthur, 73
Walvis Bay, 51, 52, 65–87, 90, 91, 125, 126, 127, 129, 132, 133, 139, 145, 167, 173, 190, 197, 249, 252, 254, 256, 259, 260, 300 (Plate 4)
Walvis Ridge, 71
Warmbad, 134, 201, 244, 250
Wart-hog, 181
Wasteland, The, 162
Waterberg, 38–9, 134, 255
Waterberg Reserve, 198–9, 201, 221
Water-collecting Devices, 155
Wellington, Duke of, 78
Wells, H. G., 137
Welwitschia, 108–9
Wesleyan Missionary Society, 250
Whales, 71–2, 181
'White Lady of the Brandberg', 113–17, 166
White Peoples of South West Africa— see European Peoples
Wikar, H. J., 248
Wild Duck, The, 215
Wildebeest, 178, 179
Wild Melon—see *Tsama*
Wild Pumpkin—see *Naras*
Wilhelm II, Kaiser, 39, 133, 176
Williams, Alpheus, 146
Williamson, Dr., 265–6, 269, 279

307

Index

Pascal, 40
Paterson, William, 249
Petrified Forest, 109
Pienaar, Piet, 249
Piketburg, 54, 139, 244
Plastic Gnomes, 171
Plautus, 92
Pomona, 145
Port Nolloth, 267, 271
Portugal, 101-3, 193, 294
Post, Laurens van der, 222, 232
Potgieter, Hendrik, 253
Powys, John Cowper, 121
Powys, Theodore, 121, 148
Prehistoric Cultures, 223-4
Pretoria, 31, 48, 62, 280
'Probity Fever', 215
Proconsul, 223
Propliopithecus, 42, 223

Quiver Tree—see Kokerboom

Rabinowitz, Sol, 33
Rainfall, 121-2
Rath, Rev., 251
Ravel, Maurice, 166
Reenen, van, Brothers, 249-50
Rehobothers—see Basters
Rehoboth and Rehoboth Gebiet, 196, 201, 249, 251, 288
Reiter von Südwest, Der, 30
Reitz, Denys, 147
Rensberg, van, 253
Reserves, 198-203, 211-13 (See also Bantustans)
Retief, Piet, 253
Rhenish Missionary Society, 251
Rhodes, Cecil, 78, 133, 137, 142, 193, 214, 263, 264, 265
Richardson, Henry Handel, 143
Riebeeck, Jan van, 236, 239, 243
Robben Island, 207
Rooibank, 75, 251
Rousseau, J-J, 298
Runtu, 204

Sahara Desert, 74, 105, 138
Salt Industry, 97-8

Samp, 12
Sander, Willi, 27, 47
Sanderburg, 25
Scheibe, Doctor, 144, 145, 147, 269, 282
Scheppman, Rev., 251
Sching, Heinrich, 238
Schlenters, 131
Schmelen, Heinrich, 250-1
Schönberg, 41
Schools and Schooling, 209
Schutztruppe, 28, 121, 144, 195
Schweitzer, Albert, 217
'Sea-bed Diamonds', 284
Seal, A Dying, 162
Seals and Sealing, 94-5, 289
Seeckt, General von, 136
Selection Trust, 173
Selous, Frederick, 173
Semi-precious Stones, 169-71
Separate Development—see Bantustans
Sesfontein, 110
Sharpeville, 208
Shaw, Rev. B., 250
Sheep-rearing, 288-90
Skeleton Coast, 103-4, 110, 113, 121, 147, 177, 254
Smuts, Field-Marshal Jan, 34, 94, 135, 138, 139, 147, 168, 211, 256
Socialism, Arrogance and Complacency of, 218, 298
Sonnichsen, Dr. C. L., 213
South West Africa Company, 173
South West Africa Native Labour Association—see SWANLA
Soviet Union, 180, 265
Sparrman, Andrew, 245-8
Spee, Admiral von, 131
Spencer Bay, 145
Spender, Sir Percy, 294
Sperrgebiet, 49, 119, 121-5, 130, 147-62, 261, 283, 284, 285, 287, 292 (Plate 11)
Spinoza, 94
Springbok (Town), 54, 100-1, 130, 147-8, 243, 268
Star of India Diamond, 280
Stauch, August, 141-5, 147, 269, 282
Steatopygia, 226-7, 236
Steinbok, 178

Index

Mariental, 288
Marine Explosions, 88-9
Maritz, General, 147, 148
'Martiens', 147-58, 282-3
Masson, Francis, 108
Mathers, Powys, 73
Maugham, Somerset, 47
Melville, Herman, 72, 299
Meob Bay, 145
Merensky, Dr. Hans, 268-9, 270, 271
Millin, Sarah Gertrude, 11, 175
Milner, Lord, 11, 78
Minerals, 76-7
Miners and Mining, 174-6
Missionaries, 36, 39, 81, 194, 199-201, 238, 250-2, 288
Moltke, von, 28, 137
Montecuccoli, Count Caprivi de, 193
Mouth-breeding Fish, 185
Morris, Donald, 239
Mozambique, 193
Mwadui, 265

Nachtigall, Doctor, 134
Nama—see Hottentots
Namib, 12, 31, 54, 74, 90, 92, 93, 97, 100, 104-10, 121, 122-5, 129, 144, 147-62, 176, 177, 194, 251, 260 (Plates 7 and 11)
Namibia, Republic of, 11
Namaqualand, 12, 33, 54, 132, 147, 172, 242, 243, 260, 267, 271, 285
Namaquas, 237
Namutoni, Fort, 176, 177, 178, 186-8, 189, 204, 221, 225, 254, 255, 256, 260, 299 (Plate 14)
Napoleon, 138
Napoli, Captain, 127
Naras, 107, 229
Nazis in South West Africa, 134-40, 168
Nehru, 294
Nel, Commandant, 247
Newmont Mining Company, 173, 174
Ngami, Lake, 183, 221, 225, 252
Niagara, 299
Nicholson, Sir Harold, 295
Nigeria, 40, 43, 132
Noble Savage, 246

North American Indians, 175, 212-13, 214
Nosob, River, 53

Obermeier and Kühn, 233
Odendaal Plan, 83, 192, 201, 214-15
Okahandja, 56-9, 132, 184, 199, 209, 251
Okavango, River, 53, 110, 183, 192, 225, 242, 254
Okavango (Tribe), 192-3, 204
Olifants River, 243, 269
Oliver and Fage, 83
Omaruru, River, 53, 100
Ombindi, 22, 23
Ondangua, 204
O'Okiep, 12, 54
Oorlams, 57, 350
Oppenheimer, Sir Ernest, 33, 146, 261, 263, 265-7, 269-70, 271-2, 275, 282-3
Oppenheimer, Mr. Harry, 272, 286
Orange River, 53, 54, 118, 130, 133, 142, 147, 172, 179, 194, 236, 237, 242, 243, 244, 249, 250, 259, 267, 268, 269, 270, 299 (Plate 3)
Orange River Project, 259-60
Oranjemund, 167, 175, 190, 205, 216, 260-3, 270-87 (Plate 15)
Orloff Diamond, 280
Oryx—see Gemsbok
Ossewa Brandwag, 135-6, 138, 139
Oshakati, 192
Otavi, 172, 173, 255, 256
Otjikoto, Lake 184-5
Otjimbingwe, 29, 183, 201, 251
Otjiwarongo, 97, 117, 164-71, 256, 299
Ovahimba, 185
Ovambo, 34-5, 41, 93, 96, 125, 159, 160, 172, 173, 177, 185, 186, 187, 189-92, 195, 197, 198, 237, 239-40, 249, 250, 252, 275
Ovamboland, 190-3, 195, 197, 204, 251, 254, 255

Padrãos, 102-3, 131
Palgrave, Dr. William Coates, 132
Parapithecus, 42, 223

305

Index

Hobbes, Thomas, 93
Hofmeyr, Jan, 34
'Homelands'—see Bantustans
Hop, Hendrik, 244–5, 249
Hope Diamond, 280
Hospitals, 209
Hottentots (Namas), 29, 35, 39, 41, 57–60, 81, 104, 107, 110, 114, 118, 125, 132, 133, 134, 175, 191, 195, 196, 197, 221, 226, 234, 235–7, 238, 239, 240–1, 242, 244, 245, 246, 247, 249
Humpata, 255

Ibsen, 215
Illicit Diamond Buying (IDB), 285–6
India, 280, 294
International Court, 48, 292–95, 296

Jackpot, 156, 157, 268
James, William, 40
Jews in South West Africa, 31–4
Joel, Solly, 33
Johannesburg, 31, 35, 48, 54, 263, 284, 288
John II of Portugal, 101–3
Jonker Afrikaner, 29–30, 57–60, 226, 242
Jonker Afrikaner, Jan, 59–60, 183, 185
Jonker Diamond, 280
Jordaan, W. W., 254, 255
Jubilee Diamond, 280

Kaffirs, 238 (See Bantu)
Kalahari Desert, 12, 31, 38, 54, 105, 195, 221, 222, 229, 230, 236, 242, 245, 254
Kambabezi, Chief, 200, 201
Kambonde, Chief, 255
Kano, 31, 43, 45
Kant, 10, 211
Kaokoveld, 12, 22–3, 54, 110, 115, 164, 177, 178, 194, 198, 255, 257, 296
Karakul Sheep, 48, 167, 180, 288–90
Karibib, 60–4
Katatura, 209–10
Keetmanshoop, 118, 119, 124, 125, 126, 134, 167, 251, 290

Kimberley, 54, 142, 145, 263, 264, 270
Kimberlite, 269–70
King Lear, 281
Kinshasa, 31, 44, 45, 65
Kipling, 47, 187
Kleinschmidt, 58, 60, 251
Koh-i-Noor Diamond, 280
Kokerboom Tree, 107–8, 109, 119, 260 (Plate 7)
Kolmanskop, 142, 143, 144, 145, 158
Korab, Peace of, 134
Korana, 237
Kroeber, A. L., 222, 225
Kudu, 45, 181–2, 260 (Plate 12)
Kürle, Adolf, 30

Lautwein, Major von, 30
Lassmann, Sgt. Bruno, 186
La Rochefoucauld, 59, 211
Lawrence, John, 78
Lawrence, T. E., 79
Leibowitz Bros., 34, 37
Leopoldville—see Kinshasa
Levenson, Jack, 34
Levinson, Olga, 58, 142, 187
Lewis, C. S., 298
Lichtenburg, 267
Lindequist, Governor, 289
Lions, 121, 183
Lithops, 106
Livingstone, 252
Lobito Bay, 75
London Missionary Society, 250
Loreburn, Lord, 11
Lüderitz, 77, 81–3, 103, 119, 120, 121, 124, 125–9, 141–6, 158, 162–3, 167, 251, 256, 259, 267, 270, 299 (Plate 9)
Lüderitz, Adolf, 81, 82, 131, 132–4

Maack, Dr. Reinhold, 113–14
Mackenzie, General, 120
Mackinder, Sir Halford, 137
Madrid, 289
Magellan, 102, 103
Maherero, 58–9, 243
Maherero, Samuel, 59, 199
Makarikari Pan, 221
Malan, Doctor, 139, 140

Index

Egypt, Ancient, 73, 93, 116–17, 161, 263
Eland, 180, 182
Eliot, T. S., 162
Elizabeth II, Queen, 279
Elizabeth Bay, 145, 158–62
Engelhard, Charles, 266
Erasmus, Captain, 130
Erlach, Fischer, von, 91
Erman, Adolf, 73
Etosha Pan, 110, 178–83, 186, 257, 260, 299 (Plate 13)
Eucalyptus, 122
Eureka Diamond, 269
European Peoples of South West Africa, 197–8
Exploration of South West Africa, 242–52

Farson, Negley, 82, 191
Fichte, 136
Fish and Fisheries, 77, 126–7, 167, 185
Fish River Canyon, 290–1, 300 (Plate 16)
Flamingos, 84–5, 260
Forbidden Area—see *Sperrgebiet*
Fourie Dr., 225
Fossil Remains, 223–4
François, Major Kurt von, 28, 29, 30, 35, 54, 134
Fransfontein, 109
Frenssen, Gustav, 30
Freud, 183, 216
Fur Industry, 94–5, 288–90

Galsworthy, John, 11–12
Galton, Sir Francis, 172, 183–5, 226, 251
Garies, 155
Gauguin, 10, 300
Gemsbok, 179
German East Africa, 193
Getty, Paul, 284
Ghana, 265
Gibeon, 142, 288
Gide, André, 44, 45, 215
Gladstone, 11
Goa, 294
Gobi Desert, 74

Goethe, 215
Goering, Dr., 29, 35, 59, 134
Goering, Reichsmarschall, 29
Golconda, 280
Gomes, Fernão, 101
Good Old Rule, The, 40, 99, 295
Gordon, Col. R. J., 249
Graaff, Sir Villiers, 296
Grand Canyon, 290
Great Fish River, 242, 243, 253, 259, 291
Great Mogul Diamond, 280
Great River—see Orange River
Great Trek, 252–3
Green, Trader, 252
Greene, Graham, 10, 44, 45
Griquas, 237
Grootfontein, 198, 203, 204, 221, 255, 256
Groot River—see Orange River
Gross Barmen, 251
Guana Industry, 98–9, 131
Guards, Brigade of, 188

Hahn, Carl, 57–8, 59–60, 251
Hahn, Major, 192
Hahn, Rev. Mr., 226
Harris, Capt. Cornwallis, 180, 182
Hartmann, Karl Amadeus, 41
Haushofer, 136
Haythornthwaite, Frank, 84
Heart of Darkness, 286–7
Hemingway, 100, 206
Hentie's Bay (Hentisbaai), 100–1
Herbert, George, 206
Herero, 34, 35–40, 52, 56–60, 81, 86, 110, 125, 132, 133, 134, 135, 164, 175, 177, 194, 195, 196, 197, 198–205, 221, 237, 249, 251, 255 (See also Reserves)
'Hereroland', 201
Herero War, 30, 38–9, 172, 201, 214
Here's to the Next Time, 165
Herzog, General, 138, 256
Hippopotamus Steak, 181
Hiroshima, 39
Hirskorn, Dr. Hans, 134, 135, 136, 138, 139
Hitler, 136, 137, 138, 139, 168

303

Index

Bushman Poisons, 228
Bushmen, 34, 104, 106, 107, 112, 114, 116, 117, 175, 187, 191, 193-4, 195, 221-4, 235-6, 238, 239, 245, 247-8, 260, 291, 300

Cabral, Pedro Alvares, 102-3
Cairo Museum, 116
Cambridge, 42, 114
Camões, Luis de, 102
Cão, Diogo, 101-2, 103, 104, 114, 242, 256
Cape Colony, 29, 122, 235, 242, 252
Cape Coloureds, 99, 125, 142, 196-7, 209
Cape Cross, 94-5, 97, 99-101, 102, 103, 104
Cape Province, 54, 57, 77, 81, 132, 133, 223, 237, 244, 245
Cape Town, 26, 31, 48, 52, 54, 75, 127, 129, 132, 136, 242, 248, 249, 253, 254, 256, 261, 286, 288
Caprivi Strip, 193
Cardiff, 65-7, 76, 86, 128, 129, 174
Carpio-de Alva Mission, 293
Carstens, Capt. J. E., 267-8, 269, 282
Cattle-owning by Herero, 201-2
Central Selling Organization, 265-6, 273, 283, 284
Chamais Bay, 284
Chamberlain, Joseph, 78
Chapman, John, 252
Charter Consolidated, 266
Chesterton, G. K., 295
Christensen, Erwin, 232
Christuskirche, 27, 30, 47, 61 (Plate 2)
Churchill, Winston, 11, 207-8, 213
Cilliers, Sarel, 253
Cissus, 106
Coetsee, Jacobus, 244-5
Cohen, 32-3
Collier, Commissioner John, 212
Collins, Sam, 284
Committee of Seven, 293
Committee on South West Africa, 293
Conception Bay, 145
Congo, the, 12, 40, 44-5, 101, 137, 215, 223, 258, 272

Conrad, Joseph, 12, 44, 45, 47, 65, 127-8, 215, 286-7
Consolidated Diamond Mines (CDM), 122-3, 146, 175, 260-87
Cook, Edward, 250
Copper Mining, 172, 243
Copper Mountains, 243, 244
Cornell, Fred, 143, 147, 148, 156, 267, 282
Couperus, Louis, 47
Crawfish, 70, 77
Cullinan Diamond, 208, 269, 280
Cunene, River, 53, 110, 125, 182, 189, 192, 242, 254, 255, 259

Dama—see Bergdama
Damara—see Bergdama
Damaraland, 29, 81, 132, 173, 183, 242-3
Dart, Dr. Raymond, 223
Darwin, Charles, 183
Davies, Sir John, 112
De Beers, 142, 146, 173, 180, 263, 264, 265, 266, 267, 272, 273, 282, 283, 285, 286, 300 (see also Consolidated Diamond Mines, Oppenheimer, and Oranjemund)
Diamond-cutting, 279-81
Diamond Detection Department, 130-1
Diamond Exchange, 279
Diamond Producers' Association, 274
Diamonds, 48-50, 99-101, 104, 122-5, 129-31, 141-63, 175, 190, 260-87 (see also CDM, De Beers, Martiens, Oppenheimer, Oranjemund, *Sperrgebiet*)
Diamond-smuggling, 285-6
Diamond Trading Company, 265 (see also Central Selling Organization)
Dias, Bartolomeu, 102, 103, 131
Dingaan, 253
Döblin, Alfred, 136, 137
Donkies, 150-1, 153, 155, 157, 158
Drury, Allen, 207
Dunedin Star, 104
Dunes, 92-3 (Plate 6)
Dunkelsbuhler, 33

East Caprivians, 193

Index

Ackermann, Herr, 119-20
Afrikaner, Jonker—
    see Jonker Afrikaner
Aighams, 29, 57
Albrecht, Brothers, 250
Alberts, Gert, 254
Alexander Bay, 147, 148, 268-9, 270, 285
Alexander, Sir James, 251
Allantropa, 137-8
Alte Fest, 27, 30, 47
American Indians—
    see North American Indians
Anderson, Andrew A., 81
Anderson, Rev. W., 250
Andersson, Charles, 183-4, 190, 251
Anglo-American Corporation, 146, 266, 267, 272, 300 (see also Consolidated Gold Mines)
Angola, 53, 75, 101, 192, 193, 204, 205, 255, 272
Angola Boers—
    see Thirstland Trek
Angra Pequeña, 132, 133
Antwerp, 280
Apartheid, 48, 55, 207-15, 296-7
Ardrey, Robert, 228
Asab, 290
Augrabies Falls, 260, 299, 300
Aus, 121-2, 124, 142 (Plate 10)

Baastards (Baasters)—see Basters
Bach, 41
Bacon, Francis, 93
Baines, Thomas, 252
Ballarat, 143
Bantu and Bantu Peoples, 189-95, 234, 238-42, 245, 247 (see also Bergdama, East Caprivians, Herero, Okavango, Ovambo)
Bantustans, 192, 211-12, 214-15, 297

Barnato, Barney, 33, 264
Barrès, Maurice, 138
Basters, 196-7
Beer, Z. J. de, 139, 296
Behn, 182
Beit, Alfred, 33, 264
Benguela and Benguela Current, 71, 76, 102, 109, 268
Bergdama, 31, 34-5, 37, 39, 41, 59-60, 125, 195, 197, 198, 211, 237, 240-1, 249, 250
Bergdamara—see Bergdama
Bertillon, 183
Bethanie, 133, 251
Beuttner, Doctor, 134
Biederbecke, Rev. Mr., 199
Birkby, Carel, 229
Bismarck, 81-3
'Black Diamonds', 288-90
'Blue Ground', 269-70
'Blue Whites', 271-2
Boers and Boer Nation, 207-14, 236, 238-9, 252-7
Bogenfels, 145, 155
Bormann, Martin, 168
Botha, General, 26, 138
Botha, J. F., 254
Botswana, 38, 193, 211, 223, 225, 293
Brandberg, 110-17, 231, 290 (Plate 8)
Brazil, 82, 280
Brazzaville, 44
Brecht, 62
Breuil, Abbé, 113-14, 115, 224
Brink, Carl, 244
British Empire, 77-83, 180, 252-3
Browne, Sir Thomas, 12, 19
Brukkaros, 290
Buchenwald, 262
Burchell, William, 179, 181, 251
Bushmanland, 53, 54, 244, 245, 299
Bushman Painting, 116, 224, 231-4

301

Augrabies. In Bushman language, it signifies 'The Place of the Great Noise'. I listen as though in a dream to the clash and thump of the waters. My cheeks are stung by the needles of spray.

... Even so, amid the tornadoed Atlantic of my being....

I stare down into the churning cauldron where ropes of foam festoon the splintered rocks. I feel a tremor of vertigo like the tremor I felt at the Fish River Canyon, now two hundred miles to the westward, where the sun is swelling and glowering low down on the horizon.

Somewhere down there below me, hidden beneath the scarf of mist that drifts perpetually across the whirlpool, swims the *Groot Slang*—the *Great Serpent*. The Bushmen say that its coils are wound around a marvellous treasure of gold and precious stones. They say that though it is old now, older than the world, it will protect that treasure for all eternity. It may be so: but none the less I think that the *Groot Slang* ought to keep one eye open for the men of De Beers and the Anglo-American Mining Corporation....

I lift my head. I turn to go. Then I see that someone is standing opposite me, on a boulder across the far curve of the falls. A tall fair-haired figure in a scarlet shirt, its hands in its pockets. The painter I saw at Walvis Bay. The battered Citroën must be parked somewhere beyond the falls—no doubt in the middle of the road. If he has seen me, he makes no sign. He stands motionless, peering at the pattern of the water as it streams off the crest of the rocks, like the combed and spreading tresses of a brown goddess.

All at once the sun sags and crashes from sight with tropical suddenness, like ripe fruit in autumn falling through the boughs.

I walk towards the Land Rover. Klaas and Sarel are waiting. A last glance at the painter. Again no motion.

I think of Gauguin.

'*Where do we come from? Who are we? Where are we going?*'

Epilogue

... *But even so, amid the tornadoed Atlantic of my being, do I myself still centrally disport in mute calm; and while ponderous planets of unwaning woe revolve round me, deep down and deep inland there I still bathe me in eternal mildness of joy.* ...

Windhoek. Swakopmund. Otjiwarongo. Etosha Pan. Namutoni. Lüderitz. They are all far behind me now. I have come out of South West and am on my way to Upington, on the road that will eventually bring me back to Johannesburg.

I stand in the slanting late evening sunlight on a wet boulder above the Augrabies Falls, in Great Bushman Land, brooding on the words of Melville that came to me in the place where the whales make love, bending the phrases to the mute calm and eternal mildness of joy which the long bright days in South West have engendered in me. ...

Augrabies Falls. Here beneath me pours the generated soul of the Orange River. It is one of the five great waterfalls of the world, higher and deeper than Niagara.

The Land God Made in Anger

alternatives. They are a practical people—and they also possess the daring imagination and the touch of vision which is their birthright as a people in Africa. There may be grounds for a cautious optimism.

I wish for South Africa and for South West Africa what I could wish for my own country, crippled as it is by self-inflicted wounds, regimented and rendered supine by petty-minded ideologues. I wish for all three of them that rarest of blessings: good government. But what is good government? To my mind, it has best been defined by C. S. Lewis in one of his later essays:

'The loftier the pretensions of power, the more meddlesome, inhuman and oppressive it will be. Thus the Renaissance doctrine of Divine Right is for me a corruption of monarchy; Rousseau's General Will, of democracy; radical mysticisms, of nationalism. All political power is at best a necessary evil: but it is least evil when its sanctions are most modest and commonplace, when it claims no more than to be useful or convenient and sets itself strictly limited objectives. Anything transcendental or spiritual, or even anything very strongly ethical, in its pretensions is dangerous and encourages it to meddle in our private lives. Let the shoemaker stick to his last.'

I will stand on that. I could live there.

A View Across the Canyon

not resented only by the Nationalist Party and its supporters: the broad mass of white South Africans react against them. And white South Africans are both powerful and tough. They believe with justification that a good deal of the hostility towards South Africa is unreasonable and has an ulterior motive. This colours their attitude to what is reasonable and constructive, and there is little doubt that they would go to great lengths to resist what they—rightly or wrongly—regard as unjustifiable pressure.'

Very well, then. Let us admit that, in this particular case, evolution appears to present a more rational alternative than revolution. Let us acknowledge that for the foreseeable future the South Africans will remain in effective occupation of South West, and that the increasing balkanization of the states of black Africa will help them to consolidate their grip on that country. What next? The next step is up to the South Africans. It is now the duty of the South Africans to show that they can meet the requirements of their self-imposed responsibilities. It is up to them to prove that the claims of the witnesses who spoke up so glowingly on their behalf at the International court can be substantiated. They have announced ambitious schemes for the territory. Let them prove that they mean what they say. Let them clean up the shanties at Swakopmund. Let them bring hope to the reserves and the Bantustans. Let them bring justice to the downtrodden and the despairing. Let them conduct themselves like the Christians they claim to be. This is their test: and their opportunity.

There are many imponderables. There are elements of lying, of bad faith and cynicism; there are broken promises. These things are not unique to southern Africa. None the less it remains just possible that the South Africans will succeed in creating in South West a society that will eventually impress us. I hope so. I should like to think that they can build a fine nation to suit a noble landscape. I should like to think that they will gradually shed their more noxious political ideas, evolving away from them towards more reasonable and workable

One thinks of the photographs of Adlai Stevenson sitting with his head bowed in his hands after telling the Security Council a pack of untruths in connection with the Bay of Pigs incident. It seems hard that a statesman of such rare honesty and attractiveness should be compelled to perjure and destroy himself for his country—and doubtful whether he would have been required to do it in any other milieu.

Contrary to received opinion, it is not necessary to love the United Nations in order to dislike apartheid. Apartheid is offensive even as a temporary expedient to meet a desperate problem. One can only trust that the severities of apartheid will first be mitigated, then disappear, as the process of educating the African takes increasing hold. It seems inevitable that the South Africans themselves will ultimately devise a more acceptable way of dealing with their predicament than apartheid. They are by nature a people of rare stature and principle. It ought not to be forgotten that, so far from being imperialist, South Africa was the first nation on the African continent to fight an anti-imperialist war. The South Africans have as true a claim to nationhood, and have earned as great a right to national independence, as any nation in Africa. They have as much right to exist and to resist aggression as, say, Israel. And although the policy of apartheid is wrong, it would be foolish of the United Nations or any other agency to try to persuade her to give up that policy by force. There are cheap victories in the slanging-matches in the General Assembly: there can be no cheap victories in the Kaokoveld.

The United Nations frequently induces one antagonist to mistake the temper of another. The South Africans would resist. That is the reality of the matter. Sir Villiers de Graaff, the leader of the Opposition, greeted the judgment of the International Court with the words: 'This is wonderful news, which can be of immense advantage to South Africa.' Mr De Beer, another liberal and a founder of the Progressive Party, has written in his *Multi-Racial South Africa: The Reconciliation of Forces*:

'It must be clearly understood that threats from outside are

A View Across the Canyon

and that South Africa had been presented with 'an undeserved victory'. No one who reads the twenty-five closely-printed pages of the Annexes of the Nineteenth Session can doubt that the applicant nations and their supporters intend to pursue the matter by other means.

Strange to say, the Good Old Rule that controls human affairs has not ceased to operate because the United Nations Organization was founded a quarter of a century ago. In fact the Rule seems to be operating with undiminished vigour. The conduct and the very existence of the Organization appear to have exacerbated instead of lessened the normal tensions in the world. The Organization has consistently encouraged small nations to make the serious and often almost fatal mistake of behaving as if they were big ones; Egypt and her group of allies are a recent case in point. It has led transient dictators to strike injudicious and inappropriate postures, and to believe that if they made blunders they could count on the United Nations to protect them from the consequences. This has proved a deadly error for the demagogues themselves, but doubly so for their unfortunate peoples. The daily welter of words makes it impossible for the realities of a situation to be honestly assessed and appreciated. Worse, wounds that might otherwise have healed are kept open in perpetuity. Mutual hatreds, after all, are the Organization's stock-in-trade. Sir Harold Nicholson once defined the art of diplomacy as the art of creating confidence. The Organization has debased that coinage. Not much confidence can be generated in an atmosphere where the heads of great states bang with their shoes on their desks. It is a very depressing experience to sit in the chamber of the United Nations and watch intelligent diplomats, who might usefully be engaged elsewhere in quiet and private deliberations, being compelled to indulge in vulgar public tirades. It puts one in mind of the poet's prayer to be delivered—

> From all that terror teaches
> From lies of tongue and pen,
> From all the easy speeches
> That comfort cruel men.

The Land God Made in Anger

for purposes of comparison, the members should then fly on to make an inspection of Liberia and Ethiopia.

The members of the Court decided not to accept the invitation. There followed a hundred days of hearings. The South African government put before the court 3,000 pages of written evidence and presented a list of thirty-eight witnesses, of whom fourteen were later called. It fought the case every step of the way with Afrikaner tenacity. Its counsel had no difficulty in disposing of the wilder charges made by the applicant countries, such as those of oppression and building military bases. The charge that there were military installations at Windhoek, a nuclear and missile base at Tsumeb, and military airfields at Swakopmund and at a place called Ohopoho, was completely scotched. But it was fair to say that, from the start, nobody expected the South Africans to win, certainly not the South Africans themselves.

On July 18, 1966, the Court delivered its judgment. It found that the applicants could not be considered to have established any legal right or interest in the subject matter of their claims, and accordingly decided to reject them. The judges who favoured the applicants' claims were those from the Soviet Union, the United States, Japan, Mexico, Senegal, and Taiwan. The judges who favoured the South African case were those from the United Kingdom, France, Italy, Greece, Poland and Australia. The vote was tied. The president, Sir Percy Spender of Australia, was thereupon asked to deliver his casting vote. He cast it against the applicants.

The South African victory has not proved in any way final. The South Africans pleaded that the world should now accept the verdict and abide by it. It was an appeal that was bound to fall on deaf ears. After all, in 1960 the International Court had decided that Portugal held clear legal title to Goa. The decision did not prevent Nehru from sending his army to occupy it. The record of the Fourth Committee of the United Nations Assembly shows that, less than three months after the judgment, petitioners were asserting that the International Court had 'lacked the courage to pronounce on the substance of the question',

Africa and the opposing side. Two further interim opinions on technical points were handed down by the Court in 1955 and 1966.

The main battle was not joined until 1961, when Liberia and Ethiopia came forward as champions of the hostile camp. They sought to prove that the League of Nations mandate was still in force; that South Africa was accountable to the United Nations; that the policy of apartheid had broken the undertaking that the well-being and progress of the peoples of the country would be promoted; that South Africa had erected illegal military bases; and that South Africa had attempted to incorporate South West into the Republic. A charge that the peoples of South West had been subjected to oppression, terrorism and genocide was originally included but was later withdrawn.

During the next five years there was prolonged diplomatic skirmishing between South Africa and the United Nations, which was backing Liberia and Ethiopia. The fortunes of the contest swayed one way, then another. The South Africans fought a rearguard action. The representatives of the Committee on South West Africa of the General Assembly once got as far as Botswana before they were turned back by the South African authorities. South Africa survived a resolution for world economic and diplomatic sanctions against her. In 1962 came the Carpio–de Alva mission. Mr Carpio of the Philippines and Dr de Alva of Mexico were Chairman and Vice-Chairman of the General Assembly's new Committee of Seven on South West Africa. The two men were invited to visit Pretoria to discuss the territory with the South African government. Carpio issued a communiqué declaring that he was satisfied that the charges of genocide and military activities were baseless, and that the South African administration was no threat to world peace and security. Then, in March 1965, when the International Court had begun its final deliberations, the South African government played a last card. It invited the fourteen members of the Court to fly to South West Africa to make an inspection for themselves, *in loco*. It also suggested that,

For a while we played our game of inventing ways of sneaking into the *Sperrgebiet* and helping ourselves to a pocketful of glassies. What about descending into the canyon and working our way along it towards the Forbidden Area? ...

Then, as always happened, we began to talk about South West and its problems. Klaas and Sarel put the Afrikaner line; I indulged in the softer speculations open to the foreigner. The great Canyon seemed to lend our conversation stature. We talked soberly, for some reason lowering our voices.

What did the three of us want for South West?

We wanted the obvious things we would want for any country in the world, and particularly for a country in modern Africa: peace, prosperity, and good government.

The prospects for South West in this regard were long unsettled by the protracted dispute about its exact status at the International Court at The Hague. Litigation continued at The Hague with increasing acrimony from 1950 onwards—nearly twenty years. Since the case closely concerns the past history and the future of South West, I should like, briefly, to summarize the proceedings.

The League of Nations mandate, signed at Geneva on December 17, 1920, provided for South Africa to govern the ex-German colony as 'an integral portion' of South Africa. The mandatory power was expressly enjoined to prohibit slavery and forced labour, to permit freedom of worship, and forbidden to build military installations. In 1950 the International Court of Justice was asked by powers hostile to South Africa to give an advisory opinion as to whether (1) the mandate had survived the dissolution of the League of Nations, and (2) whether South Africa was under a legal obligation to place South West under the trusteeship of the United Nations. The Court's subsequent ruling gave rise to confusion. The applicants were informed that, in the Court's opinion, the United Nations had indeed become vested with the residual powers of the League of Nations, but that South Africa was not obliged to place the territory under the United Nations trusteeship system. The ruling represented a stalemate between South

A View Across the Canyon

Grand Canyon, or the Rio Grande at Big Bend in Texas, the Fish River Canyon scores by reason of the sensation it gives of utter loneliness and desolation. To reach it entails a long hot drive along a winding track across a scrub-tangled plateau. The difficulties of the drive serve to increase the effect it makes when you get there. Suddenly an unbelievable gash in the land opens up before you. You feel that you can experience one of the phenomena of the natural world absolutely on your own. You are alone in a lonely land, confronted by a tremendous cosmic event. No booths selling postcards, newspapers, candyfloss and ice-cream nibble the edge of that mighty chasm; no cars are ushered into car-parks; no juke-boxes or transistors blur the air. The only sound is the wind.

If you suffer from *horror vacui*, the canyon is no place for you. The place is baked and devilish. It is Nature flexing a muscle. You would require eight hours to climb down to the bottom of the gorge, where the brown and sulphurous Fish River coils around and around like the sluggish rings of a python. (The Fish River of South West, of course, is a different river, and has no connection with the Great Fish River of South Africa.) The mud-curdled water flows fitfully, often dwindling to a trickle; but over the millennia it has carved for itself a deep channel in the rock. Once it must have been a wide and irresistible torrent; now, for a moment of Time, it slumbers.

The vision of the canyon makes the mind reel. The impression it gives is too vast, too callous, too indifferent. Standing on its rim reminds one of the view from an aircraft over the great red-raw plain of Castile—except that the plain of Castile is humanized by an occasional dot of a whitewashed house or pueblo.

The Fish River Canyon is the world without people, the world before the Bushmen. It is the world as it will be when the people have gone. Through it will pour the Phlegethon of flame and lava which will cover the face of the earth in its last agony.

After I had rejoined my companions, we sat on boulders on the lip of the pit, frowning down into it.

ruining it; the matador makes a dozen panic-stricken jabs with the *estoque*, a dozen more with the *descabello*. Horrible. And yet ... stumbling over the rocks to drag the young seals away from their parents ... clubbing and booting them to death, tearing off the pelt while the creatures are still alive ... or caressing the throat of a lamb, slicing the windpipe, oh so delicately, in order not to damage a fleece still sticky with the uterine waters. ...

Producing furs, like producing diamonds, would be regarded in a less mercenary world as one of nature's random gifts, a felicitous by-product: not an implacable commercial enterprise. How are the Africans to be persuaded not to exterminate lions and leopards when they see the white men stalking among seals and sheep with clubs and knives?

It seems a stiff price to pay for a little thoughtless finery.

Fortunately, there are other sights to stretch the mind as you travel towards Keetmanshoop.

At Brukkaros, near Ses, is an imposing extinct volcano, over 5,000 feet high; and near Asab, away to your left, is a remarkable sandstone pillar, a hundred feet high, weathered out of the rock, a great upthrust minatory block balanced on a slender attenuated pedestal. It dominates the desert in the guise of a mourning figure, a presage, a secret sign. Like the Brandberg, it is a presence: and whoever gave it the name by which it has come to be known—'The Finger of God'—was alive to the immanent life of that uncompromising landscape.

But the volcano and the pillar are only incidentals on your path to the most awe-inspiring of all the natural spectacles offered you by South West: and it is right that you should have saved it until last. This is the great Fish River Canyon, fifty miles south-west of Keetmanshoop, and sixty miles north-west of Karasburg.

The Canyon is often spoken of as rivalling the Grand Canyon. The Grand Canyon is 400 miles long, whereas the Fish River Canyon is forty: but the comparison is not unjust. I have seen both: and if it lacks the fantastic shapes and colours of the

he had come across the flocks which furnished the fine pelts known in the trade as Persian lamb. These are the flocks of sheep, with tight, curled fleeces, that roam the steppes of Uzbekistan, Turkmenistan and Kazakhstan, and the high mountains of Kirgizia and Tadzhikistan; there is a town called Karakul fifty miles south-west of Bukhara, almost on the river Amu, the ancient Oxus. Thorer brought back a number of the sheep and tried to acclimatize them in Germany. Conditions there were unfavourable: but a similarity had been noted between the climate and conditions of Uzbekistan and those of South West Africa. The German governor at Windhoek, von Lindequist, was approached, and was eager to try to establish the breed in the new colony.

Progress was slow, but breeders and farmers persisted. By the early 1930s fifty farmers were keeping flocks of karakul. The first batches of pelts were sent for auction in England and America, and in 1934 the Hudson's Bay Company bought an interest in South West. From 20,000 in 1920, when South Africa took over the mandate, the number of pelts produced had risen to 2 million by 1960. In 1965 there were 3 million karakul sheep in the territory, and the industry yielded £7 million ($17 million) a year.

Like sealing and diamonds, the mode of culling karakul sheep is depressing. As with the seal pups, only the young lambs have fur which is reckoned fit enough to be draped round a lady's shoulders. In the case of the karakul, the newly dropped lambs are slaughtered within twenty-four hours of their birth; after that time the close pattern of the curls is lost, and the whorls loosen and slacken. The lambs are skinned and their small skins stretched tightly on wooden frames, like so many miniature crucifixions.

Allow not Nature more than Nature needs. . . . It seems inconsistent to be squeamish about killing seals and sheep. At the Fiesta de San Isidro in Madrid I have for some years sat through seventeen or eighteen corridas on successive afternoons. Bullfights too can be dispiriting. The picador hits the bull too far back, puncturing the lungs, leaning on the animal, deliberately

THIRTEEN
A View Across the Canyon

You can depart from South West Africa by the easy route.

You can fly out from Windhoek to Cape Town or Johannesburg by Suidwes Lugdiens.

You would be missing some interesting sights.

The journey by road south from Windhoek, through the small townships of Rehoboth, Mariental and Gibeon (good missionary names), is not in itself particularly eventful. The southern half of the country is not fertile. Rainfall is low, vegetation sparse. It is not cattle country: but as you travel you will catch sight of flocks of white and black sheep, tended by a Hottentot boy who shares their life on the veld. They bring immense wealth to their owners.

They are the famous 'Black Diamonds' of South West, and have an unusual history. They were originally introduced into the territory in 1907. Five years earlier one of the adventurous German merchants of the era, Paul Thorer, who had extensive interests in the fur-trade, had visited Central Asia. In Uzbekistan, near the magical townships of Bukhara and Samarkand,

Close Goods

I would not go as far as that to describe the operations of C.D.M. But when you stand on the tortured beaches of the *Sperrgebiet*, watching the trucks and scrapers bumping and grating across the dunes, the words of Marlow come vividly to mind.

'A taint of imbecile rapacity blew through it all, like a whiff from some corpse. By Jove! I've never seen anything so unreal in my life. And outside, the silent wilderness surrounding this cleared speck on the earth struck me as something great and invincible, like evil or truth, waiting patiently for the passing away of this fantastic invasion.'

the stones and swallowing them again. Such is the romance of diamonds. The record in this respect was held by a worker at Kimberley who swallowed twenty-one large stones. His photograph holds a well-merited place on the walls of the De Beers offices. He is shown carrying a plate on which are displayed ten of the larger stones. They weigh an unbelievable 348 carats. These are the stones which he was compelled, as it were, to cough up; the eleven others were never recovered. He looks thoughtful.

Today the fluoroscope makes it unnecessary to search the more intimate orifices of the outgoing employee or visitor. You are simply requested to empty out the contents of your pockets on a tray, where they can be separately examined and will not interfere with the main operation. Then, minus coat and tie, you are placed behind a screen and the fluoroscope is run over your body. The attendants are quick, polite, and thorough. Careful records are kept.

Everyone who leaves Oranjemund, be he high or low, is subjected to fluoroscopy. It is said that Mr Harry Oppenheimer himself submits to it, *pour encourager les autres*. I suppose it is less distasteful than being fingered and prodded: but I noticed an undertone of resentment towards it on the part of the staff. If you have to go through the procedure each time you want to spend a week-end in Cape Town it must become irksome. It has the same irritant effect as an examination by the customs: a minor irritant, but an irritant all the same. Most people shrug it off; it comes with the job. But to others it seems to represent a petty but cumulative humiliation. It reminds them that Oranjemund, in spite of the shops, the church and the golf club, is a prison.

'To tear treasure out of the bowels of the land was their desire, with no more moral purpose at the back of it than there is in burglars breaking into a safe.' Thus Marlow, in *Heart of Darkness*, describes the operations of the Eldorado Exploring Expedition. 'It was an inextricable mess of things decent in themselves, but that human folly made look like spoils of thieving.'

to the human race, instead of mere peddlers of bits of burnt carbon. They have committed the crime of daring to set themselves up against the state, and against the state within a state that is De Beers. They have been outrageous enough to defy the official machine. Their ingenuity, far from commanding good-humoured admiration, is regarded as *lèse-majesté*.

Some of the methods which have been used to smuggle diamonds out of the *Sperrgebiet* and Namaqualand have been extremely imaginative. At Oranjemund and Alexander Bay stories are told of bags of diamonds being thrown over the protective wire fence: or, when this was made impossible, of diamonds being inserted in revolver bullets and fired through the fence into sandbags. There is the story of how the wife of one of the employees used to take a packet of diamonds with her on the bus that made a weekly shopping expedition to the nearest town; the journey across the desert was a long one, and at the half-way stage was a hut fitted up as a toilet where the ladies would stop to refresh themselves. Here the wife would leave the diamonds in the lavatory cistern, to be collected later by one of her husband's confederates. Diamonds have been smuggled out embedded in plasticine stuck in the backs of books or in some other object, the plasticine being impervious to X-rays and preventing their tell-tale shape showing up on the screen. Another trick was to feed the diamonds to a pet dog or pet monkey which could be sent through the wire at night. It is said that the company cat was once subjected to this treatment.

Illicit Diamond Buying or I.D.B. was a serious problem to the industry as far back as the 1870s. In Rhodes's time, African labourers were already being penned up in compounds for the duration of their contracts. On leaving the diggings, they were isolated for several days in a detention cell, to make sure they passed the diamonds they may have swallowed. Swallowing stones was the most time-honoured dodge of all. A bowel-opening medicine of a peculiarly thunderous character was put in their mealie-meal to speed the process up, and their hands were bound in special gloves to prevent them from retrieving

good for the diamond business—it is good for South Africa.

I thought it curious, talking to people in the diamond industry in Oranjemund, Johannesburg and elsewhere, to discover that there is a marked dog-in-the-manger attitude even on the part of the leading producers. C.D.M. controls 99.3 per cent of the diamond production of South West—yet how bitterly they grudge the few diggers outside their control a thin spatter of diamonds. The big boys want them all—every one. That outstanding .7 per cent irks them; they take it almost as a personal affront. There is not much spirit of live-and-let-live in the diamond industry. A veritable frenzy was created a few years ago by Paul Getty, when he started prospecting for diamonds in South West Africa in connection with his Tidewater Oil Company. He was followed by a Texan, Sam Collins, who fitted out a barge with a perilous mass of equipment and started dredging for alluvials at Chamais Bay. He argued that although C.D.M. might have title to the *Sperrgebiet*, and to most of the beaches of South West, he was legally free to explore the sea-bed beyond the low-tide line. This was cheeky and highly ingenious. Then he announced that he was finding 250 carats of diamonds a day. The thought of all those diamonds being raked in an inch beyond the tips of its fingers was agony to C.D.M. The wailing of the shorn was pitiful to hear. Collins next compounded his crime by cocking a snook at that sacred idol, the Central Selling Organization. He began to sell his 'sea-bed diamonds' at £10 ($24) a carat. The wails grew louder. Collins, in true Texas style, and alone of the great ones of this world, had refused to be overawed by De Beers. He did not care a damn. He was enjoying himself. Finally De Beers had to buy him out at a thumping price. It was a neat and uproarious bit of manoeuvring.

Perhaps these major scares curdle the temper of the large monopolies, and account for the savagery with which they treat minor offenders. You might expect them to regard the exploits of the occasional smuggler with a certain tolerant amusement. Not at all. I have heard these small fry denounced with an anger that would lead you to think they were a menace

building in a big, drab city? Or could it have been silly old Martiens, huddled in his blanket in the lee of the Kowisberg, under the proper motion of the stars, playing his mouth-organ to Lord Roberts? ...

I was made welcome at Oranjemund; I do not like to abuse the hospitality which C.D.M. offered me. But I must admit that the air of the model township was unmistakenly uneasy. Suspicion is endemic in the diamond business, and the attitude of the members of the staff towards each other, let alone towards the casual visitor, was wary. I was surprised to learn that, with the exception of a privileged few, none of the white employees at Oranjemund would ever dream of picking up a diamond and taking charge of it. The blacks were regarded as more trustworthy in this respect than the whites. If a white supervisor spotted a diamond lying in a cranny in the bedrock, during the sweeping process, he would point it out to one of the African workmen: under no circumstance would he touch it himself. Diamonds might have been radioactive, as far as the members of the staff were concerned. To be found in possession of one, even if you were on your way to the office to hand it in, would lead to endless questioning and possible dismissal. Only the senior men in the heavy media plant and the security branch are allowed actual physical contact with the end-product of the operation. And these men too are discreetly scrutinized. Diamonds exert a very potent and very special temptation. Nobody is immune. I might add that the ban on possessing uncut diamonds extends beyond the *Sperrgebiet*. It applies throughout South West and South Africa, and every other territory where the writ of De Beers runs. It is an offence to be caught in possession of an uncut stone. The golden rule, if you find a diamond, is—throw it away. Unless you have a licence, as an authorized prospector or dealer, the thing can only bring you trouble. There is nothing light-hearted or easy-going about the gentlemen of the Central Selling Organization. They make the law of the land. The God-fearing Afrikaner might not relish the prostration of his rulers before the Golden Calf with its diamond eyes: but what is good for De Beers is not only

The Land God Made in Anger

My father, an inexpugnable romantic, was once the part-owner of a goldmine in West Wales. It was said to be the smallest and was certainly the worst goldmine in the world, and my father was no Ernest Oppenheimer: but I can speak as one who has had a goldmine in his family. Nevertheless, I cannot help feeling that Oranjemund takes the business of furnishing superfluities to lengths which are absurd. In a hungry and suffering world it is painful to contemplate such elaborate and self-perpetuating foolishness. De Beers has made a multi-million pound industry out of what ought to have been one of nature's casual gifts. Oranjemund represents a perversion of healthy values. It gives substance to that uneasy feeling I touched on earlier that somehow, somewhere, the development of civilization has taken a wrong turning. I found Oranjemund invigorating, fascinating: but all the time I was conscious of a sensation that the entire effort was misconceived. A diamond ought to represent a glow in the eye of the chthonic deity, of the earth-goddess who is the mother of us all. The grim process at Oranjemund has reduced it to the mercenary twinkle in the eye of a whore.

Sir Ernest Oppenheimer was a very remarkable man. It would be ridiculous to belittle his achievements, which were of a quite exceptional magnitude. He demonstrated gifts of character and intellect of an undeniably superior order, amounting to nothing less than genius. He must have enjoyed moments of satisfaction, on the conclusion of his successive coups, which are beyond the imagination of those of us who are not and never can be financiers. The abilities of a hundred Stauchs, Scheibes, Cornells and Carstens would not add up to a tenth of his overwhelming talent. He was a great man. By contrast, old Martiens was childish and dim-witted. A failure, a fantasist, at times a transparent liar; a man of no possible importance or account. Why, then, I wonder, do I feel a lively warmth in the thought of a man like Martiens, and no warmth at all in the thought of a man like Sir Ernest Oppenheimer? And I wonder who, in the final account, felt the keener satisfactions? Who came closest to bedrock? Was it Sir Ernest, in the boardroom of a big, drab

Close Goods

West Africa, for all its fecundity, has not yielded an individual stone of comparable size.

The technique of diamond-cutting does not concern us here. But it is worth noting that the main shapes into which diamonds are reduced by this most exacting and hazardous of artistic occupations are, like the art itself, traditional. The object is to cleave, saw and polish the individual stone in such a way that its natural qualities will shine to their best advantage, and its defects will be removed or concealed. The principal shapes, inherited by modern cutters from antique originals, include Brilliant (round-cut with fifty-eight facets); Marquise (boat-shaped); Baguette (straight-sided); Emerald-cut (oblong or square with facets polished diagonally across the corners); and Pear-shaped.

It is not easy to associate these small, sophisticated, aristocratic objects with the crude slogging of the rotary excavators and the treatment plants. One hundred million parts of earth are being dug, dumped, transported and sorted to produce one part of diamond. Thousands of men toil under that broiling sun on those scalped sands to unearth a few inconsequential specks of glorified glass. There must be times, after a gruelling day on the beaches, when the tired employee of C.D.M. returns to his bungalow, fetches a can of beer from the icebox, and asks himself how he came to be caught up in such a vast network of insanity, such a colossal exercise in triviality and irrelevance. What lasting benefits to mankind, what scientific advances or technological fall-out, can justify the antics at Oranjemund, Kimberley and Hatton Garden?

I like precious objects. As Lear replied to his daughters, when they asked him why he needed such a magnificent retinue:

> O reason not the need! Our basest beggars
> Are in the poorest things superflous.
> Allow not nature more than nature needs,
> Man's life is cheap as beast's. Thou art a lady:
> If only to go warm were gorgeous,
> Why, nature needs not what thou gorgeous wearest,
> Which scarcely keeps thee warm!

On monthly sale-days these are offered to prospective buyers to accept or to refuse. There is little trading or arguing: the buyer is given a take-it-or-leave-it proposition. He usually takes.

After purchase, the stones are sent for cutting. Here too the operations are highly specialized. The majority of stones will be cut in Antwerp, which maintains the leading rôle it has exercised in this field for more than three centuries. America, which buys three-quarters of the world's output of diamonds, cuts most of the really choice stones, and Israel has come to the fore in the cutting of melées. England, France, the Netherlands, and South Africa also maintain firms of skilled cutters.

The art of cutting, which will reduce the blue-whites of Oranjemund to their final form, is of course, an ancient one. It has been practised for at least a thousand years, from the time when the goldsmiths and jewellers of India learned to produce facets which would enhance the beauty of their gems. They discovered that diamonds are the hardest substance in the world: ninety times harder than the next substance in hardness, corundum, a class that includes sapphires and rubies. The Indians therefore worked out how to cut one diamond by using another. India had been the world's first great producer of gems, her diamonds coming from the famous Golconda mines on the Kestna River. The Great Mogul, the Orloff, the Koh-i-noor and the Hope Diamond were all products of Golconda. In the eighteenth century, when the Indian mines were failing, finds were made in Brazil; and for a century the Brazilian mines of Tejuco and Minas Gerais were paramount. And when the Brazilian mines became exhausted, in the 1870s, the initial discoveries had already been made in South Africa. The South African stones far surpassed their predecessors in point of size. The Cullinan, found almost casually at Pretoria, weighed 3,106 carats uncut, and furnished nine large gems and ninety-six brilliants. Cullinan I, 'The Star of India', weighs 530 carats, and is mounted in the Queen's Sceptre. Cullinan II, III and IV are also part of the royal regalia. Other celebrated South African stones are the Jonker (uncut 726: cut 125), the Jubilee (uncut 650: cut 245), and the Tiffany (cut 128). South

plant, it is silent and restful, furnished in dark woods, its walls surrounded by brightly lit display cases. A sedate, almost religious air prevails, as is appropriate to the contemplation of great riches. Here, on a tray on the counter, the diamonds which represent the week's takings are spread out before you. They are a thought-provoking sight. They have been roughly buffed up with the rest of the concentrate in the attrition mills, to make sure that they will present dry and non-conductible surfaces to the sorting machines; they have therefore lost much of the dirty brown integument that shrouds them in their natural state. They shine under the lamp against the velvet-backing. They are of all sizes and shapes, the larger specimens basking amid a shoal of smaller ones. Their outlines are sharp but irregular. There is an astonishing variety of colours, from the pure blue-whites, through a marked scattering of yellows, down to a sprinkling of 'fancies'. 'Fancies' are coloured diamonds, produced by eccentric conditions of chemical content or of firing in the volcanic pipes. There is a wide range of hues—amber, pink, green, mauve. Fancies are not favoured by the public, and are therefore not greatly sought after by the trade: although when Dr Williamson presented Queen Elizabeth II with a magnificent circular-cut pink specimen on the occasion of her wedding in 1947, pink stones at least were given a certain vogue.

In their natural eight-sided shape, diamonds are known in the industry as 'glassies'. If, as often happens, they are twin stones or triangles, they are called 'maccles'. There are also special terms for diamonds classified by weight, 142 carats being reckoned to the ounce. Small diamonds of less than a carat are known as 'melée', while broken stones are described as 'chips' if of melée size, and 'cleavages' if larger. In their rough state, diamonds are sold to only two hundred dealers throughout the world, and most sales take place in London, through the Diamond Exchange in Hatton Garden. Nine-tenths of the world's uncut diamonds are marketed in London. The vendors make up 'sights' or parcels of their wares, trying to arrange roughly equal selections of stones of different weight and quality.

silicon powder. The media have a specific gravity of 3.0, which means that they are three times as heavy as water. Only the diamonds and heavier concentrates sink to the bottom and are removed for further treatment, while 95 per cent of the remaining materials are floated off and dumped. It will then be seen what an infinitesimal proportion of all the gravels collected from the diggings has now been retained. Nevertheless, the waste-material has a beauty of its own. The visitor can stand in the sunlight beside one of the humming conveyor belts, with its cargo of wet concentrate, watching the newly cleansed stones sparkle invitingly: and now and again he cannot resist lifting from the belt a piece of garnet, agate, sard or chalcedony which is otherwise destined to be thrown away.

The material is now graded into four sizes: oversize, coarse, medium and fine. These are put through an attrition mill, then subjected to two ingenious process that bring about the final elimination of the waste material. The three larger fractions are passed, while wet, over eight moving belts coated with a special grease—an abominable and evil-smelling material. Diamonds are by nature hydrophobic, or water repellent, and their dry surfaces cling to the grease-belts, while the useless material drops down and is washed away. All that is then necessary is to scrape the diamonds off the belts and boil them to remove any residual grease. As for the finest of the four fractions, which is too small for the grease-band treatment, it is sorted by means of electrolysis. Subjected to an electrostatic field of high intensity, the waste is immediately attracted by the positive electrodes, while the diamonds, another of whose characteristics is to be non-conductive, are deflected into a pipeline straight into the sort house.

Just as the first step in the operation required the delicacy of the human eye and hand, so does the last. The diamonds are separated by means of spatula or trowel from any remaining gravels, given a last soak in hydrofluoric acid, and are then ready for conveying to the building where they are packaged for despatch to Kimberley. A visit to this building is deeply absorbing. After the factory-floor atmosphere of the treatment

factory substitute for the human hand and eye, although experiments have been made with a gigantic vacuum-cleaner, its probing snout resembling the trunk of an outsize elephant. A platoon of Africans moves across the bedrock in line abreast, teasing the last vestiges of gravel out of the crevices with broom and hand-brush. It gives you a strange little flick at the nerve-ends to see an African worker suddenly stop brushing to pick something up, with a smile and a grin, and tuck it with broad fingers safely in an inner pocket. He will take it back to the compound, and at the end of the day a security-man will call to collect his haul. His stone or stones will be weighed, and he will receive a bonus, usually in the form of a chit on the company stores. A grateful company might reward him with, say, a bar of carbolic soap for a diamond worth three or four hundred pounds. But it is only just to remind oneself that it was the company, after all, that got him down to the diamonds in the first place....

There are almost a score of field screening plants sited at strategic points on the beaches. They can be dismantled and re-erected where required. With the incessant banging and clattering which is characteristic of Oranjemund, the gravels are unloaded from the ten-ton trucks and hauled up a series of conveyor belts over what are known by the piquant terms of vibrating screens, rotary scrubbers, and vibrating-bar grizzlies. All the sand and big rocks and pebbles are hived off and spilled on to the dumps. When this trash has been discarded, about 15 per cent of the gravels is left. This is loaded on to electric or diesel locomotives and carried away to the Central Treatment Plant. All roads on the beaches lead ultimately to the Central Treatment Plant.

The Central Treatment Plant, technically known as a heavy media separation plant, represents the fifth distinct stage of the enterprise. It is a nexus of brightly painted sheds, surrounded by a latticework of scarlet and yellow conveyors. It stands at the core and centre of the whole operation. The gravels are unloaded from the locomotives, washed, then passed through the so-called heavy media, which are a mixture of water and ferro-

16 Fish River Canyon

15 Oranjemund: trenching by hand

Oranjemund: sweeping the bedrock. Behind the diggers is the gravel terrace, and beyond the terrace the sand overburden

into stacking conveyors that drain it off on to the dumps. The dumps themselves, like everything else at Oranjemund, are outsize. They constitute a small range of mountains. An engineer took me up one of them in a jeep. From the top we had an unparalleled view of the whole thirty or forty-mile battlefield. In comparison with the sight of the Promised Land or the Kingdoms of the Earth, it was a miserable vista: but there was no doubt about its wealth or its power to tempt.

When the overburden has been removed, and the lighter, coarser diamond-bearing gravels have been exposed, the scrapers and Lübeckers are withdrawn. The third phase now opens. The gravels usually overlay the bedrock to a depth of three to three-and-a-half feet. If it is thin enough it is bulldozed into stockpiles, otherwise bucket excavators and front-end loaders are used to load it into ten-ton rear-dump trucks. A skein of these big lemon-painted trucks then carries the gravel to the field screening plant, where the first stages of the sorting process will take place. Adding these ten-tonners to the scrapers, the rotaries, and the squadrons of other vehicles on the beaches, it is easy to understand what the bill for fuel, maintenance and spare parts must be, what problems of sheer logistics and supply the planners at Oranjemund are called upon to face.

With the gravels on their way to be treated, the bedrock is now visible. It is whale-grey, puckered into channels and runnels, punctured with potholes, dotted with boulders worn smooth in the ancient rivers that flowed over them for uncountable aeons and have been dead as long. Looking at those scoured terraces is like looking at the original floor of the world. They are scored with incomprehensible runes. That naked stone is the reality—the true bedrock. In some ways it seems indecent to disturb it—like laying bare your mother's body in order to rip the ornaments off it.

The bedrock is examined, at least, with a certain reverence. Though most of the diamonds are found in the gravels, some of the heavier ones will have worked their way through the scree into the holes in the rock. Once again there is no satis-

diamond business. In these first and vital investigations there is still no substitute for the human eye, hand and brain. De Beers have gone far to make human tissue redundant: but at the base of the whole pyramid is a European engineer or African supervisor running his fingers through the sludge at the bottom of a pan. Whenever I saw one of those little groups of men clustered round the battered tools of their trade, surrounded by a collection of tin buckets and rusty oildrums, my spirits would rise. They had a cheerful, brotherly air about them. They rattled about happily with their well-worn sieves and rickety sorting-tables, a pleasant contrast to the martial efficiency of the scene all around them. It was like coming across a pub or a fish-and-chip shop in the middle of a stuffy financial district.

When it has been decided to begin work in earnest on a particular area, the heavy brigade is brought in to tackle the job of removing the overburden. The mule-and-cart days were over long ago. Most of the work is done by a force of giant four-wheel scrapers. It is exhilarating to watch these bright yellow monsters dashing about on their huge pneumatic tyres, scoring abstract or op-art arabesques in the orange sand. On their sides is the mysterious but appropriate legend: EUCLID. They are driven by white-shirted Ovambo—magnificent men with noble heads, their shoulders plated with muscle, the glistening skin of their necks and forearms corded with sinew. They manoeuvre their gigantic machines with astonishing speed and precision. Hour after hour, in teams of three, they work with a concentration and élan which seem scarcely to diminish. Ernest Oppenheimer enjoyed another unlooked-for slice of luck when he found a tribe of men as virile and intelligent as the Ovambo close at hand to work his mines.

The scrapers tear away the overburden, transferring the sand to dumps on worked-out areas, at the rate of almost 200 tons an hour. Where the sand is unusually thick, reinforcements in the shape of Lübeckers or rotary bucket excavators are ordered up. These creatures are like figments from science-fiction, crawling forward like animated buildings, chewing up 600 tons of sand an hour and evacuating it in a dung-coloured stream

The Land God Made in Anger

I doubt if there is another open-cast mining operation in the world to match it. The men who direct it are kept up to the mark by the very rigours of the problems that cofnront them. They have estimated that to win their annual toll of diamonds they have to remove 15 million tons of sand, 6 million tons of beach terrace, and treat nearly a million tons of diamondiferous gravel. Thus to produce a million-and-a-half carats of diamonds, which weighs upwards of 400 pounds avoirdupois, they are called on to shift and sift more than a hundred million tons of earth.

The complete process at Oranjemund, from the preliminary survey on the edge of the beach to the final despatch of a parcel of stones to the offices of the Diamond Producers' Association in Kimberley, is divided into five distinct phases. The whole object—remember—is to dig down to the bedrock. The diamonds lie in the scatter of gravel spread across the ancient marine terraces: but to reach them it is necessary to strip away the deep drifts of sand that have accumulated on top of them.

The first stage is to prospect the chosen section by means of soundings. Prospecting is carried out at Oranjemund in the most systematic way, and every strip of beach is tested. The soundings show the depth at which the gravel terrace and the bedrock are located. Subsequently the overburden of sand is removed and the gravel terrace laid bare. A trench is then cut through the gravel terrace down to the bedrock. The trench is only two or three feet wide, but it may extend for a hundred yards or more. The gravels are sorted on the spot, and the proportion of diamonds to gravel and the character of the gravel concentrates determines whether or not the area is worth exploiting.

In some ways this earliest stage of the entire process is the most interesting to the visitor. It is carried out by means of very elementary equipment. The samples of gravel are treated in the simple jigs and hand-cranked trommels which were used a hundred years ago by the first diamond-prospectors. To see them at work is to catch a glimpse of the heroic age of the

Close Goods

for De Beers is good for the Central Selling Organization. De Beers usually scoffs at the idea that it hoards diamonds in the so-called 'buffer pool'; it denounces as a myth the popular notion that its strong-rooms are bulging with diamonds which it deliberately withholds from the market. It likes to paint a pathetic picture of a world-wide diamond-hunger which it is valiantly struggling to satisfy. Nevertheless the diamond-field at Oranjemund is divided into a number of subsidiary blocks, each with its own quaint designation—Chameis, Affenrucken, Kerbe Huk, Mittag, Uub-Vley, Area G: and if the company norm, as it were, looks like being exceeded, then work is periodically slowed down on the more productive blocks and attention is turned to the less developed. Production and demand are thus kept satisfactorily in balance. Of course, as I said in a previous chapter, should the political situation in South West ever threaten to turn sour on C.D.M., then the rate of production would be doubled and trebled, and no bones made about it.

When you witness it, you do not doubt C.D.M.'s ability to step up its activities any time it feels like it. C.D.M. is an army in action. The four-wheel scrapers are the heavy tanks; the rear-dump trucks are the medium tanks; and the big bulldozers are the light tanks. Behind them come the weird paraphernalia and rocketry of a modern army, in the shape of giant mobile stackers, Lübeckers, and monstrous vacuum cleaners, fifty feet high. And behind the machines come the men, the battalions of infantry, armed with shovels and pick-axes, brooms and brushes. From dawn to dusk every day the dunes and beaches around Oranjemund roar and crackle with activity, with the spectacle of men and machinery marching and counter-marching as far as the eye can see. It is as if the battles around Derna or Tobruk were being re-enacted every twenty-four hours for the benefit of some megalomaniac general. The sight is undeniably exciting and impressive. A brief glance is enough to convince you that the campaign is being waged not only with huge resources, but with an altogether uncommon imagination, ruthlessness and pertinacity.

thirds of the total cash turnover. There is money in diamonds—all diamonds; but most of the money is to be made in the diamonds that can be mounted in rings, bracelets or necklaces. So if you want to start a diamond mine, start one that produces gem-stones.

Of the thirteen major diamond-producing areas in the world, Oranjemund is the only one where the proportion of gems to industrials exceeds 50 per cent. Oranjemund is ludicrously fertile. In the number of carats produced annually it is outpaced or liable to be outpaced by other regions: South Africa itself, Angola, Ghana, Liberia, the Congo, Sierra Leone. But the value of production in these territories is reduced by the high proportion of industrials. The Congo, for example, produced in its heyday nearly 15 million carats annually, but only 5 per cent of this massive total were gems. However, South West's neighbours on the West African seaboard, Angola, Liberia, Ghana and Sierra Leone, yield fine 'blue-whites' of the same character and structure as the gems of Oranjemund, and it is thought that these fields are linked in a common geological system. The diamonds were washed out of the African heartland by the same ancient river or net of rivers, and were then caught up in the fierce icy sweep of the Benguela Current and deposited on the ancient strand-lines. An alluvial diamond found in Sierra Leone in 1945 weighed 770 carats. Anglo-American—De Beers has made a predictable and largely successful effort to extend its monopoly over these other fields. Even Oranjemund will not last for ever. Mr Harry Oppenheimer learned at his father's knee the lesson that, in the diamond business, when one door is closing another must be made to open.

At Oranjemund a million-and-a-half carats of diamonds, give or take a hundred thousand, is extracted every year. The fluctuation is only partly accounted for by the actual difficulties of mining. In an artificial industry, output must be artificially regulated. Oranjemund is given its individual target, adjusted to suit the overall requirements of De Beers: and what is good

Close Goods

line involved a colossal effort and expenditure. The diamondiferous gravels lay beneath a protective blanket of sand that was anywhere from thirty to seventy feet thick. The entire process of 'alluvial' digging, as it had to be practiced at Oranjemund, demanded a completely fresh approach. And at the end of it, as Oppenheimer's critics expected, there might lie disappointment and failure. Alluvial diamonds might turn out, after all, to be nothing but a series of erratic deposits, profitable to the casual digger but ruinous to a company with heavy overheads.

In those early months and for many years to come the only way to shift those hundreds of thousands of tons of overburden was by means of mule-drawn carts. Not the most spectacular of beginnings. But within a few years the South Western venture proved to be the most triumphant and profitable of all Oppenheimer's undertakings. Today the fifty-mile strip of coast above Oranjemund produces a greater profit than all its sister-fields in the Republic. It is the world's largest source of gem diamonds. As the mines in the Transvaal and the Free State dwindle, Oranjemund continues to wax fruitful. C.D.M. has also enjoyed the ironic victory of being made responsible for working the Government sites south of the river, below Port Nolloth, called Kleinzee and Annex-Kleinzee, which were in the original Merensky country. C.D.M. surveyors range deep into Namaqualand, and the company is buying up large tracts of land there.

Most important of all, the diamonds of South West Africa are majestic in size and appearance. Their quality is superlative, yielding a high proportion of 'blue-whites', the purest and most sought-after stones of all. They are what in the trade are known as 'close goods', merchandise of the first quality. Moreover, as a bonus that even the supernaturally far-sighted Sir Ernest could not have foreseen, the preponderance of gem stones over industrial stones is in the region of 90 per cent. The staggering profitability of Oranjemund can therefore be appreciated. Every year gem stones amount to only 20 per cent of total world production: but their sales account for more than two-

Pretoria, which weighed 3,106? And what about the deep mines at Kimberley—Wesselton, Dutoitspan, Bultfontein, the 'Great Hole' itself? What about nearby Koffiefontein, or Jagersfontein?

The idea of a switch away from 'blue ground' to 'alluvials' was radical and revolutionary. But Oppenheimer's success was not based on being afraid of new ideas. He was an outstandingly tough minded and prescient man. Almost alone among his fellow members of the Syndicate, who were content to jog along without peering too far in to the future, he was willing to face the fact that the supply of 'blue ground' diamonds would not last for ever, and that a yard-by-yard investigation of the land-surface of South Africa had failed to reveal promising new sources.

He sent his survey-teams hurrying down from Lüderitz to the mouth of the Orange. They were instructed to search for the 'oyster-line' near which Merensky had made the bulk of his finds at Alexander Bay. The 'oyster-line' marked the point at which the fresh-water flood of the ancient river was believed to to have met the salt water of the sea.

Once more Oppenheimer's shrewdness and intuition produced rapid and uncannily rewarding results. Immediately north of the mouth of the Orange, only a matter of yards from the trial trenches dug by the German Regié before the first World War, the C.D.M. surveyors found rich diamond-bearing deposits. At that moment Oranjemund was born.

It is easy today, when you drive out into the desert to watch C.D.M. at work, to forget what a bold decision Oppenheimer made. The whole operation is now so gigantic, so monolithic and well-established, that you would imagine you were looking at a factory for making diamonds instead of an instrument for finding them.

Merensky had wandered along the shore—to adapt Isaac Newton's famous phrase—picking up diamonds as if they were pebbles. On the opposite bank of the river the case was very different. To reach the buried gravels on the prehistoric shore-

With the glorious exception of Williamson, Merensky was the last of the great free-lancers, the really successful pioneers. His expedition had been a triumph of individual courage and enterprise.

Merensky's discoveries led to a drastic reappraisal of the whole business of diamond production. The area of his investigation was south of the Orange, across the river in Namaqualand. Alexander Bay was a mile or two beyond the borders of Oppenheimer's *Sperrgebiet*, the land which had belonged to the old German Regié. Oppenheimer was therefore unable to lay hands on it, and had to stand aside while Merensky's concessions were bought up by the South African government. Merensky asked for and received a million pounds.

Oppenheimer's colleagues, though not Oppenheimer himself, regarded the strikes of Carstens and Merensky, as earlier they had regarded the strikes of Stauch and Scheibe, as a flash in the pan. They remained loyal to the thesis that the prime source of diamonds had been, and would always be, the diamondiferous rock that had come to be known as Kimberlite or 'blue ground'. It was in the 'blue ground', which represented the material in the necks of circular pipes of extinct volcanoes, that the specks of carbon which were to become diamonds had been trapped in streams of molten lava, and there subjected to such intense heat and pressure that their structure had been changed and they had become precious stones. It was acknowledged, of course, that in the course of ages the lava had been worn away, and that in some instances the diamonds had been washed into rivers and carried enormous distances from their place of origin. But these river-born diamonds were simply sports or freaks: it made more sense to search for 'blue ground' than for ancient beaches or river-terraces. Diamonds had always been mined far inland in South Africa. True, the first diamond ever found in South Africa, the Eureka, had been picked up in 1867 on the banks of the Orange; but who would compare the Eureka, a diamond of a mere 21 carats, with the Cullinan, found in 1905 in the famous Premier Mine near

Orange, and fifty miles north-west of Springbok, there is very little else to do except look for diamonds.

Much more significant were the investigations made in the following year by Hans Merensky. Merensky, like Williamson, was a professional. A doctor of geology, he took a team to the south bank of the Orange, in the vicinity of Alexander Bay, and began a search conducted on scientific principles. He worked on the assumption that in ancient times diamonds had been washed down the Orange from volcanic pipes situated in the interior of the continent. They had then entered the current of the Atlantic—but the current had promptly washed them back again towards the shore. Merensky believed that in that far-off era the prevailing current had been flowing from north to south, not from south to north as it does today. He therefore settled on the area around Alexander Bay as the likeliest site. As it happens, scientific opinion considers that he was mistaken in both his main contentions. The Orange could not have been the primaeval river along which the diamonds were carried: the Orange as we know it today is of relatively recent formaation. There is no doubt that an ancient river existed, but its bed has never been located, in spite of the most exhaustive searches. Nor did the Benguela Current run in the direction Merensky thought it did. However, the errors in his calculations made no difference. Like many scientists, he did the right thing for the wrong reasons. What mattered was that he had formed ideas which were informed, inspired, and in many respects sound. They served to enable him to work systematically and confidently towards a definite goal.

He hit the jackpot. He had scarcely begun to dig his trial boreholes when he uncovered a tremendous clutch of large diamonds, some of them so big they would not pass through the neck of his water-bottle. He had to return to base to fetch a wide-necked Eno's Fruit Salts bottle. Even that would not take the number of diamonds which he and his party, in a state of euphoria, began to pick up from the beach. He had to make a hurried dash for the nearest general store to buy a square sweet tin of large capacity.

Close Goods

The figures are almost too titanic to grasp. Anglo-American-De Beers appears unassailable and indestructible. It is very hard to realize that only a generation ago Sir Ernest Oppenheimer was deeply exercised by local difficulties in South West.

He was busy nailing the lid on the diamond business, making it duly watertight, when the barrel suddenly sprung a number of leaks. At Lichtenburg, only a hundred miles west of Johannesburg, there developed a good old rousing, primitive, free-for-all diamond rush. The situation became distressingly untidy. As we have seen, the discovery of a new diamond field, like the discovery of a million penny blacks, is not an event to be welcomed with handsprings and shouts of joy. Oppenheimer put the stopper on Lichtenburg by acquiring a controlling interest in the strikes. He also took action to secure the situation that threatened in South West Africa and the contiguous territory of Namaqualand.

For in a few short days, in 1925, the focus of attention in South West had shifted dramatically southwards. There was no warning. Oppenheimer's juggernaut was grinding away at the sites up at Lüderitz, when those awkward, irrepressible, impertinent people, the independent prospectors, made two sensational discoveries at the mouth of the Orange River.

Fred Cornell had travelled along the coast and in the wastes of the Richtersveld in 1910, during the course of his compulsive wanderings. He had scraped around with his usual great-hearted lack of luck. It was not until fifteen years later that an equally vivid personality, Captain J. E. Carstens, found the long-sought deposits. There is a romantic story to the effect that many years earlier, when he was a subaltern in a Gurkha regiment on the North West Frontier, an Indian fortune-teller in the bazaar had told Carstens that one day he would discover treasure in a distant country. He had not the remotest interest in diamonds at that time, and only took up diamond-hunting years later as a desultory pursuit when he was staying at Port Nolloth, where his father kept a store. At Port Nolloth, an excessively grim little town fifty miles south of the mouth of the

he was taking diamonds out of the ground without being able to get rid of them. He was seated on a fabulous and ever-mounting stockpile of some of the finest diamonds in the world —and he was going broke. His diamonds were useless to him. The result was that, with the costs of recovery snow-balling, he had to knuckle under. He was bitter. When he died at the age of fifty-one, in 1958, only a few months after Sir Ernest Oppenheimer, half the shares in the Williamson Mine were bought by Harry Oppenheimer. It was thus brought into what De Beers, in its jocular way, likes to call its 'family'.

Under Sir Ernest and his equally remarkable son, the De Beers family has grown to proportions which even Cecil Rhodes would not recognize. Its interests and those of the Anglo-American Corporation to which it is wedded have been diversified to include not only diamonds, but also, of course, gold, with its by-product or co-product, uranium. The Anglo-American–De Beers–C.D.M. giant owns coal, copper, steel and vanadium. It operates in Zambia, Rhodesia, the Congo, Angola, West Africa, Mauritania, and a dozen other African countries. It is intimately connected with companies in England, Luxemburg, Sweden and Canada—its principal vehicle outside South Africa being the booming new Charter Consolidated—and with the Engelhard group in America (which we have already encountered in connection with the mines at Tsumeb and Otavi). Charles Engelhard is in fact a member of the executive committee of Anglo-American. In 1966 the net profit of Anglo-American was £15½ million ($37 million), a rise of more than 5 per cent on 1965. £6¼ million was placed to reserves, and the value of investments increased by £35 million to £245 million. As for De Beers, the amount of diamond sales for which the company was responsible through the C.S.O. came to £177 million, and in 1967 has amounted to a record £87¾ million for the first half of the year alone. The diamond production of De Beers Consolidated in South Africa and Consolidated Diamond Mines of South West Africa now run together at a joint profit of well over £70 million ($168 million) a year.

Close Goods

forced Barnato out. Thereafter Rhodes was the richest and most powerful man in Africa.

Oppenheimer determined to apply the same medicine as Rhodes. He got his chance when he became chairman of De Beers in 1929, in the panic that followed the collapse of the Wall Street Market. It took him four years to steer the industry into safe waters, and in 1933 he was ready to establish the Diamond Trading Company. The Company was designed to be the only outlet through which the South African diamond producers could market their stones. Today, known as the Central Selling Organization, it handles 85 per cent of the diamonds of the entire world, maintaining the price per carat at a level decided by itself. In March 1963 the price of uncut diamonds was raised by 5 per cent; in July 1966 by $7\frac{1}{2}$ per cent. There was no appeal from the retailers, and little discussion with the producers. The C.S.O.'s decrees were absolute. In 1961 Ghana, a major producer, struck an attitude of defiance and tried to break away; by 1963 the revolt was over and she was back in the fold. Even the Soviet Union, when it sells diamonds outside its own borders, channels them through the C.S.O. It has to. Not only is the price fixed by the C.S.O. favourable to the producer, but if the Soviet Union tried to undercut the C.S.O. and flood the market it would be unable to do so because C.S.O. controls all the outlets. A diamond-dealer who defied the C.S.O. would not last long. The C.S.O. would see to it that any traders who bought from him were blacklisted.

An entertaining example of the power of C.S.O. was demonstrated in the 1940s. In 1940 the famous Dr Williamson discovered his tremendous pipe of diamonds at Mwadui in Tanganyika. By all accounts Williamson, a Canadian geologist, was a maverick—lively, pugnacious and bloody-minded. He fondly imagined he was going to market his diamonds himself, at a price that suited him. In the gentlest possible way—his manner was always gentle and unassuming—Sir Ernest Oppenheimer strove to disillusion him. Williamson was obstinate. He persisted. The word went out from the C.S.O., and merchants and retailers shunned Williamson. Every day

that at no time will the value of their investment be threatened or destroyed by the flooding of the market. Diamonds are by no means the scarce commodity the public supposes or that the producers pretend. There are plenty of diamonds in the world. But disposing of them is even more complicated than producing them. The difficulty is not so much to find buyers: people are always anxious to buy diamonds. The problem is how to find buyers at the right price. And the right price is the artificial price fixed by the diamond monopoly.

Suppose you were a stamp dealer, and had been selling the 1840 British Penny Black at a generally accepted price of £1. Then suppose you heard that a man in Shropshire had found a million Penny Blacks in his father's deed-box, and was proposing to sell them to all comers at 3s 6d. What would you do? You would club together with your fellow-dealers and buy the whole lot from him at a price of, say, 8s. 6d. a piece. An expensive operation—but necessary if you are to protect the value of your own stocks. Then, when you have got the million Penny Blacks in your own hands, you agree with your fellow-dealers that—pretty as the stamps undoubtedly are—you will burn them. Unless, that is, you can trust your colleagues enough to share the stamps out, hoard them, and dribble them back on to the market at the regulation price of £1—or, say, 25s., the increase representing your expenses in the recent deal. In Sweden, in the summer of 1967, it was decided to kill off all the existing stock of mink. Full length sapphire-mink coats had been selling in Scandinavia for as little as £200. The only solution was to gas two million mink kids, as the young are called, and start again. Mink had become common and had to be made scarce.

Rhodes was faced with the same problem in the late 1880s, when he was chairman of De Beers. The price war he was waging with Barney Barnato, who controlled the rival Kimberley Central Mining Corporation, had resulted in the price of diamonds plummeting to a pathetic 10s a carat, whereas they cost 15s a carat to produce. Backed by Rothschild and Alfred Beit, Rhodes went after Kimberley, and in 1888 captured it and

told me that clubs proliferated: sailing clubs, cricket clubs, bowling clubs, amateur theatricals, even golf clubs—anything that is bright and busy and binds people together, or possesses any possibility of keeping boredom at bay. The work at Oranjemund is absorbing, and the wages are high: but there are still left many hours in the day to kill, and nothing can hide the fact that existence in such a place, in spite of all the ingenuity of which human beings are capable, must be soul-destroying and terrible.

Beyond the church and the hydroponics farm, beyond the football field and the abattoir, rise the huge unforgettable yellow triangles of spoil from the recovery plants on the edge of the Atlantic. The pyramids of Egypt without their mystery and faith. Monuments of an empty and mechanistic philosophy.

When Oppenheimer bought out the German Régie in 1920 for £8½ million, and set up Consolidated Diamond Mines, it seemed to the financiers in Kimberley and Johannesburg that he was taking a great gamble. But very soon C.D.M. (an offshoot of De Beers, and linked to Oppenheimer's own parent corporation, Anglo-American) was accounting for 20 per cent of South African diamond production. The fields around Lüderitz, however, started to show ominous signs of exhaustion.

Pickings had been relatively poor in the diamond business during the depressed period after the First World War. Under the determined leadership of Oppenheimer, the mine owners of South Africa had begun to band together and to practise the tight, unashamed monopoly which in later years was to make them so incalculably rich. Oppenheimer had grasped at the outset of his career the simple point that Rhodes had grasped before him. Rhodes had realized that diamonds have no value in themselves, but only the value that merchants can persuade the public to put on them. Buying diamonds is like buying stamps, coins, pictures, or Louis Quinze furniture. Without doubt there is a genuine aesthetic element involved in the transaction, but that is well and truly a secondary consideration. Diamonds are a financial investment. What both producer and purchaser want is a restricted supply: they want to be sure

fluoroscope or X-ray apparatus on the other side of the room; but there was no need to use it at the particular moment. What is brought into Oranjemund is of much less concern to the security branch than what is taken out.

After the desert, the green island which is Oranjemund, tacked like a square of baize to the sand, is unexpected and gratifying. The green is somewhat moth-eaten, for there is no turf or grass-seed in existence which could honestly thrive beneath that brassy sun; but as you drive down the main thoroughfare a squad of Africans are hosing down the trees and arranging the sprinklers on the lawns. The nearby river supplies all the water needed to soak the top-soil which the company has imported. Many of the staff scarcely bother with their gardens. Others, particularly the English, haunted by nostalgic dreams of the Chelsea Flower Show, have transformed their little plots into pocket-handkerchiefs of scent and colour which would do credit to a corner of Kent or Sussex. Oranjemund, like all the other Oppenheimer gold and diamond mines, is notable for the determined efforts that have been made to deck it out with plants and flowers. The attempt is praiseworthy, although nothing can conceal the fundamentally stark and ruthless appearance and purpose of a mine: and in more jaundiced moments I was reminded, as I watched the Ovambo and the Englishmen busy with hoe and spray, that the inmates of Buchenwald had been great gardeners too.

The three-roomed guest-house in which I was installed was comfortable, and my hosts had thoughtfully stocked the ice-box with cans of beer and soft drinks. The soft drinks, like most of the amenities of life at Oranjemund, had been manufactured in the town itself. The house, white-painted, green-roofed, surrounded by its own wooden fence, was conveniently situated for exploring the town. There were, I found, a row of shops, a church, a cinema, a primary school, a swimming-pool, a clubhouse—all the appurtenances which make life more or less tolerable for this unique community, whose members are stuck out in the desert together for weeks or months at a time. The notice boards dotted about the town

Close Goods

fetch the price of a small diamond: yet in my memory the flash of an almond-pink feather is as ineffaceable as the flash of a gem. Nevertheless a visit to Oranjemund is undeniably awe-inspiring. The place makes an impression on the most sinewy mind. It certainly provides a rousing climax to any trip through that extraordinary country.

If you are accompanied by a diamond detective, you can drive down to Oranjemund through the *Sperrgebiet*. The track is rough and in places totally undefined, used only by infrequent patrols. You keep the honed white knife-edge of the surf square on your right-hand side, and scamper across the cracked landscape as quickly as you can. The more usual way to approach Oranjemund by road is through Namaqualand, across the Ernest Oppenheimer bridge that spans the river south of the town. The bridge is ugly but substantial: as it needs to be to stand up to the batterings of the river, which has been known to wash it away.

You will not be able to drive your car or Land Rover over the bridge. No motor vehicle is allowed to enter or leave Oranjemund. You must park your machine in a lock-up compound on the south bank and cross the bridge by foot or in a company car. Thus the severity of the precautions against diamond smuggling is made clear to you before you even set foot in the town. Oranjemund is crowded with vehicles and cycles of every type: but once they are on the premises they never leave it. The private cars of the employees, in which they make the long drive down to Cape Town for holidays and occasional week-ends, spend their entire lives in the compounds on the far side of the river.

The security man who had been detailed to greet us and escort us over the bridge was uncommonly friendly and forthcoming for one of his persuasion. All the same, I was intrigued to notice from the puffiness of his ears and the thick, shiny tissue around his eyebrows that at one time he had been a professional fighter. The first place to which he led us was the reception centre, where the contents of our pockets and our baggage were carefully inspected and noted. We could see the big

River, and the system of power created will stretch from the Atlantic to the Indian Ocean. For Namaqualand and the south of South West Africa, the Project will ultimately entail the establishment of no less than six generating stations in the 250 miles between Augrabies Falls and the sea. These will bring into being vast newly irrigated areas. Altogether the Project will give rise to the irrigation of 750,000 acres.

New townships with synthetic names like Oviston (Oranje-Vistonnel) and Oranjekrag (Orange Power) have been created to house the workers and technicians engaged on the undertaking. None of them, however, are ever likely to match, in size or amenity, the town of Oranjemund (Orange Mouth), the headquarters of Consolidated Diamond Mines of South West Africa.

Oranjemund, founded thirty years ago, is today the third biggest town in South West. It lies on the north bank of the wide, sandy estuary of the river, within sight of the sea. In its early days it was nothing more than a collection of flimsy huts, but its growth has kept pace with the phenomenal boom in diamonds which has taken place since the war. From this one town flow $1\frac{1}{2}$ million carats of diamonds a year, representing a profit for their owners of 40 million rand (£23.5 million, or $56 million). The wealth of Oranjemund outgrosses the wealth of any other industry in South West: more than mineral production, fishing, sheep or cattle raising. It can only be compared, in its ceaseless, swollen garnering in of wealth, to the Arab oil-sheikdoms of the Persian Gulf.

South West Africa offers the traveller an unparalleled diversity of sights and sensations. The flamingoes of Walvis Bay, the kudus of Etosha, the kokerbooms of the Namib, the Bushman rock-paintings, the German forts. But the most clamorous and overwhelming sight of all is the diamond-city of Oranjemund. One must not be confused, of course, by considerations of mere size and monetary value. Who is to judge between the absolute or the relative value of, say, a diamond and a flamingo? Who can tell what place each occupies in the eye of the beholder, or the Eye of God? All the feathers of a flamingo cannot

TWELVE
Close Goods

FEW countries in the world can be bounded by two such stately rivers as the Cunene and the Orange. The Orange is the greatest of the rivers of South Africa. It rises in Lesotho, among the snow-capped ranges of the Drakensberg, and winds westwards for 1,300 miles, fed by a score of tributaries. One of its many offshoots is the Vaal, South Africa's second largest river, and the principal river of the Orange Free State and the southern Transvaal. It empties itself into the Atlantic 400 miles south of Walvis Bay and 160 miles south of Lüderitz.

In 1963 the South African Government initiated one of the most ambitious engineering projects of our time. The Orange River Project, according to its sponsors, will take thirty years to complete and cost at least 450 million rand (£265 million, or $630 million). It will entail building three major dams, nine smaller ones, a fifty-mile tunnel, twenty hydro-electric generating stations, and the longest continuous aqueduct in the world. The Orange River will be linked to the Great Fish

the drops splash on his upturned face. *God se dank, dit reent! Dit reent!*[1] A rain to make him break out into a hymn. *Hy laat my neerle in groen weivelde na waters waar rus is, lei my heen . . . !*;[2]

The downpour drummed on the roof of the Land Rover like a tattoo of Number One shot. Above the buzzing of the thunder I could hear the veld gurgling and choking beneath the weight of the water; the wasplike flashes of the lightning showed me a landscape sagging beneath the deluge. A tropical storm. A storm from the Congo.

From time to time the high, satisfying, soothing note of the engine was interrupted as we wallowed into a sheet of water. Long sections of the road were awash. We kept going, trying to keep up our speed on the softening surface.

With dawn the storm died away. Or rather it stopped as if cut with a knife. One minute it was pouring down in torrents: the next there was nothing but a hot, scented, cavernous stillness lit by big wet stars. Africa never does anything by halves.

The dawn was just as sudden. The first lemon streaks of light struck the gunmetal surface of the Land Rover and revealed that at places the water was nearly up to the level of the headlights and the handles of the doors. But the engine sung on and the wheels hugged the churned red earth as we went swinging from one side of the road to the other, weaving a swift path between the glistening pools.

The sun grew stronger. The world shone. A tart breeze with a tang like the hide of lions billowed through the windows and made our cheeks tingle.

Suddenly the world was young. We were wide awake. We delved into a big bag of lychees the size of your thumb. The Land Rover bucketed merrily this way and that, and we all bawled 'I Dream of Jeannie with the Light Brown Hair' at the top of our lungs.

[1] 'Thank God, it's raining! It's raining!'
[2] 'He maketh me to lie down in green pastures! He leadeth me beside the still waters.'

Muskets and Assegais

hazards and disabilities that have been removed from the life of the modern labourer and office-worker. The *voortrekkers* endured the extremes of thirst and hunger, heat and cold. They were never able to put down roots. They were compelled by circumstance and their own restless character to set out across the plain that started where the last plain ended.

They grew old before their time. The men were worn out by the continual hunting, by the ceaseless casting-about for a meagre patch of grazing for their scrawny cattle. The women soon lost the strength and confidence of their adolescence and became round-shouldered drudges. The smooth white foreheads beneath the high Cape caps grew wrinkled and blistered. The blue eyes were reduced by the glare of the sun to washed-out slits.

There was no water to spare for them to wash their bodies, so they stank like goats. They bore their children in the stifling interior of the wagon that contained the only possessions they would ever own—a few pots and pans, a wooden stool, a chest with their Sunday dress. When they were sick in pregnancy, they ate red earth. They treated their children's sores and rashes with axle-grease. When their children died, they lowered them into their lonely grave in the veld in coffins made from the supply of planks they carried for the purpose slung from the bed of the wagon.

I have seen the graves in the Kaokoveld. Wind-scraped, sun-chapped, nameless slabs of schist, beside a pool of *brak* water in the desert, a hundred miles from nowhere.

A terrible life. A terrible death.

Then why is it possible to feel for them a dim and cloudy sense of envy? What did they have? Nothing. A dream, a desert, a jealous God. But was there some mystery there? Something the *voortrekkers* knew, or came to know, that we can no longer unravel?

We drove down from Etosha through the night.

It rained. How it rained. The kind of rain that would have brought a Thirstland Trekker tumbling out of his wagon to let

14 Fort Namutoni

13 Etosha Pan: birds on the salt flats

The trekkers who returned to Angola remained there on this second occasion for fifty years. Their children and their children's children were born there. They had grown fearful of the horrors of a long trek: and where was there, now, for them to trek to? They had reached the limit. None the less they were not contented. When Smuts, as Minister of Justice in the Herzog government, offered to 'bring them home' and make them citizens of South West, as part of his Afrikaner counterbalance to the growing influence of the Germans, they agreed. So between 1928 and 1940 a steady trickle of the Angola Boers, 2,000 in all, 'came home' and were settled on farms between Otavi and Otjiwarongo.

Smuts' experiment was not a success. The Angola Boers resented the South West African authorities as they had resented the Portuguese, and as their parents had resented the British. There could be no 'coming home' for people whose only real home was a creaking ox-cart. One by one, family by family, they slipped away into the bush, and died off.

They detested government and all its ways. They chafed beneath the yoke of civilization. They were in their deepest nature anti-social. They were wanderers. Bushmen with white faces.

What can you do with such ungrateful, cross-grained, unteachable, untameable, magnificent people?

Suidwes Lugdiens will carry you to Windhoek from Cape Town or Johannesburg by any one of a dozen weekly flights. It will fly you from Windhoek to Walvis Bay. You can charter a two-seater to take you from Windhoek to Lüderitz, Grootfontein or Namutoni.

Today you can cover in six hours the distance which only ninety years ago it took the Thirstland Trekkers six years to traverse.

There are now no ox-carts swaying over the plains, a line of little barques with leather sails, like the ships of Diogo Cao, beating across the brown immensity.

The life of the *voortrekker* was terrible. It consisted of all the

Cunene. Somehow they crossed that tremendous flood. They were in Angola now. Still they felt they had not travelled far enough. They journeyed on to Huila province, and settled down to graze their cattle on the plateau of Humpata, near present-day Sá de Bandeira, 200 miles north of the Cunene.

They had come 1,200 miles in their ox-wagons, across some of the most desolate terrain in the world. It had taken them six years.

It would be pleasant to report that they had attained the *lekker lewe*. But the *lekker lewe*, of course, is one more mirage; it is not a state that men can ever achieve, or were meant to achieve. Human life is a Thirstland Trek, and even the plateau of Humpata is no more than a temporary resting-place. Perhaps Jordaan's people had become too accustomed to the wandering life; perhaps the authority of the Portuguese was as irksome to them as the authority of the British. No matter. After a brief interlude the whole party packed up and trekked back to the Cunene, across the Cunene and the Kaokoveld, past Namutoni, to their ultimate destination at Grootfontein.

Here, in 1884, Jordaans proclaimed the Republic of Upingtonia. It consisted of three ragged and half-starved groups of trekkers, living respectively at Grootfontein, Otavi and the Waterberg. They bought the land for their Republic from Chief Kambonde of the Herero for twenty-five muskets, a salted horse, and a keg of brandy.

They held out for four years before the fates, whom the trekkers had defied at the outset, and had flouted outrageously for a dozen years, decided that their time had run out. The Herero became antagonistic; fever broke out; Jordaans was killed in Ovamboland on a hunting-trip.

The Republic collapsed. Its members disintegrated. Half of them trailed back to the Western Transvaal, to the scenes whence they had set off so many years before with such hope and determination. By now they were dispossessed and long forgotten. The other half made its way once more to Humpata. By 1890 the houses they had built for themselves at Grootfontein were in ruins.

down on an uninterrupted view of the limitless veld in front of him.

They crossed the Kalahari and the marshes of the Okavango. By the beginning of 1878 they were in northern Botswana, and the track across the desert was littered with their graves. It is impossible not to be awed by the slow, fanatical persistence of such people. They went on. The hated British were plotting to annexe the Transvaal, and even a death in the desert was preferable to living under British rule. They entered South West Africa, led by J. F. Botha, and for a while ungraciously accepted the protection offered them by the British Commissioner and laagered at Namutoni. This was, of course, nearly thirty years before the German fortress was built on the same spot.

They sent an eight-man force under Gert Alberts ahead of them to find the Cunene. Perhaps it was beyond the Cunene that the *lekker lewe* was to be found. Alberts returned with the news that he had discovered water at Gauko-Otavi in Ovamboland, a hundred miles south of the Cunene. Again they girded themselves and went on. It took them sixteen stages to reach Bauko-Otavi from Namutoni.

They stayed there for over a year. The story of their tribulations had reached Cape Town, and public imagination had been stirred. A distress fund was opened, and a ship was chartered to take succour to them. The ship was unable to make a landing on the Skeleton Coast, and put back to Walvis Bay. Scouts were sent from Walvis Bay to try to reach them and report whether they were still alive. There was immense jubilation when it was learned that the scouts had found them and were bringing them back to Walvis Bay.

The *trekkboers* accepted the goods which had been bought for them in Cape Town. But they found even the Walvis Bay of the 1870s oppressively overcrowded. They decided to resume the trek. Ignoring all entreaties, they returned to Gauko-Otavi. The call of the Good Life, the vision of the land flowing with milk and honey, was too strong. Led now by W. W. Jordaans, they harnessed their wagons and trekked north. They reached the

Muskets and Assegais

The Great Trek began in 1835, the year after the news that the British parliament had abolished slavery had reached Cape Town. Louis Trichardt and a dozen families, followed by Van Rensberg with ten, bumped off towards the east with their horses, slaves and cattle. Both parties crossed the Vaal, and Trichardt reached the Drakensberg; but Van Rensberg and his party completely disappeared, swallowed up by Africa. In the following year two more groups of pioneers set forth, led by Hendrik Potgieter and Sarel Cilliers. The idea of escape into the open spaces was growing irresistible, and in 1837 Piet Uys was off, on the heels of Piet Retief, who had taken with him no less than 120 families. In June a rendezvous and grand conference of 4,000 *voortrekkers*, representing the separate groups of Retief, Maritz, Uys and Potgieter, was held at the Vet River, far to the north-east, 650 miles from Cape Town. Their attempt to hammer out a common policy and a common area of settlement was a failure. They could not agree with the British, and they could not agree with one another. The parties split up once more: and the price of disunity was soon paid. At the Ncome River, a branch of the Buffalo River, the Zulu chief Dingaan fell on Piet Retief's waggons on February 6, 1838, and massacred 96 men and women and 186 children. Retief died with the rest. Thereafter the Ncome has been known as Blood River, and February 6 as Dingaan's Day.

The *voortrekkers* were an admirable and pig-headed breed. It was inevitable that sooner or later a few of the more intractable members of that intractable race should get it into their heads to defy the rigours of South West. When they came, however, they came not from the Cape but from the Transvaal. In 1875 the members of what was later aptly named the Thirstland Trek left the Western Transvaal in search of the ever-evasive *lekker lewe*. It was to be the last of the classic treks, setting out a full forty years after the first treks had crossed the Great Fish River. Its leaders were in the grip none the less of the same simple, patriarchal vision. They sought a place where a man could sit on his own *stoep*, smoking his pipe, sipping his coffee, his Bible on his knees, while the sun went

deserve mention. Thomas Baines, who had earlier been associated with Livingstone, landed at the embryonic port of Walvis Bay in 1861 and made an epic journey to the Victoria Falls by way of Lake Ngami. He published his *Explorations in South-West Africa* in 1864. Meanwhile his friend John Chapman undertook a journey in precisely the opposite direction, travelling from Natal to Walvis Bay, recounting his adventures in his *Travels in the Interior of South Africa* (1868).

But the number of Europeans who arrived on the doorsteps of the poky little mission-houses were very few and very far between.

Nothing that the Boers of Cape Colony had ever learned about South West, from the expedition of Simon van der Stel onwards, encouraged them to consider a trek northward. They would have heard of the tribulations of the missionaries; they would have heard of the fate of the hunter and trader Green, whose little party fought to the last against 800 Ovambo.

By the 1830s, however, the Boers at the Cape were ready to undertake mammoth journeys in another direction—journeys which, like the opening up of the American West, brought a great nation to birth. They were sick of British tutelage and its pettifogging restrictions. The Boer's idea of what he called the *lekker lewe*, the sweet life, was the free and easy life of the frontier. He was beginning to feel that Cape Colony was growing overcrowded. The old-time Boer used to feel he was monstrously hemmed in if he could see a single campfire on the horizon; he felt suffocated, and had to move on. There was plenty of space in Cape Colony: but with every Boer possessing sons who felt that they had a right to a minimum holding of 60,000 acres when they came of age at sixteen, the supply of land would clearly not last for ever. What was more, the British, not satisfied with questioning the system by which the Boers controlled their 36,000 slaves at the Cape, had had the impertinence to introduce a tax of £5 a year on every farm. It was more than flesh and blood could stand. The ox-waggons were brought out and the teams were harnessed up.

ways. The Schmelenhaus at Bethanie, which he built between Lüderitz Bay and Keetmanshoop in 1814, is the oldest existing building in South West.

In 1840 the English missionary societies, as a result of a mutual adjustment of territories, handed over their task to their brothers of the Rhenish Missionary Society. The famous names here include those of Hugo Hahn and Friedrich Kleinschmidt, who married the daughter of Heinrich Schmelen. Hahn worked among the Herero at Gross Barmen near Okahandja, while Kleinschmidt stayed with the Hottentots at Rehoboth. Others soon followed. Scheppmann opened a mission at Rooibank near Swakopmund; Rath opened a fourth at Otjimbingwe. In 1862, while the so-called 'Second Herero–Hottentot War' was in full swing, a Christian mission was started at Gibeon. Slowly the mission-stations became the nuclei of the warring tribes. They were centres of calm and common sense at the heart of the storm-clouds. The Finnish missionaries, entering Ovamboland in 1870, strove to add a further element of stability to the distracted territory. The missionaries of South West had to tread a thorny path. Their mission-houses were burnt down around their ears; they were hounded and humiliated; they succeeded in making only a derisory number of actual converts. Few groups of men have had such great need of faith, and few have ever shown so much of it.

The missionaries, living out their lives in loneliness and obscurity, must have been overjoyed whenever they received a visit from another European, bringing them a breath of a world they once knew. Sometimes they would struggle across the Namib to visit one another; at rare intervals a roving naturalist or hunter would tap at their door. John Barrow and William Burchell were active on the banks of the Orange in the opening years of the century; Sir James Alexander reached the site of the future city of Windhoek in 1837, giving its springs the patriotic but transient title of Queen Adelaide's Baths; and the years 1852–7 witnessed the wanderings of Galton and Andersson, which have already been described. Two other explorers

vleis of the Kuiseb and the Swakop, but after twelve days were forced to set sail again for the south without encountering any Herero.

The Van Reenens and their predecessors had been seeking ivory, copper, cattle, scientific information, or a glimpse of the fabled Bushman capital of Vigiti Magna, whose battlements were said to be studded with precious stones. In 1799 the Reverend William Anderson crossed the Orange River in search of souls.

He came on behalf of the London Missionary Society, which established its first mission station at Warmbad in 1805. He was the first of a tiny band of missionaries who gave their health and often their lives in South West in the nineteenth century. There is no doubt that, in many parts of the world, the missionary movements had an unfortunate influence on native peoples. Too often, instead of mitigating the harshness of imperial rule, they acted as its agents. They instilled a sense of sin and damnation that robbed many peoples of their confidence and energy, and by clumsy and ill-considered actions tore the whole fabric of tribal life apart. But it is only just to state that the sad pageant of history in South West Africa would have been far sadder had it not been for the intervention of the missionaries. Blessed indeed, at that time, were the peacemakers. Coming in with the Hottentot Oorlams, who began to cross the Orange in strength from 1800 onwards, the missionaries quickly made contact with the peoples in the north—the Bergdama, Herero and Ovambo.

At first the heat and burden of the day was born by the London Missionary Society, who shared the work with the Wesleyan Missionary Society. Outstanding names, in addition to that of Anderson himself, include those of the brothers Albrecht; the Reverend B. Shaw and his wife; Edward Cook (dead at thirty-six); William Threlfall (murdered in 1825); and particularly the famous Heinrich Schmelen. Schmelen translated the New Testament into Khoisan and opened up the roads and trackways which later became the regular high-

pardon from the Governor. In the following year Colonel R. J. Gordon, a soldier of mixed Scots and Dutch blood, commander of the troops at the Cape, reached the Great River and gave it the name by which we know it today. He called the river the Orange—not, as is often assumed, on account of its turbid and muddy colour, but in honour of the royal house of Orange. Parting from his companion, the Englishman William Paterson, Colonel Gordon then made a hazardous 500-mile journey up-river, almost as far as the junction of the Orange and the Vaal.

Finally, in the eighteenth century, the three van Reenen brothers, who farmed at the Olifants River, made two extremely determined attempts to penetrate the unexplored interior of South West. Willem van Reenen deserves to be better known, as he made a truly astounding journey. In 1791 he travelled 400 miles further than Hendrik Hop had done thirty years earlier. After surviving the attacks of lions and hostile tribesmen, he appears to have got as far as Rehoboth—only 63 miles from Windhoek. He was nearly 800 miles away from his starting-point. What was more, he sent his companion, Peter Brand, on ahead. Brand travelled north for a further fifteen days with seven Africans. He lost all his oxen: but he succeeded in making contact with the Bergdama. He was the first European to do so, and to enter the country beyond Windhoek. He found that the Bergdama were already beginning to suffer at the hands of the Hottentots. They complained that the latter were raiding their kraals and stealing their stock. The cauldron of the succeeding era was on the boil.

Peter Brand saw nothing of the other Kaffirs, the Ovambo or the Herero, whom he and Willem van Reenen had particularly wanted to meet, having heard stories about their phenomenal herds. There is therefore a strong supposition that the Bergdama must have constituted the spearhead of the Bantu descent into South West. The following year Willem's two brothers and a farmer named Piet Pienaar made another unsuccessful attempt to reach the cattle-rich Herero. They sailed up the coast, landed at Walvis Bay, and sought to move into the interior from this new point of ingress. They explored the

betray him still. In his wild state the Bushman hides from the marauding European or African farmer because he knows that, once he is drawn into conversation with the strangers, he is lost. His curse is that he can never say no. The farmer paints a glowing picture of life on the settlements, and holds out a handful of tobacco. The next thing the Bushman knows is that his wife and children are being lifted over the tailboard of a truck and the whole family is being whirled through a cloud of crimson dust to a life of captivity. The Bushman nation has by no means finished treading its *via dolorosa*; perhaps that road will end only with the death of the last Bushman.

Today in captivity the Bushman still reveals the characteristic noted by Sparrman of escaping into the bush whenever he has the chance. His employers complain that they can never tell when he will abscond. For nine or ten months he will give excellent service, seeming cheerful and contented. Then the spring comes: and one morning the boss finds that his Bushmen, with their wives and babies, have scurried off in the night. There are pools of water on the plains; the yellow buffalo-grass has shot up a foot in the night; the *veldkos* is waxing fat; the buck and the birds are growing sleek and plump and glossy. It is said that the Bushman's hearing is so acute that he can actually hear the grass growing. His instincts are irresistible. The tides in his blood respond to the rustle of grass, the whisper of water, the sigh of the soft damp wind, the belling of the kudu. When the frosts come and the grass withers he will often, fearful of cold and hunger, creep back to his master: but during the spring he feels his ancestral kinship with nature. Even the strollers in St James's Park or Central Park, released for an hour from their offices, can be seen on a fine April day lifting their faces towards the moist emerald buds on the swaying boughs.

In 1778 one of Sparrman's fellow-countrymen, H. J. Wikar, ran away from his desk in the offices of the East India Company at Cape Town and spent two years in the wilds, living the life of a hunter on the banks of the Great River. Like the Bushman, when hard times came he stole back to captivity to ask a free

degree of cheerfulness to the colonist's place of abode. There this luxurious junketting upon meat and fat is exchanged for more moderate portions, consisting for the most part of buttermilk, frumenty and hasty-pudding. However, he soon finds his good living embittered by the maundering and grumbling of his master and mistress. The words *t'guzeri* and *t'gaunatsi*, which, perhaps, are best translated by *young sorcerer* and *imp*, are expressions that he must frequently put up with, and sometimes a few curses and blows into the bargain. So that, having been used to a wandering life, subject to no control, he most sensibly feels the want of his liberty. No wonder then, that he generally endeavours to regain it by making his escape: but what is really a subject for wonder, is that, when one of these poor devils runs away from his service, or more properly bondage, he never takes with him anything that does not belong to him.'

Bribery by belly is an effective gambit. It is surprising how much liberty men will surrender in return for a bit of fillet steak. What is interesting about Sparrman's account is that, although treated to 'a few curses and blows', the Bushmen were not at that time subjected to the campaign of mass murder that was to follow. It was not long delayed. Commandant Nel, who took part in thirty-two murder commandos between 1793 and 1823, once headed an expedition that slaughtered in the coldest of cold blood no less than two hundred Bushmen. The Hottentot and Bantu expeditions were similarly effective. Hunting Bushmen and enslaving their women and children was a sport, more exciting and profitable than hunting wild animals. Shooting a Bushman was not a crime but a public duty, and the pious Boer farmers were men who took their duty seriously.

The greater part of the surviving Bushmen still live in semi-slavery today, either as servants of the European farmer or of the African farmer on the reserves. The Bushman remains the low man on the African totem-pole. The good-nature and candid appetites that betrayed him two hundred years ago

perhaps, the reason, why in a Hottentot's craal or village, the huts are all built exactly alike; and that one meets there with a species of architecture, that does not a little contribute to keep envy from insinuating itself under their roofs. The equal of fortune and happiness in some measure enjoyed by these people, cannot but have a singular effect in preventing their breasts from being disturbed by this baneful passion.'

Clearly Andrew Sparrman subscribed to the belief of the Enlightenment in the Noble Savage: the uncorrupted Child of Nature, living out his life in ease and tranquillity. A citizen of our own century might wish that it ever had been, or ever could be so. But Sparrman does seem to confirm that even as late as the 1770s the social pressures were not extreme; that in spite of their disputes with the Bushmen and their preliminary brushes with the Bantu, the character of the Hottentots had not yet been demoralized and disfigured by the impact of the coming wars with their neighbours. I have not seen it suggested that the eighteenth century formed its view of the Noble Savage because at the date when it first encountered him there were no acute population problems, and most native peoples existed in tolerable peace and isolation. It would be an idea worth investigating. Certainly the view of the Noble Savage, or the noble anything else, disappeared in the surging, grating pressures of the century that followed.

It was Sparrman who gave the earliest account of the enslavement of the Bushmen. He described how the Hottentots and the Cape Colonists rounded them up and coaxed them to forsake the hazards of hunting and gathering *veldkos* for the benefits of a humdrum existence and three square meals a day:

'The prisoners are at first treated by gentle methods; that is, the victors intermix the fairest promises with their threats, and endeavour to shoot some of the larger game for them, such as buffaloes, seacows (hippopotami) and the like. Such agreeable baits, together with a little tobacco, soon induce them, continually cockered and feasted as they are, to go with a tolerable

journey, and because their draught-oxen were totally exhausted, and especially because of the report received of the road ahead that hardly any water was to be found, and that this deficiency would grow with the heat that was increasing daily, they therefore judged it inadvisable to remain here any longer. In order to avoid suffering through lack of water on the return journey, they considered that they ought to return to the Cape as soon as possible. They added that they hoped that the Supreme Authorities, taking into account with what patience, toil and peril they had so far completed the journey, would rest assured that had it been possible they would have travelled further inland with cheerful readiness.'

It was little wonder that the Supreme Authorities concluded, on Hop's return, that there was no point in sending further expeditions into South West Africa; and for the remainder of the eighteenth century the country was visited by no more than four or five adventurous spirits of the calibre of Jacobus Coetsee. Andrew Sparrman, a Swede who had sailed as a naturalist with Captain Cook aboard the *Resolution*, travelled widely in Bushman Land and the Kalahari between 1772 and 1776. He left an entertaining and admirably detailed account of his friendly exchanges with the Hottentots, 'Caffres' and 'Boshiesmen' in his *Voyage to the Cape of Good Hope* (1785). He was one of the most scholarly and observant of early ethnologists.

For the Hottentots in particular Sparrman had a soft spot. In the beautiful eighteenth-century English of the London edition of his *Voyages* he gives the following account:

'Their habitations are as simple as their dress, and equally adapted to the wandering pastoral life they lead in those parts. In fact, they scarcely merit any other name than that of huts; though, perhaps, as spacious and eligible as the tents and dwelling-places of the patriarchs, at least they are sufficient for the Hottentot's wants and desires; who may therefore be considered as a happy man, in being able in this point likewise so easily to satisfy them. The great simplicity of them is,

Jacobus Coetsee, a burgher, farmer and spare-time ivory-hunter of the town of Picketberg, eighty-five miles north of Cape Town. In 1760 (and this, after all, is a bare two centuries ago) he rode out of the pleasant, sleepy, sheltered little town, reached the Copper Mountains, pressed on through the glaring wastes of Bushman Land beyond them, and got to the banks of the Groot Rivier. This he not only forded, but went on another fifty miles to the Hottentot camp at Warmbad, the hot springs that were to become the site of the first white settlement in the country.

The following year this brave and indefatigable adventurer returned to South West as the guide to a full-scale expedition. The expedition had been created as a result of the account of his travels he had rendered to the authorities at the Cape. It was under the command of Hendrik Hop, a *heemrad* of Paarl and an officer in the Cape Burgher Cavalry, and consisted of seventeen Europeans and sixty-eight Hottentots. A lively diary of its progress was kept by Carel Brink, a surveyor and map-maker who accompanied it on the orders of the Council of Policy. It reached Warmbad on October 5 and slowly bumped its way over the dry dusty country northwards, beset by a continual anxiety about water. Coetsee rode on ahead, casting about for watering-places, sometimes absenting himself from the main body for as much as three days. By December 5 they had covered only thirty-three miles—thirty-three miles in sixty days—and were somewhere in the region of the modern town of Karasburg. They had done their best, but they had still not found water, and they were worn out. Hendrik Hop considered the reports of Coetsee and the other scouts, and then called the Europeans together and asked them for their decision. It was to become a familiar sight in South Africa, this group of bearded, weary, travel-stained men in troubled conference among the battered ox-wagons. On December 6 Brink wrote:

'The company unanimously declared that, because their wagons had become completely useless by the long-continued

the prisoners whom they captured. Struggling eastwards across the Great Fish River and confronting the Kaffirs—that was worth it. Everyone knew there were rich lands for farming there. But as for Damaraland, even when you got there the grasslands were reputed to be sour, sparse and waterless.

For 400 years after Diogo Caõ landed at Cape Cross, and 200 years after Jan van Riebeeck landed at the Cape, South West Africa remained a sealed, secret country. The energetic Commander of the Cape, Simon van der Stel, made a remarkable journey to the Copper Mountains of Little Namaqualand in 1685, after Hottentots had brought him specimens of copper ore. With twenty wagons, two field pieces and fifty-seven Europeans, he set out from Cape Town on August 25, crossed the Olifants River, and reached the Copper Mountains on October 21. He was a brisk and efficient organizer: but it took him fifty-eight days to travel 370 miles, or a little over six miles a day. Such was the pace of African travel in those times. The figure also helps to rub in the fact that, once the traveller had left his home base he was, to use a modern word, 'committed'. There was no such thing as a speedy turn round and a quick canter homewards. If you ran into trouble on the trek, you were as good as finished. It was quite common for a column of wagons to vanish into the thin African air as if it had never existed.

Simon van der Stel duly discovered his deposits of copper, and founded the settlement which is now the town of Springbok. But he did not venture the further seventy-five miles that would have brought him to the banks of the Orange River, then called the Groot Rivier. That, after all, would have entailed a further two weeks' journey, to no specific purpose; and possibly he doubted whether the Groot Rivier even existed. Like a sensible Dutchman and a practised trek-leader, he took his wagons, his copper and his two field-guns back to Cape Town.

Another seventy-five years were to pass before the first white man is known to have reached the Groot Rivier and actually crossed over it, into what is now South West Africa. This was

These quarrels, as the Irish say, were private. They were exclusively the concern of Bushman and Hottentot, Damara and Herero. They took place largely in the north of the country, a long way from the formidable frontier of the Orange River.

Nor were the Europeans, until the Germans annexed the not-much-wanted territory in 1884, greatly concerned about events in South West Africa. The inhabitants of Cape Colony were sufficiently occupied by their own disagreements. While Bushman was fighting Hottentot, Briton was fighting Dutchman. Cape Colony was formally ceded to Britain in 1814: but the British, reluctant as ever to lose contact with the sea, clung to Cape Town and discouraged the efforts of the Boer farmers to extend the boundaries of the Colony. Movement eastwards across the Great Fish River, the semi-official boundary between European and Kaffir, was slow and cautious. Bands of adventurers got into Natal, but it was not officially annexed until 1842, and the first declarations of what were to become the Orange Free State and the Transvaal were not made until 1848 and 1850.

The direction of migration from the Cape was always eastward, not northward. The area to the north of Cape Colony was ignored. Up there was nothing but desert—one desert succeeding another. There was the desert of the Roggeveld, followed by the deserts of the Hantamsberg, Little Namaqualand and Bushman Land, followed by the even more terrible deserts of Great Namaqualand and the Kalahari. Desert, always desert, all the way up to the Cunene and the Zambesi. Where was the incentive to trek north? True, there were rumours of grazing-grounds in Damaraland. But to reach Damaraland a man would have to transport his family and cattle 300 miles to the Orange River, through the first succession of deserts, and then another 500 miles, through more deserts, before he reached his goal. He would probably be drowned and his ox-carts swept away in the ordeal of crossing the Orange River. If not, he would be disembowelled and decapitated by the Herero or the Hottentots. He had heard grim accounts of the barbarities committed by Tjamuaha and Jonker Afrikaner on

part of the enemy, nor from any especial cowardice on their own. Stalwart warriors might be seen paralysed with fear at the sound and effects of the muskets with which the Hottentots were armed, and it was no uncommon occurrence for a Damara soldier to stand still in fear and trembling while a little Hottentot, at twenty paces distance, deliberately loaded his weapon and then shot him down. Being ignorant of the construction and management of fire-arms, the Damaras had no idea that guns were harmless after they had been discharged, and therefore allowed themselves to be deliberately shot, while the enemy was really at their mercy.'

Such is the ultimate argument of weaponry, from the crude flint hand-axe to the atom bomb.

The aftermath was horrible. Wood continues:

'If the men suffered death in the field the fate of the women was worse. Whenever the Hottentots came upon a Damara woman, they always robbed her of every ornament, tearing off all her clothing to search for them, and, as the metal rings could not be unclenched without some trouble, they deliberately cut off the hands and feet of the wretched woman, tore off the rings, and left her to live or die as might happen. Strangely enough they often lived, even after undergoing such treatment; and, after stanching the flowing blood by thrusting the stumps of their limbs into the hot sand, some of them contrived to crawl for many miles until they rejoined their friends. For some time after the war, maimed Damara women were often seen, some being without feet, others without hands, and some few without either—these having been the richest.'

Having settled the hash of the *Chou Daman*, the 'filthy blackskinned people', as they called the Bergdama, the Hottentots turned to the major encounter with the Herero. These too they smashed, as I have previously related. It took the genius of a Maherero to raise his people from the dirt and set them on their feet again.

The Land God Made in Anger

most dignified and agreeable peoples on earth, emerged from the long turmoil unscarred. They were the only people of their race who did. There seems to be a virtue in staying out of the limelight and cultivating your own sweet potatoes.

South West Africa, with so much of its surface blanketed by rock and sand, had always been a backwater. No one except a handful of missionaries and explorers paid it any attention during the decades that followed. The Hottentots and the Bantu were able to get on with the serious business of trying to exterminate each other without the outside world either knowing or bothering about what was happening. The Hottentots, aided and in some cases now actually intermarried with their cousins the Bushmen, waged war on the Bantu with the ardour of one cattle-ranching community on another. The issue was deepened by differences in custom and appearance. Between Bantu and Hottentot, in the circumstances of the time, there could be no peace.

In Chapter Two I dealt at some length with the strife between them. The Hottentots were lucky in that the Ovambo and the Okavango stayed in the far north, remaining neutral. This meant that the Hottentots only had to deal with the two Bantu tribes who, shut out by the Ovambo, came filtering south. These two tribes were the Herero and the Bergdama, the latter being more commonly known at that time as the Damara or Dama. The Hottentots, though heavily outnumbered, were an exceptionally courageous and combative breed. They crushed the Bergdama, enslaved them, even imposed the Khoisan tongue and Hottentot customs on them. It must not be thought that the Bergdama lacked bravery, even though they had long had a reputation for being peaceable. They fought as hard as they could, but their assegais and knobkerries were no match for the superior weapons of their adversaries. Wood gives a pathetic picture of their plight:

'In their conflicts with the Hottentots the unfortunate Damaras suffered dreadfully. They were literally cut to pieces by inferior forces, not through any particular valour on the

Africa one of the more grisly epochs of human history. By the century's end the plains of Southern Africa were in places literally piled high with the bleached bones of the dead. Driving gradually down from the north, perhaps from an original homeland 10,000 years earlier in Mesopotamia, the Bantu increased and multiplied and their huge herds increased and multiplied with them. Land hunger dragged them south—although when Jan van Riebeeck was founding Cape Town in 1652 the name of the Kaffirs came to his ears as no more than a thin whisper. The hordes of the Bantu were still hundreds of miles off. Donald Morris puts the position succinctly in *The Washing of the Spears*, his monumental account of the rise and fall of the Zulu nation: 'The Bantu tragedy was that history had offered them a continent, and had given them 10,000 years to fill it; and because they did not know they were in a race, with a continent for a prize, the Bantu lost it. The hare, in a twinkling of a century, had outstripped the tortoise.'

The shock of the meeting between Bantu and European occurred in the 1770s. In distant South West Africa it had taken place between Bantu and Hottentot only a little more than a century earlier, for such arid country was not immediately inviting to the Bantu. South West had been the main theatre of the Hottentot invasion, because the latter were relatively few in number and had been content to amble down the central grasslands of South West towards the Cape: but the Bantu, when finally they woke up and quickened their pace, rolled in a vast jolting mob straight for the juiciest prairies—and these lay due south and south-east. One of the largest Bantu tribes, however, did enter South West Africa. This was the Ovambo. As we have seen in an earlier chapter, they settled without delay and without undue fuss in the territory where they have remained ever since. They had found a place to live and to feed their cattle that appeared to them to be the most fertile and well-watered available; there they settled down, minded their own business, and extended a helping hand whenever necessary to the refugees who took shelter with them from the wars to the south. It is pleasant to record that the Ovambo, one of the

early missionary Heinrich Sching, to the effect that 'Anyone who for any length of time has travelled in the company of Hottentots, and has suffered starvation and thirst with them, has shared their joys and sorrows, will doubtless discern under that rough exterior a good heart, and will learn to appreciate them.'

The troubles of southern Africa did not begin in earnest until the ingress of the second body of invaders. These were the Bantu, whom the Boers called Kaffirs, an Arab word for infidel which the Boers had borrowed from the Portuguese. The Bushmen had to fight against the Bantu or Kaffirs even more fiercely than they had fought against the Hottentots. The Bantu invasion was not a haphazard stroll down the west coast, like the Hottentot invasion, but a tremendous folk-movement that came pressing down along the entire breadth of the continent, east, west and centre. Again the rock-paintings tell the story. This time the tiny Bushman is opposed to hordes of warriors of immense physique and truly gigantic stature. The Kaffirs carry huge cowhide shields and flourish knobkerries and six-foot-long spears with a six-inch steel tip. From their ears dangle monstrous copper ear-rings the size of a Bushman's head; from their scalps rise two prongs of stiffened hair almost as tall and sharp as the horns of a gemsbok. They cover the ground with enormous strides, chest thrust forward, muscles quivering as they raise their arms to hurl their spears bigger than two Bushmen standing on each other's shoulders. The artist has captured the terrifying energy of the Bantu warrior in full cry. It was a sight that daunted not only the Bushman and the Hottentot, but soon brought fear into the souls of the Europeans. Only ninety years ago the stark charge of a Zulu impi overwhelmed a British column at Isandhlwana. Six full companies of the Warwickshires, a thousand strong, died to a man. The Warwickshires killed twice that number of Zulus: but that was the kind of price the Zulus were prepared to pay.

This is not the place to chronicle the clashes between the innumerable branches of the Bantu, and between the Bantu and the European, that made the nineteenth century in southern

an educationalist and the territory's leading historian, has an interesting comment on the character and temperament of the Hottentots, among whom he worked for many years. The Nama of South West, be it noted, remained somewhat purer in race than their brothers who crossed the Orange River to the Cape. The latter became the bastard races of the Griquas, the Namaquas, the Korana, and other tribes with makeshift names that have since largely disappeared from the stage of history. The South West African Nama came together under the leadership of the Khauben tribe, whose own name of *Rode Natie* or Red Nation was extended to cover the allied tribes. The Nama you see today, in the European clothes that they have worn for well over a century, are not greatly different from the Nama whom Dr Vedder first encountered in the 1890s:

'The Nama is above all an emotional being. It is not difficult to rouse him to transports of joy and he who is able to rouse his joyous instincts has won his heart. In this state the Nama is willing, kind and hospitable; he will share his last crumb with his visitor and reveals clearly that he is indeed capable of noble sentiments. In this state, too, he is susceptible to religious impressions and the indiscrimination with which he surrenders to his emotions makes him an easy victim and a ready follower of visionaries. It need scarcely be added that dreams, visions, supernatural voices, etc., are fruitful seed in minds of such psychological structure. As far as rapidity of thought and imagination are concerned, the Nama takes first place in South West, leaving the Herero, Berg Damara and Ovambo, even the so-called Bastards, far behind. On the other hand, under the influence of disagreeable passions the Nama presents an altogether different and almost unrecognizable aspect. He is then sulky, unapproachable, impudent, faithless, unmerciful and cruel. He can no longer be trusted and is capable of quite unsuspectedly evil actions.'

But Dr Vedder endorses, in conclusion, the verdict of the

pearance. Like the Bushmen, they were not negroid but yellow-skinned, with the same bridgeless noses, wide thin lips, diminutive ears, mongoloid eyes and peppercorn hair. They shared the Bushman's slanted eyes, his tendency to steatopygia and to excessive wrinkling in middle-age. Where they differed was in a vital element in their culture: the Hottentots were cattle-drovers, the Bushmen were exclusively hunters. The Hottentot herds ate up the pasture on which the game had lived, and the game was further reduced by Hottentot hunting activities. The Bushmen struck back. Their poisoned arrows wreaked havoc with the Hottentot cattle; there were bitter fights over the possession of the waterholes and the fitful streams. Gradually the Bushmen were forced to take the first backward steps into the Kalahari.

It was a lengthy process, and in many cases the two peoples, being cousins, were able to come to terms with each other. The Hottentot incursion started about a thousand to fifteen hundred years ago, becoming significant about A.D. 1300. The invaders clung to the west coast, and took their time about uncoiling through South West Africa, across the Great River or Orange River, and into the Cape. They were foolish to have dawdled. Only a few years after they reached the south-western tip of the continent, the Europeans arrived. On April 6, 1652, Jan van Riebeeck landed in Table Bay, with orders from the United Chartered East India Company to establish a settlement. That day, honoured today as a holiday throughout South Africa, marks the founding of the Boer nation.

The Boers (the word is the Dutch word for farmer) had no difficulty in driving back the eleven Hottentot tribes who had made the journey to the Cape. The advance guard of the latter thereupon swung east and milled around aimlessly in Cape territory, but beyond the well-policed borders of the Europeans. Eight large tribes of the Hottentots had remained in South West Africa and the upper reaches of the Cape; but as yet there were no extreme tensions. For a century and a half the Hottentots and Boers existed side by side in reasonable amity.

Dr. Heinrich Vedder, one of South West Africa's great men,

ELEVEN
Muskets and Assegais

THE Bushman was doomed from the day when the first Hottentot set foot in the south. His art reflects his brave but losing battle against the newcomer. All over southern Africa there are rock paintings that show him stubbornly contesting the advance of his lofty, heavily-armed adversary. The little naked Bushman, his body striped with war-paint, can be seen facing the onrush of the thickset Hottentot hefting his long spear.

South West Africa was the highway down which the Hottentots gained access to the lush grazing-lands of the Cape. No one knows where the Hottentots, ancestors of the 32,000 modern Nama of South West, originally came from. They were simply the first wave of that endless, leisurely flow of pastoralists into the tempting grasslands of the south. Ironically, they were related to the Bushmen; at some stage there had been contact and mingling between the two peoples. They shared the same language, Khoisan, and were of much the same physical ap-

235

zebra skin belt around the dead man's small body were the horn pots containing his colours.

It is seldom that one is able to date with such cruel finality the ending of a great school of art. The tradition of painting which the Bushman practised had come down from the beginnings of man's time on earth; it had survived—indeed, been nourished by—thirst, hunger, natural cataclysm, and the accidents of a hunting life. It had survived for a hundred thousand years. It could not survive the last two centuries. It could not survive the spears of the Hottentots and Bantu, nor the rifles of our own white grandfathers, the first lethal promptings of the cult of order and progress stirring in their hearts.

The art of the Bushman was innocent and intuitive. It was a simple song, but a joyous one, springing from a source that was undefiled. It was a hymn to creation. Its destruction represents the shattering into even smaller pieces of the mirror of the earth's lost youth.

W. B. Yeats once wrote:

> God guard me from those thoughts men think
> In the mind alone;
> He that sings a lasting song
> Thinks in a marrow-bone

The Bushman artist thought in and by and through the marrowbone. He exercised happily and by natural right the values our own artists have had to struggle so hard to shield and preserve. It is some consolation that tens of thousands of years must pass before the sand and wind can scour the Bushman's record from the rocks.

Wild Honey

the figures were filled in was applied, according to Hugo Obermaier and Herbert Kühn in their *Rock Paintings of South-West Africa*, with a bone spatula, giving the figures their wiry, springy appearance. The effect which the artist aimed at was linear: he wanted to create figures which would be tense, vibrant. In the case of the human figures, he grossly exaggerated his own diminutive stature, presenting hunters that were impossibly tall and proud. Not that his colours, when he employed them, were dull. He had a rich palette at his command. From hematite or limonite he got his reds, yellows, browns, and purples; from kaolin he got his white; from charcoal, his greys and blacks. These pigments he mixed with fat, usually the marrow fat of the eland, whose long shoulder-blade also provided him with material for his bone burins. On occasion, too, he worked the colours with his fingers; and no doubt from time to time he used the technique of other prehistoric painters and used his mouth as a spray-gun.

Nobody now alive has watched a Bushman painter at work. The Bushmen artists lost their skills, letting them lapse as a result of the discouragement and despair of the last two centuries. We have to remember that the beating heart has been torn from the Bushman nation; all that exists today is a timorous wraith. Miss Thomas asked each group of Bushmen she met to paint pictures for her with materials which she provided. The results, though instructive, did not approach the full-blown Bushman art. The latter-day Bushman can do no more than scribble a few hieroglyphs on an ostrich shell or on the bark of a tree.

The last attested example of the high art of the Bushman appears to date from 1869, in which year George Stow watched a Bushman delineate a group of Boers on horseback. It is to Stow that we owe the first copies of Bushman painting, and the first attempt at a definitive study: and it is Stow who has recorded the death of the last Bushman artist. He tells us that the artist was shot down in Basutoland during the course of one of the murder commandos which brought about the systematic extinction of the Bushman nation. Hanging from a

worked with a special delight that is beautifully conveyed by
Laurens Van der Post:

'There the animals of Africa still live as he knew them and as
no European or Bantu artist has yet been able to render them.
They are there not as quarry for his idle bow or food for his
stomach, but as companions in mystery, as fellow pilgrims
travelling on the same perilous spoor between distant life-
giving waters. . . . He alone of all the races of Africa, was so
much of its earth and innermost being that he tried constantly
to glorify it by adoring its stones and decorating its rocks with
painting. We other races went through Africa like locusts
devouring and stripping the land for what we could get out of
it. The Bushman was there solely because he belonged to it.
Accordingly he endeavoured in many ways to express this
feeling of belonging, which is love, but the greatest of them was
in the manner of his painting.'

Bushman art is an art of action, of movement. Erwin
Christensen points out in his *Primitive Art* that the Bushmen
painters were obsessed with hunting, dancing, fighting, not
with quiet domestic scenes or the representation of inanimate
nature. They painted animals as they painted human beings,
noting in an extraordinary way the character of each individual
beast, its personal quirks and habits. Their technique was not at
all abstract or formalized but sharply realistic and anecdotal.
Looking at the scenes where the huntsmen run to earth the
valiant rhinoceros or the princely gemsbok, you feel you are
seeing a record of the actual death of an actual animal, that
the event took place not far from the actual kopje where
the painting was executed, and that the figures of the huntsmen crowding round the dying animal are portraits of
actual men, behaving as they behaved on that particular
occasion.

The sharpness of the impression is heightened by the fact that
in most cases the outlines are not painted but incised, often to a
depth of a full inch. This was not a brush art: it was the art of
the bone burin or the stone chisel. Even the paint with which

of his dreams. The Bushmen are great singers, dancers and instrumentalists. They will dance the night away around their fires to the accompaniment of gourds and rattles; they love to comfort themselves with intricate and melancholy part-songs; they will put their hunting-bows on an empty tsama melon, to give it resonance, and tap out a delicate string-music on the sisal cord. They possess an astonishingly wide oral literature, a characteristic blend of the humorous and the tragic, of blistering topicality and the shadowy half-world of the gods and daemons who to the Bushmen are more real than reality. Their stories, like their inventors, are mischievous, witty, and spiced with a gentle malice. They contain the pith and seed of the later epics—Gilgamesh, Wenamun, the *Iliad* and the *Aeneid*—and tell of arduous and incredible journeys and adventures. They tell how a Bushman discovered the far-off land inhabited by the People with No Knees, who sleep propped up against the trunks of *mopani* trees; how a Bushman discovered that the sun was made of good red meat—and ate it; how a Bushman climbed down a waterhole to visit the paradise beneath the earth, where roam the silver herds of buck, and where the lakes of cool sweet water stretch clear away to the horizon....

But it was as a painter and graver, above all, that the Bushman revealed himself and showed his genius. I have explained how I was unfortunate enough to miss the monumental frieze that is the hidden glory of the Brandberg; but elsewhere I was able to feast my eyes on many prime examples of their art. Although different in style and content, the work of the Bushmen of Southern Africa has been compared in its sweep and intensity with that of the Aurignacian hunters of Altamira and the Magdalenian huntsmen of Lascaux. This is, of course, the highest praise. The Bushman's rendering of the animals and birds he hunted is so subtle, so animated, that it is probable that he drew them from life. Most of the sites of Bushmen paintings are situated high up the mountainside, on outbreaks and overhangs of dolerite, as though he stood there and sketched on the stone the creatures that grazed in the valley below him. He

up. Ants and their eggs ('Bushman rice'), insect larvae, snakes and scorpions, rats and field mice, lizards, frogs and locusts—all are served up in a multitude of ways: boiled, baked, broiled, or roasted. But the delicacy which the Bushman most relishes is wild honey. The bees of the Kalahari are remarkable for their virulence when disturbed, yet to secure their combs the Bushmen will climb a hundred feet into the branches of a tree to smoke them out of their hollows, often breaking a limb or even his neck to do so.

Water is the chief necessity, and for lack of it an entire Bushman family will frequently perish during the summer months. Some Bushmen groups are fortunate in that they possess waterholes on their hereditary territories; but most must rely on a plentiful supply of the wild melon. Spare water is carried in ostrich-shell containers, plugged with grass, which can be buried out of the hot sun deep under the sand. A Bushman can literally smell out water, and sometimes if he is in dire straits he will dig up another man's cache or put down a reed tube, pierce the shells, and draw off the water without disturbing the overlying sand. However, this is considered not merely a contemptible but a criminal act, meriting complete social ostracism. A valuable source of water is the first stomach or rumen in which wild animals such as the gemsbok store up their own spare supply of water; thus hunting furnishes the Bushman with drink as well as meat.

They are cunning and resourceful, the First People. They show us how our forefathers survived in the wilderness, how they fed themselves, and how they laid the foundation of such essential skills as a knowledge of medicine. The Bushman know how to compound ointments from insects and reptiles, and how to make poultices from the *duwweltje* and other plants. I was told of an ingenious manner of suturing wounds by allowing a number of giant red flesh-eating ants to bite the lips of the wound; the ants' bodies are then torn off, leaving the ants' jaws rigid in death to serve as clamps.

The Bushmen also helped to lay the foundations of the arts, that wild honey of man's hard existence, the fragile containers

Wild Honey

They are capable of fantastic feats of eating. Carel Birkby recorded in 1936 in his *Thirstland Treks* that he had heard of cases where a single Bushman had gorged a hundred pounds of meat at a sitting. However, it ought to be borne in mind that Bushmen do not gorge from simple greed: they *have* to eat an animal at one session, before in that fearful heat it begins to decompose.

Meat is supplemented by *veldkos* or 'field food', of which they have an extraordinary knowledge. The Kalahari supplies these foods in abundance in the brief rainy season, between December and March; and their existence has to be detected and marked so that the family can survive the terrible Kalahari summer, when the temperature rises to 120° Fahrenheit, and the equally terrible cold season, when the temperature drops night after night below freezing. The Kalahari is not a desert in the sense of the Namib or the Sahara: its blood-red, brick-red, jeweller's-rouge-red earth is covered with parched yellow grass and little low stunted dried-up trees. It is a vast empty undulating plain almost devoid of hills or scarps, where the landmarks are an occasional grove of mangetti or *n'tambuti* trees and the lonely eminences of the baobabs. The baobab is the Bushman's fixed mark, a mountain or a whole grove of trees in itself, a pink beacon rising 200 feet high and with a girth of thirty feet. Elizabeth Marshal Thomas has recorded that the Bushmen possess a truly remarkable sense of location; they can tell exactly where they are at any given moment, and find their way across the seemingly featureless desert with complete confidence. Thus a woman out gathering *veldkos* will note the position of a buried root, and when she passes that way the following year she will go to it unerringly and dig it up.

Tsi roots and *ointjie* bulbs are two of the delicacies for which a Bushman woman, accompanied by her children will grub around with the aid of her sharpened digging-stick. She will gather nuts, berries, tubers, tree gums, wild figs, above all the *tsama* melon and the fruit of the spiky *naras* plant. These she throws into the fold of her *kaross* or pops into the two skin bags which she invariably carries with her. From the exiguous resources of the desert a whole rich *à la carte* menu is conjured

of the Bushmen people is the family, never consisting of more than twenty persons, and they seldom bother to erect permanent dwellings. Occasionally the Bushman *werf* or dwelling-site will consist of a few flimsy *scherms* or shelters built of grass and interwoven branches; but usually the family will do no more than hang up its scanty possessions in the boughs of a tree, scooping out individual sleeping-pits around the trunk and close to the central hearth. It is none the less interesting to note that, even if they seldom build huts, the Bushmen obey the fundamental territorial instinct of human beings, recently studied by Robert Ardrey in a stimulating book, by carefully marking out the corners of each imaginary hut with twigs.

Bushmen families roam unceasingly from one spring, hunting-field or food-patch to the next. The men are magnificent huntsmen, and when they come up with an animal they combine together in a well-ordered team to club it, hamstring it or shoot it with one of their poisoned arrows. Incredibly fleet of foot, they can keep pace in the heat of the day with a bounding duiker or herd of steenbok, and will run beside a wounded animal for hours or even days until it drops and dies. The Kung in particular are noted meat-eaters and hunt with marvellous cunning; they tip the detachable heads of their reed or wooden arrows with barbs of tin or wire, which they trade with farmers for pelts, rather than with the customary reed or bone. They do not shoot to kill outright, but to wound, and let the poisoned arrowhead break off and do its work. All Bushmen anoint the upper part of the shaft of their arrows with a deadly poison; they never anoint the actual tip, because of the danger of an accidental scratch, especially to children. The Kalahari Bushmen extract the poison from snakes, spiders, the bulbs of certain euphorbias and amarylli, and the grub of the Cladocera beetle, *Comiphora dinteri*, or the grub of another beetle known as *Diamphidia simplex*; while the tribesmen farther south in Namaqualand also use the juice of the cactus known as the Bushman's Candle, *Candelabra euphorbia*. When the animal is killed and brought back to camp, they eat every part of it but the hide and tail—eyes, ears, even the hard gristle that lines the nostrils.

'This remarkable protruberance, which shakes like a jelly at every movement of the body, is not soft as might be imagined, but firm and hard. Mr Christie, who is rather above the middle size, tells us that he has sometimes stood upon it without being supported by any other part of the person. This curious development does not cause the least inconvenience, and the women find it rather useful as affording a support whenever they wish to carry an infant.'

Two other unusual physical features of the Bushmen are the permanently half-erect penis of the men, and the flap of flesh known as the *tablier Egyptien* that covers the genitals of the women. Their most distinctive physical feature, however, is their extreme slenderness, grace and sprightliness. They lack entirely the squat and clumsy air of the Hottentot, and give an impression of creatures of the utmost lightness and delicacy. Their limbs and faces are sharp and vivid.

The externals of the lives of these elusive people are simple. Their enemies, seeking to justify their own barbarity, stigmatized them as dirty, slovenly and uncouth. Nothing could be further from the truth. Their possessions are as neat and trim as their owners, though kept as few and light as possible, as might be expected in view of the fact that Bushmen must travel many hundreds of miles each year in search of food and water. Both men and women wear a plain leather apron, and the costume is completed by a skin cloak or *kaross*. However, archaeologists have shown that the desire for adornment is almost as old as the Australopithecines themselves, and the women set off their appearance with a profusion of bangles, necklaces and elaborate pendant hair ornaments made from ostrich shell, amber wood, and pieces of gourd, strung together on a tough cord which the Bushmen manufacture from wild sisal. Around their necks hangs a box consisting of the empty shell of a baby tortoise, containing scented animal fat, and they anoint their limbs with the powdered leaves of the graceful *n'tambuti* tree, which gives off a haunting and lingering scent.

Their living-arrangements are equally simple. The basic unit

their buttocks, which then stick out like shelves. They share this characteristic, called steatopygia, with their cousins the Hottentots; but in the Bushmen it is not so exaggerated, and disappears entirely in normal seasons, leaving the buttocks smooth and flat.

In connection with steatopygia, I cannot resist quoting once more from the irrepressible Francis Galton, who described a 'Hottentot *Venus*' he encountered among the household of the missionary Hahn:

'I was perfectly aghast at her development, and made inquiries upon that delicate point as far as I dared. The result is, that I believe Mrs Petrus to be the lady who ranks second among all the Hottentots for the beautiful outline that her back affords, Jonker Afrikaner's wife ranking as the first; the latter, however, was slightly *passée*, while Mrs Petrus was in full *embonpoint*. As a scientific man, I was exceedingly anxious to obtain accurate measurement of her shape; but there was a difficulty in doing this. I did not know a word of Hottentot, and could never, therefore, explain to the lady what the object of my foot-rule could be; and I really dared not ask my worthy missionary host to interpret for me. I therefore felt in a dilemma as I gazed at her form, that gift of bounteous nature to this favoured race, which no mantua-maker, with all her crinoline and stuffing, can do otherwise than humbly imitate. As I was considering the problem, the object of my admiration was standing under a tree, turning herself about to all points of the compass, as ladies who wish to be admired usually do. Of a sudden my eye fell upon my sextant; a bright thought struck me, and I took a series of observations upon her figure in every direction, up and down, crossways, diagonally, and so forth, and I registered them carefully upon an outline drawing for fear of any mistake. This being done, I boldly pulled out my measuring tape, and measured the distance from where I was to the place she stood, and, having thus obtained both base and angles, I worked out the result by trigonometry and logarithms.'

J. G. Wood also has a comment on steatopygia:

an unusually Harmless People. Authorities are agreed that they lived at peace with themselves and the world around them, and that it was their contact with other, hostile peoples which at last prompted them to acts of uncharacteristic brutality.

Today they can be divided into a number of groups distinguished by differences in language—that extraordinary Bushman language that consists of clicks, wheezes and explosions that together constitute a kind of oral assault and battery. In the heart of the Kalahari live the Naron and Ko Bushmen; then, closer to its western edge, sometimes spilling over into South West, live the Gikwe Bushmen, whose territory extends right across the desert to the eastern frontier of Botswana. In the north, between Namutoni and Lake Ngami, taking in the many salt-pans of the north-east corner of South West Africa, live the Kung Bushmen. Other groups in South West include the seldom-seen River Bushmen, who paddle their dug-out *makorros* on the Okavango, and the so-called Saan people. The latter are an ancient stock, taller and darker than the normal Bushmen, who linger on in a small tribe called the Heikom, whose home is situated on the northern fringes of the Etosha Pan. Fourie, writing forty years ago, divided the Bushmen into seven groups, belonging to two main branches, the Ngami Bushmen and the Kaukau Bushmen. He also listed five tribes that once existed elsewhere in South West at one time, but which had already become extinct.

The Bushmen, as Kroeber said, are of distinctive race. The women are under five feet in height, and their menfolk only a few inches taller. Their skins have the sheen and colour of a beautiful fine gold, darkened in the heat and dust of summer to a dull copper. Their hair is crisped and tightly curled, and has the strange property of becoming so dry and brittle that it need not be cut but can be broken off. Their faces, smooth in youth but volcanically wrinkled and puckered in age, are flat and curiously Chinese in character, an appearance heightened by the epicanthic or Mongoloid fold of flesh across the inner eye. They tend to have pot-bellies, and in the summer season when they gorge themselves with food they have the capacity to store fat in

12 The Windhoek kudu

11 Boundary of the *Sperrgebiet*

A diamond prospector's claim in the Namib

The stone tools he made, and still makes today, have affinities with the prehistoric cultures which archaeologists call the Wilton and Smithfield cultures, after the sites where they were first identified. The two cultures are distributed over enormous areas of Southern Africa. Bushman-type tools are also very closely identified with the Magosian culture, which extends from the north of South West Africa, down through the Orange Free State into Basutoland (now Lesotho) and Natal. The past and present domains of the Bushman can therefore be shown to overlap.

A resemblance between the Boskop skull and a skull found at Singa on the Blue Nile in the Sudan has led some scholars to suppose that the first home of the Bushman race was in north Africa, and that they set the pattern for later races by drifting gradually down the empty continent until they reached the south. Alleged similarities between the Bushman language and the Hamitic languages of the upper Nile have also been brought forward to support the theory; and we have seen that the Abbé Breuil believed that Bushman art had been executed by men in contact with Ancient Egypt and the eastern Mediterranean. Physical connections have also been adduced between the Bushmen and the Congo pygmies. None of these theories, however, has been accepted, and the likelihood remains that the Bushmen, alone among the peoples of Africa, were born and bred in the surroundings that were to witness their later torment and decline.

In their Golden Age they roamed at will over the open country from the Congo to the Cape. The land was theirs. They neither sowed crops nor kept cattle. They had no need to. They wandered at will through a landscape teeming with wildebeest, hartebeest, eland, kudu, boar, giraffe, elephant, zebra, gemsbok, antelope, and every kind of bird and fish. Lacking gunpowder, they were unable to destroy the wild life in an insensate way; nor would they have wished to. Their relationship with brute creation was too intimate for them to kill indiscriminately; this was at the dawn of the world, when men and beasts were brothers. For the most part they were indeed

Wild Honey

and a tattered pair of pants. All their ancient virtues, their loyalty, gaiety, courage, skill and intelligence, have in the end availed them nothing.

It is incredible to reflect that in all probability they and their ancestors have occupied the same territory continuously for 25 million years. They are the oldest sitting tenants on earth. The rest of us are usurpers of other peoples' homelands, our usurpation legitimized by nothing more than the passage of time: but the Bushman's right to southern Africa is sovereign. It seems more than possible that they are the lineal descendants of man's proto-human forbears, who were cradled in Bushman country. Twenty-five million years ago, in the Oligocene era, little ape-like creatures like *Parapithecus* and *Propliopithecus* were scampering about in southern Africa. Five million years later, in the Miocene era, they were succeeded by the still primitive but now genuine ape *Proconsul* and its collaterals, who spread from their homeland in central Africa throughout the whole of the old World. And finally, in the Pliocene era, the great race of the Australopithecines made their appearance in Bushman territory, and found their way eventually as far afield as northern Europe.

The Australopithecines were apes, but they were certainly evolving in the direction of men. They left the forests to live in the open, among the dolomite hills and peripheral grasslands of the Transvaal and Botswana. They were given their present name by Dr Raymond Dart, who found the first skull of the type at Taungs in South Africa, in 1925; later he found material of a similar type elsewhere in the Transvaal, at Sterkfontein and Kromdraai. Twelve years earlier fossil deposits in the Transvaal had also yielded a skull from Boskop that had manifestly belonged to a direct ancestor of the Bushman. The Boskop skull can be dated to the Middle Stone Age in Africa, that is to say 10,000 to 50,000 years ago, corresponding to the Upper Stone Age in Europe. Thus the Bushman's title-deeds to southern Africa, even as represented by this late skull, are of a very respectable antiquity. The original size of his kingdom can be traced in addition by the wide distribution of his handicrafts.

South West are divided by one of those absurd straight lines, with quaint cranks and angles, which I mentioned in the last chapter. But the Kalahari takes no cognizance of straight lines.

It is time, now that I have described the different ethnic groups of the country, together with their numbers and distribution, to describe a little more of its history. And this history must start with the Bushmen. Indeed, not only the history of South West Africa, but the history of the whole continent, the history of the world itself, might be said to begin with the Bushmen. Laurens Van der Post, in his *Lost World of the Kalahari*, calls them by the felicitous and respectful name of 'the First People'.

They are a unique folk. A. L. Kroeber speaks of them as 'one of the very few peoples on earth possessing at the same time distinctive race, distinctive speech, and a distinctive culture'. They are the descendants of one of the basic stocks—probably *the* basic stock—of mankind. They represent the human original. And now, like superannuated members of the household, they have been relegated to the attic or the back-yard. Contrary to popular superstition, they never cast off their old folk to starve and die: but this is precisely what the other races, white and black alike, have done to the Harmless People. There is something sinister and alarming in the spectacle of their long martyrdom. Sometimes it would seem—the Tibetans are another case in point—that a people's inoffensiveness and contentment are the very things that arouse the fury of its neighbours. Only the pathetic remnant of the once numerous Bushman nation now survive, and fewer still live in true Bushman style. Of the 12,000 to 14,000 Bushmen listed in the latest returns as living in South West, only 4,000 appear to be following the way of life of their forefathers. The rest are farm workers or domestic servants. You can see one or two of them on most of the farms or factory establishments in the country—tiny, wizened, furtive, good-humoured creatures, frail and sad and diminutive as captive Hobbits. They are as highly valued as servants as they are grossly ill-treated and underpaid; for a year's work they might get a handful of tobacco, half a crown, an old shirt,

TEN
Wild Honey

THERE is a people in South West which has been more unlucky than the Herero, Nama or Bergdama. The American anthropologist Elizabeth Marshall Thomas wrote a book about them which has become a minor classic, and which she called by the name they call themselves: *The Harmless People*. It could have been called *The Luckless People*.

If you stand on the ramparts of Namutoni and face towards the east, you are looking towards their homeland. But you must look beyond Tsumeb, beyond Grootfontein, beyond the concrete blockhouses of SWANLA, beyond the reserves of Waterberg, Epikuro and Otjituo. You must travel in imagination 500 miles to Lake Ngami and Makarikari Pan, heartland of the territory which is all that remains—because nobody else yet wants it—to the Bushman nation. They have been pushed back during the course of the last 300 years into the Kalahari desert, which occupies almost the whole of Botswana and the entire north-eastern region of South West Africa. Botswana and

pendence, nationhood, or at least a decent way of life, without undergoing the bloody, wasteful and consuming struggles taking place to north and north-east of it. Sometimes it may be necessary for a nation to wage a war to gain its nationhood. Nations, like people, tend to value only what they have had to win for themselves. But, in the case of South West, surely the price in blood has already been paid.

South West deserves a smooth passage to acceptable status and enlightened government. More than most countries in a troubled continent, it has long been due for a slice of luck.

The Wa-benz and Others

Africa, of all places, in such terms. Everywhere one looks, Africa is in chaos. The democratic regimes are going down one after the other. Bloodshed is widespread. No one would deny that the difficulties facing the African leaders are formidable. Somehow the blood-letting must be halted. Then the Wa-Benz must be prised loose and more suitable forms of government introduced. It is understandable that democracy on the Westminster Model has been rejected: after all, democracy on the Westminster Model has demonstrated its drawbacks even in Great Britain. This may be painful to our *amour propre*, but it has happened because democracy on that pattern neither chimes with the character nor fulfils the needs of the new African nations.

The whole problem is immensely complicated by the insanity of the present boundaries of almost every state in the continent. These boundaries are one more handicap bequeathed to Africa by the former colonial powers. England, France, Germany, Italy, Spain, Portugal—the Europeans merely drew a series of straight lines on the map. They drew them to suit themselves and their own interests. Tribal and linguistic areas were cut down the middle, whole peoples and nations arbitrarily and irrationally sundered. The mischief will take generations to undo. It has taken Europe a thousand years of warfare to settle into its present boundaries: and even now many of these boundaries are only temporary and approximate. It seems hard that Africa too has been condemned to many years of warfare because a set of lines was drawn on the map in a matter of minutes at the Berlin Conference of 1878.

Nevertheless, no one who has lived or travelled in Africa has been untouched by its splendour, its grandeur. No one who has been there will think it altogether fantastic to suggest that in this distracted continent there lies something that we need: something more valuable than the diamonds, copper, zinc and vanadium we take from it. They will not think it fanciful to suggest that some of the qualities of the old world should be brought in to redress the balance of the new.

As for South West Africa, I hope that it can reach inde-

'do good' to their subjects and allow them to be free at the same time. The administrators of the Welfare State in Britain, for example, have seen that they cannot look after a man and simultaneously let him wander around loose. It is too untidy.

The child of nature inside us, in Africa as elsewhere—even in Socialist Britain—fights hard to retain his freedom in face of an arrogant and complacent bureaucracy. The struggle for independence on the part of an emergent nation often implies a recognition that its character and self-respect are threatened by the onset of 'civilization'. The struggle represents a people's attempt to reaffirm an older and more dignified mode of life, moulded over the ages, and to repudiate the more deadening aspects of the 'civilizing' mission. The struggle for nationhood can be a struggle to retain one's own soul.

Frequently, of course, the battle for independence can degenerate into nothing more than a bid for power on the part of a band of crooks and demagogues, led by some gifted gangster, who use the slogans of freedom, equality and prosperity to further their own ends. This is a characteristic of the present phase of African history. But can there be some reason to hope that in a century or two—and what is a century to Africa?—this phase will pass? A future generation of leaders may find a way to adopt the more positive elements of industrialization without permitting it to dry up their spiritual roots and cut them off from their past, as it did in Europe. Perhaps they will be able to avoid the cultural impoverishment that so often accompanies the 'civilizing' process. With luck they may be able to spare the body of Africa the leprous rash of a thousand Dagenhams, Coventries, Sheffields and Wolverhamptons. If the old and complex personality of Africa succumbs in turn to the mechanizing mania, where will the battered and humiliated soul of man find succour and refreshment? In a sense Africa represents the last chance of the human spirit, one of its few remaining opportunities of returning to the place whence it came, to retrace its journey to a point before the wrong path was taken, to seek out some new point of departure.

It may appear visionary, even profoundly naive, to talk of

The Wa-benz and Others

At the present moment Africans are dazzled by our cars, jet-planes, telephones, air-conditioners, washing-machines, television-sets—all the useful adjuncts to living that we are apt to mistake for living itself. It would be foolish to belittle these products of human ingenuity, or to indulge in facile criticisms of 'materialist society'. These things were invented for our use, and use them we should. In particular we should applaud the advances of modern medicine, especially when we recall the hideous catalogue of African maladies recited by Albert Schweitzer in his *On the Edge of the Primeval Forest*. Nevertheless we should bear in mind that these mechanical gadgets and medical advances of ours are apt to prove costly in more ways than one. They can carry a spiritual as well as a financial price-tag. We are increasingly aware that they can exact a heavy toll in terms of social and psychic well-being. Uncritical worship of our western technology—what Gerald Sykes calls 'technolatry'—can be vulgar, shallow, and dangerous. In Africa it has already brought to birth a brand-new tribe called the *Wa-Benz*—'The People of the Mercedes-Benz'. The term was invented to describe the corrupt ministers of Tanzania, where the breed is particularly numerous: but it has already engendered progeny throughout the entire continent.

Imperialism used to come in the frank and simple guise of direct colonial rule: now it comes in the guise of remote economic domination. In both guises it demands the imposition of standardization and uniformity. Standardization, after all, is the hallmark of 'civilization'. Without standardization there can be no efficient industry. You standardize the size of nuts, bolts and screws. You standardize doors and window-frames and houses. Ultimately you standardize people. 'Civilization' increasingly demands the sacrifice of individuality. Even civilized leisure and civilized pleasure tend to become standardized. As Schweitzer put it with regard to the African: 'The child of nature becomes a steady worker only so far as he ceases to be free and becomes unfree.' The citizens of westernized states passed this particular point long ago. The rulers of civilized modern countries have increasingly realized that they cannot

On the other hand, if the maintenance of order implies the steady increase of westernization, is that altogether what one wants? Is that really what we desire for Africa? Do we wish that wild and noble continent to be filled with little Sheffields, Liverpools, Wigans, Newports, Crewes, Manchesters and Swindons? With Chicagos and Pittsburghs? Essens and Dortmunds? Is that what life is about? Is a man, especially an African, the inhabitant of a continent which is the great mother of us all, to finish as no more than a lathe-operator, a trades-unionist, a social-security number? Must we duplicate in Africa the worst features of an industrial society that we ourselves find increasingly unsatisfying and oppressive? 'I have endeavoured,' wrote Freud in his *Civilization and its Discontents*, 'to guard myself against the enthusiastic partiality which believes our civilization to be the most precious thing we possess or could acquire, and thinks it must inevitably lead us to undreamt-of-heights of perfection. I can at any rate listen without taking umbrage to those critics who aver that when one surveys the aims of civilization and the means it employs, one is bound to conclude that the whole thing is not worth the effort and that in the end it can only produce a state of things which no individual will be able to bear.'

As Gerald Sykes puts it in his recent book, *The Cool Millennium*: 'Man rushes first to be saved *by* technology, and then to be saved *from* it'. This is how I felt when I visited Tsumeb and later Oranjemund. There must be another and a better way to live. Perhaps the Africans will help us, in the years ahead, to discover what that way is: we have always suspected that deep inside itself this most venerable of continents contained some ancestral germ of wisdom. At a deeper level than the cruelty and the suffering, the heart of Africa may perhaps be made to yield us a balm, an unction. Medicinal remedies often derive from the unlikeliest of sources. Freud believed that 'many systems of civilization—or epochs of it—or possibly even the whole of humanity—have become "neurotic" under the pressure of civilizing trends'. Perhaps the Africans will assist us in finding if not a cure, at least a palliative for that alarming neurosis.

community, then it may well prove a first step towards a more settled future for the territory. When each ethnic group has a plot of land that it can call its own, and to which its title is clearly established, some of the ancestral tensions which are a legacy from the centuries of habitual and distracted wandering may lose a measure of their virulence. One might have to face the fact that, in South West Africa as elsewhere, it may be many centuries, if ever, before human groups of different race, colour and background can be persuaded to live in amity with one another. In the meantime they might really be much better off if they were made to live apart.

Hypocrite lecteur, mon semblable, mon frère. How you view these matters is your own affair. For my own part, I long ago gave up the business of being an oracle. I have become highly distrustful of people or nations who rush about the world trying to do good. The Americans (they say) have been doing good in South-east Asia. Perhaps they would have been better occupied cultivating their own back garden. I agree with Doctor Relling, in Ibsen's *The Wild Duck*. He was the diagnostician of that most horrid of all diseases, 'probity fever'. He has the last word in the play, after the disaster has occurred. 'Oh, life wouldn't really be so bad,' he declares, 'if we could only get rid of those infernal duns who keep pestering us poor folk with their claims of *the ideal*. . . .'

Today, in the heart of Africa, the same obscure and terrible happenings are taking place as when Mister Kurtz came down the river, eighty years ago. When Gide saw Belgian rule in the Congo, he wrote on his return to Europe that: 'Henceforth an immense lamentation dwells in me.' Is it likely that the lamentations of this most compassionate of men would have been lessened had he been able to return to the Congo at any time since its 'independence'? Are there in fact certain cases in which one has to say with Goethe that one prefers an injustice to disorder? Would one want to hazard even the limited freedom which the peoples of South West Africa possess at the present time for the torture and massacre of the Congo?

white might be eased if the other countries of the world, including some that ought to know better, could resist visiting their individual and collective guilt on South Africa and stop making her the moral scapegoat for their own shortcomings.

The Bantustan concept, open to many objections though it is, is at least a vast improvement on the rigid concept of apartheid. What else can one hope for, in an imperfect and slow-moving world? As I said earlier, all that a sensible man can hope for is that, during the continuous crisis which constitutes human history, man's natural antagonisms may be at least in some degree mitigated. If Bantustans can help to do this in South Africa and South West Africa, then they are well worth entertaining. It is also worth noting that the theory is not an abomination specially created by the South Africans: at various times it has worked, and worked reasonably well—American Indian Reservations excepted—elsewhere in the world. Cecil Rhodes proposed a not unenlightened form of it in his Africa Act. The Germans, as we saw, were already experimenting with the possibility of organizing reserves in South West Africa in 1902, mainly with the object of preventing the Herero and the Hottentots from tearing one another to pieces. If they had succeeded, some of the tragedy of the Herero Rising might have been softened.

Since 1923, when the South African government began the task of establishing the reserves, the ethnic groups of South West Africa, described by one writer as the most heterogeneous population of any country in the world, have lived ever since in more or less unbroken peace with themselves and their neighbours. To keep the peace in any part of the African continent for forty years, albeit in a somewhat miserable way, is an incontestable achievement. In 1964 the South African government took a further step. Acting on the recommendations of the Odendaal Commission, it tabled a motion proposing the setting up of ten different African 'homelands'. If the partitions are effected intelligently and equitably, and if they do not turn out—as is so often the case with partitions—to be a camouflaged land-grab on behalf of an already dominant section of the

crucifixion of the American Indian, from the days of such mindless brutes as Colonel Hatch and General Carleton to the present time, is well-documented. Of such incidents as the transportation to Florida prison-camps of the Arizona Apaches even such a clement and judicious historian as C. L. Sonnichsen has been moved to write, in his *The Mescalero Apaches*: 'A more disgraceful display of callousness and bad faith cannot be found in our annals, and white Americans still remember it with shame and regret.' There were hundreds of such incidents. Most of them took place within living memory. It would therefore seem reasonable to expect the Americans to allow a decent interval—say, of several centuries—to elapse before seeking to reproach the South Africans or any similar people with abusing the rights of their coloured citizens.

It is not my intention, as I have said, to offer solutions to the problems which face the white South Africans. I am not qualified to do so. The issues are too cloudy and complex. Nor do I share the puerile modern faith in the efficacy of what is called 'thinking things through', as though the process of arriving at some cheery conclusion about some difficult problem would thereupon make it vanish in some magical manner. The problems of South Africa are ancient ones. As Churchill told the House of Commons in 1907: 'I would ask the House to remember for one moment the figures of the South African census. In the United States the proportion of white men to natives is eight to one, and even there I believe there is something sometimes approaching to racial difficulties; but in South Africa the proportion is one white man to five natives. The House must remember these things in order to appreciate how the colonists feel towards that ever-swelling sea of dark humanity upon which they, with all they hate and all they love, float somewhat uneasily.' Not an easy situation: hard then, and hard now. The proportion of white man to black man still remains steady at one to five. All I would suggest is that, if the Africans deserve our sympathy, then the white South Africans deserve a little sympathy too. And it seems to me that a little of the pressure down there on both black and

posals are automatically greeted with howls of fury, has already brought discredit on this policy. Yet it is worth noting that the present South African government was by no means the first to introduce the concept, even in their own country. The English, after introducing the system of pass laws into the Cape as early as 1819, moved the Natal Kaffirs bodily into eight well-demarcated reserves between 1845 and 1850. They did this with the entirely laudable intention of protecting the Kaffirs from the rapacity of the white man.

Nor is the South African record in establishing and administering the policy of reservations and separate areas unworthy of being compared with the record of the United States: for what, after all, are the Indian Reservations but areas of apartheid or Bantustans? The Americans, having successfully encompassed the deliberate and almost total extermination of the original owners of North America, did not even play fair with the derisory amount of land which they grudgingly allotted to the broken survivors. Year by year the Reservations were whittled away. Between the General Allotment Act of 1887 and the Indian Reorganization Act of 1934 the land owned by the remnant of the North American Indians shrank from 137 million acres to under 48 million, and most of what remained consisted of desert and semi-desert. As a great American, Indian Commissioner John Collier, put it as late as 1935: 'The historic policy: That Indian property must pass to whites; that Indian organization must be repressed and prevented; that Indian family life must be dismembered; that Indian cultures must be killed; and that Indians as a race must die.' Apartheid with a vengeance, and with a savagery with which it has never been applied in South Africa. In the year in which Collier wrote, only 375 Indian students were receiving high school or college education throughout the entire United States. It took such belated measures as the Soil Conservation Program, the Game Co-ordination Act and the Indian Arts and Crafts Act to improve the picture a little: but even today the long martyrdom of the red man is not at an end, as one can see from the passing of Public Law 280 during the Eisenhower Administration. The

The Wa-benz and Others

A man would have to be a skunk if, during a tour of South Africa and South West Africa, he were not affronted by those universal signs of '*Non-Europeans Only—Slegs vir nie-Blankes*'. The separation between white and non-white is as rigorously enforced as the Jim Crow regulations in America a few years ago. It makes you feel ashamed when another man, even if he happens to be the dirtiest, lousiest, most pox-ridden man in the world, is not allowed to ride on the same bus with you, walk through the same door, buy a postage-stamp at the same counter, or even sit on the other end of the same park-bench. Such prescriptions are not only against Christian morality, they are against that much more important moral intuition which Kant in his *Critique* called *Practical Reason*: that subliminal apprehension of what is right and good that lies at the root of the nature of every unperverted man.

In part the Afrikaners, with their pious Dutch Reformed background, are the victims of their own honesty. As La Rochefoucauld pointed out: 'Social life would not last long if men refused to be taken in by one another.' Hypocrisy is an emollient and by no means contemptible ingredient of human relationships. But the Afrikaners scorn to tell the little lies and half-lies that elsewhere make life supportable. If any people ever insisted on calling a spade a bloody shovel, it is the Afrikaners. No government in the world has ever so blindly put weapons into the hands of its foes as the South African. What other government would have had the appalling frankness and stupidity to coin and circulate the very word apartheid?

I am a convinced opponent of the current theory and practice of apartheid. Nevertheless I will risk shocking you by stating that I believe that the wider and more flexible policy of 'separate development' represented by the concept of *Bantustans*, or semi-autonomous African homelands within the borders of South Africa, is at least worthy of serious consideration. Any idea that was entertained by such a perceptive and humane statesman as Jan Smuts surely deserves more than superficial examination. Unfortunately, the South African government, having put itself into a position where even its altruistic pro-

down, stinking and insanitary dwellings of the Industrial Revolution which are still normal housing in Battersea and Bermondsey, Salford and Wigan, and in the mining-valleys of Wales. The relationship between Windhoek and Katatura is in many respects no more abnormal and a good deal less sordid than the relationship between the rich and poor suburbs of any large city.

Yet in one vital respect Katatura and the 'model' townships like it are infinitely discouraging to the visitor from abroad. They are discouraging because apartheid itself is discouraging, and because the townships are an extension of it. Life is made tolerable for a boy born in Bermondsey because he may one day be able to translate himself, if not to Belgravia, at least to Blackheath. He does not feel permanently condemned to a deprived and circumscribed life. And he can always comfort himself with the warm and hopeful feeling that, even if he himself never escapes from his wretched surroundings, at least his children and his grand-children may well come to occupy better ones. He lives in an open society, where there is contact and free exchange between different social groups. This is not the case in Katatura. A boy from Katatura will never in any circumstances move across the mountain to Windhoek to live in the fashionable Block Twenty, or be elected to the smart Sport-Klub Windhoek.

The South Africans, like their enemies the Communists, are trying to deprive people of a social mobility that is a necessary part of human relationships. Like the Communists, they will fail, and probably fail in a painful way, because such a restriction is against the natural order of things. You may have no particular desire to visit Scotland or Antarctica: but this is entirely different from being officially forbidden to do so by meddlesome officials. You like to feel that you can go if the fancy takes you, and if you can raise the fare. To feel otherwise is to feel that you have been put in a cell. Nor are the South African bureaucrats merely stifling the primordial right of people to indulge in an easy commerce and natural *va-et-vient* with one another: they are doing it in a highly offensive way.

lightened. In South West Africa they are building schools, hospitals and houses for the Africans. The other side of the picture is so obnoxious that it is hard for them to convince the world of the truth of this: but it is so. The hospitals and health-service of South West Africa outstrip anything which African regimes to the north are doing for their own people. The number of doctors to patients in South West is one to 5,000, compared with one to 25,000 in Ghana, and one to 40,000 in Liberia. The schools in South West are excellent, and several of them, like the Augustineum at Okahandja, are outstanding. They are attended by 46 per cent of South West's children of school age, and by 1970 it is expected that the figure will rise to 60 per cent. This is no small achievement in a country where groups and families are widely disseminated and children must be brought to school from enormous distances. The clumsiness and obstinacy of South Africa's rulers have enabled her enemies to claim that her non-white policies are entirely cynical and tyrannical. Nevertheless she possesses a cadre of administrators, sociologists and anthropologists who care for the African and are devoting their skill and energy to helping him. It is a tragedy that these admirable men receive little recognition for their endeavours.

Why, then, having said all this, was I so depressed by the spectacle of such places as Katatura, the new black African township laid out on a hill outside Windhoek? Like the nearby Cape Coloured township of Khomasdal, Katatura is methodically planned, well constructed, and a thousand times superior to the conditions in which its 10,000 inhabitants existed when they used to live in their old shanty-towns. The inhabitants occupy decent, soundly built homes, some of them own their own cars, and they enjoy such amenities as well-stocked shops, cinemas, sportsgrounds, an assembly hall, a concert hall, a library, a post-office and a bank. The houses of Katatura are better houses, better furnished, and with better services, than many of the houses in which hundreds of thousands of people live in Europe or America: certainly I would rather live in one of them than in one of the back-to-back, two-up-and-two-

years earlier he had been a prisoner of the Boers, and knew what he was talking about. In 1907 the South Africans offered King Edward the Seventh, as a gift, the enormous and newly unearthed Cullinan Diamond, the largest diamond ever found, and in August of that year Churchill wrote to urge the King to accept 'this genuine and disinterested expression of loyalty which comes from the heart of this strange and formidable people.' The South Africans have been made strange and formidable by the rough circumstances of their history: and only a zealot or a mischief-maker would refuse to take notice of that fact and make due allowance for it.

The South Africans, and in particular their leaders, are often humourless, slow-thinking and insufferably self-righteous. They have therefore got themselves a thoroughly bad press—much of which they deserve, and much of which they do not. We should remember that at Sharpeville, in 1960, sixty-eight people were killed; while in Indonesia, in 1965–66, hundreds of thousands of Communists and Chinese were conservatively estimated to have been hunted down, hacked to pieces, and their bodies thrown into wells or rivers. In the Sudanese province of Equatoria 500,000 people were estimated to have been massacred also during the course of 1965–66; and in the first three months of the Nigerian civil war the *Manchester Guardian* quoted an official estimate of 50,000 dead. None of this excuses Sharpeville: a nation which calls itself civilized is under a correspondingly great obligation to behave in a civilized way. But the relative indifference towards worse barbarities being enacted in less accessible countries—genocide in Tibet, poison gas in the Yemen, the Wall in East Berlin—does suggest that a double standard is in operation.

I admire the South Africans deeply. I remember that in the last war they came to the help of my country when help was sorely needed; they were brave soldiers and good comrades. The South Africans are a strong, industrious, pioneering people, who in less than three centuries have created a homeland out of a wilderness. Contrary to common belief, many aspects of their policies towards the non-Europeans are generous and en-

The Wa-benz and Others

When I was turning over the shape of this book in my mind, I resolved to cut politics to the minimum. This is not a book about politics or political theory: it is the story of a personal excursion; it is about the land, about nature, about such things as history and prehistory. But in Africa today politics takes you by the throat and demands to be discussed. Politics is inescapable. Therefore—at last and most reluctantly—I am compelled to grasp the political nettle. It will be evident that I do not do so with any great eagerness.

Let me confess straight away that my feelings are cloudy and ambivalent. Who am I to set myself up as an expert on such matters? I can provide no confident and clear-cut answers, such as you are accustomed to receiving from the more assertive kind of commentator. I am merely an observer.

I must state straight away that I am not—emphatically—anti-South African. The South Africans have their faults, like everybody else: but they are not the monsters or Nazi-type thugs that the propaganda of their enemies paints them. Only people with closed minds could believe that. Nor, in spite of what large numbers of people have been persuaded to think, is South Africa a police-state or a dictatorship, in the classic sense of Nazi Germany or Soviet Russia. There are certainly some mean and brutal manifestations of the police-state, such as the suspension of Habaeus Corpus, the law permitting arbitrary detention for ninety days, and the existence of such notorious prisons as Robben Island. But no ban exists on freedom of expression, and views that are critical of the government or in opposition to its policies are aired in an uninhibited way, in private, in public, and in the press. South Africa is a democracy: a very strange sort of democracy, and one with obvious and lamentable imperfections. But South Africa is a very strange country. As Mr Allen Drury's young professor in Pretoria observed: 'We have a very strange society.' Mr Drury later took the last four words as the title of his book on South Africa. Winston Churchill had delivered exactly the same verdict sixty years before, when he was a thirty-two year old Under Secretary for the Colonies in a Liberal administration. Seven

own countrymen—we think we know them, but we never really do. We never know ourselves. How then can we ever hope to know people of another colour, another culture, another continent? One thinks of George Herbert's lines, in his *Travels at Home*:

> Make no pretence
> Of new discoveries, whilst yet thine own
> And nearest little world is still unknown. . . .

We are busy with the exploration of outer space: perhaps it is inner space that we ought to be exploring.

The problems of the African bear little resemblance to our own problems. The boss-boy in his white overalls at Tsumeb: what can you grasp of that man's loves and hates, his troubles and ambitions? Can you picture the inner reality of his leisure hours in the compound, or his life in the distant kraal among the *oshanas*? The nexus of his life is remote from yours. What can you do beside stepping across to him, shaking him by the hand, nodding to him, giving him a smile? He will smile back. A smile isn't much, though it is something: but it represents the full extent of your contact with him. At such a moment you fetch up against the cold iron fact that one man lives cut off from another. We are social animals; we huddle together in our tribes and cities. But in spite of Donne and Hemingway and their tolling bells we remain islands. We live and die unto ourselves, shut in with anxieties and aspirations we cannot communicate. We are all of us segregated.

In what light, then, are we to view the African workers we see as we move about the country? They come of a desperate past, they enjoy a circumscribed present, and they are faced by a precarious future. To hear the white farmers and industrialists tell it, the Africans are living in a golden age of stability and affluence. To listen to the African leaders, their people are in servitude to SWANLA and the administration. The white man points to schools, hospitals, housing-estates, regular employment, rising wages. The African points to the poverty of the reserves, the squalor of the urban areas, the tyranny of the pass laws, the humbug of 'separate development'.

The Wa-benz and Others

there are steady wages and a recognized code of labour relations. However, one way or another the farmers contrive to persuade SWANLA to fill their requirements. In a busy year SWANLA will recruit about 30,000 Africans, half of them Ovambo, Herero, Nama and Bergdama, the other half Angolans. It is an impressive catch. Of these, fully one third will go to the farms of South West, slightly more than a third to its mines and factories, and the remainder to the Witwatersrand, as a concession to the all-powerful WNLA whose tentacles reach into half the countries of Africa. Contracts are normally for a year in the first instance, but may be renewed. In certain trades the government appears to discourage consecutive contracts, which would expose a man for too long to European customs and ideas; he must return for long spells to his reserve. The government has no intention of creating a cadre of the bitter, rootless *evolués* who have caused so much trouble in other African countries. A man's period of residence at Tsumeb or Oranjemund is therefore represented almost as a privilege, the peak of his career, from which he returns laden with smart clothes and mechanical gadgets, eager to offer himself again and to submit once more to discipline. Furthermore a homesick worker is a poor worker, and for the sake of his morale an African, like everyone else, needs to return at frequent intervals to his own heath and hearth. The wages he earns are difficult to determine, as they are subject to fluctuation and, at times, to the whim of the individual employer. They may vary from 7s 6d or 10s a week for an unskilled or category *C* worker to £1–£2 a week for a first-class man. Labour is in such short supply that wages are already in excess of the statutory minimum, and will inevitably rise even more steeply. Nobody will grudge a few extra pence a day to the lonely herdsman shivering in his kaross, or the face-worker sweating in his safety-helmet.

They cross their arms on their shovels as you drive by. They stare at you with impenetrable brown eyes.
What are they thinking? What is going on in their sombre heads? Impossible to tell. Our own family, our own friends, our

employer sends his request for the type and number of workmen he needs direct to Grootfontein; he also sends a capitation fee of about £13–£15. His men are thereupon selected for him from the multiple compounds at Grootfontein and despatched to him by rail and truck. Without SWANLA the economy of South West would disintegrate; the organization is as indispensable as it is soulless. It is the product of a merger in 1943 between the Southern and the Northern Labour Organizations, the second of which already had its headquarters at Grootfontein. The merger was brought about by the farmers and mining companies of the country as a result of political pressure and in response to a desperate labour-shortage. Before 1934 the cream of Ovambo, Herero, Nama, Damara and Portuguese Angolan labour was being regularly skimmed off by the Witwatersrand Native Labour Association (WNLA), which had been operating successfully for a full half-century. WNLA collected its labourers inside the Police Zone and ferried them down through Botswana to the mines and factories of Kimberley and the Rand. The creation of SWANLA put an end to poaching by WNLA, and ensured that the bulk of the country's labour was kept at home. The authorities at Grootfontein set up two new recruiting offices, one at Ondangua in Ovamboland, 100 miles north-west of Namutoni, the new 'capital' of self-governing Ovamboland, and the other at Runtu in the Okavango Native Territory, on the border of Angola. Here the Ovambo and the Angolans are gathered together and sent down to Grootfontein to be graded and contracted. They are placed after medical examination into A, B and C categories, which correspond to fitness for heavy, medium heavy, and light labour. They then volunteer for the type of work they prefer, mining and industry being the first choices, with agriculture a bad third. Work on the farms is unpopular because the pay is poor, housing mediocre, fringe-benefits uncertain, and employers frequently harsh and sometimes brutal. The prospect of falling into the clutches of a harassed and impoverished farmer in a remote area is not an attractive one. In the mines, on the other hand, and on the railways and in the canning-factories,

sisters in the towns, but household goods are fewer. There is an occasional radio-set, electric iron, sewing-machine and pressure-cooker; bicycles are on the increase, while in some reserves Africans own their own cars and trucks.

Crops are grown on the reserves, not always with much success; kitchen gardening is similarly sporadic. The Africans buy the bulk of their food from their own shops, and favour much the same meat, vegetables, tinned food, fruit and dairy products as the Europeans. They have a sweet tooth, and consume tremendous quantities of sugar. The traditional basis of their diet consists of mealie meal for porridge, boer meal for baking bread, mealie rice, and samp, or broken maize. These are the daily ingredients of the family cooking-pot. The women also wander off into the bush on the immemorial search for *veldkos*, or wild food—berries, nuts, roots and melons—and during the milking season the principal diet of the Herero is *omaere* or thick milk.

Coffee and tea are extensively drunk, in about equal amounts. In the African beer-halls, which are a feature of the reserves, and which strain at the seams during week-end celebrations, beer is brewed under the eye of the superintendent and sold by the bottle or by the mug. This official beer is made of malt, yeast and sugar, and is low on alcohol; but there is also an unofficial veer called *kari* which many households brew illicitly and which is much more deadly. *Kari* is made from split peas, sugar and yeast. Drink has been a scourge in South West ever since the Africans acquired a craving for it from their early contacts with white traders. The problem is not pressing on the reserves, where it is easy to control, but is serious in the African townships in the urban areas. The high incidence of tuberculosis among the Herero is in part attributable to the rot-gut on which they squander their hard-earned wages.

If a Herero at Waterburg wishes to leave the reserve and seek employment he has not far to go. The town of Grootfontein is the headquarters of SWANLA, the South West African Native Labour Association. SWANLA is one of the largest and most efficient labour exchanges in the world. Any would-be

have been persuaded to sell or slaughter up to 15 per cent of their animals, which has relieved the strain on grazing and supplied them with additional funds. Their spare cash they bury in the ground, or occasionally put into a savings bank; but few Herero possess savings accounts of more than £100, and most of their profits are ploughed back into their herds, or spent on buying a fine horse. Cattle still possess a ritual and social as well as an economic significance; the bride price or *ovitunja* is sometimes still paid by the groom or his family in the form of an ox, a heifer and three sheep.

A reserve is run by a board consisting of representatives of the various ethnic groups of which it is composed. Most reserves have minority groups whose interests must be safeguarded. The supreme authority is the local magistrate, but an arbiter is often closer to hand in the guise of a superintendent welfare officer who lives in the reserve. The magistrate or superintendent issues the permits that are needed before a man may step outside the reserve, even for the purpose of visiting relatives on another reserve or in one of the towns. The Afrikaners, once the most informal and libertarian of peoples, who preferred to trek thousands of miles into the wilderness rather than submit to British rule, came late to the business of bureaucracy and police supervision. But once the Nationalists seized power, they soon made up for lost time.

Housing on most of the reserves is primitive. The huts are square or round, plastered with a mixture of clay and cowdung, and either thatched or roofed with tin. A few houses have little *stoeps* or verandahs and enclosed yards. There is a single room with holes for windows, which are covered with boards in windy weather. Herero and Ovambo houses on the reserves are usually cleaner and neater than the houses of the Nama and Bergdama, who often make their homes out of paraffin cans sold to them by the local municipality. The floor of the living-room is of beaten soil, and the fireplace is in front of the house, consisting of a ring of stones or the wheel of an old car filled with earth. The dress of Africans on the reserves is the same, if slightly shabbier, than that of their brothers and

The Wa-benz and Others

European dress and European farming. The German administration was considering the creation of reserves as early as 1898, and convened a commission in Berlin in 1902 that actually proclaimed a pilot-reserve at Otjimbingwe. The outbreak of the Herero rebellion and the First World War put an end to these plans; and it was not until the onset of more settled times that the idea was once more taken up. Most of the twenty-two reserves were instituted between 1923–26. Eighteen of them are in the southern half of the country, four in the north, and they range in size from the miniature Warmbad Reserve to the gigantic acreages of the Eastern Reserve and the Rehoboth Gebiet. Waterberg dates from 1924. In common with the others, its boundaries have been enlarged and adjusted from time to time. Under the Odendaal plan it would become part of 'Hereroland', one of the ten separate 'homelands' proposed for the African population, of which Ovamboland is the first.

What is life like on the reserves? They are, of course, huge open stretches of country, and the quality of life depends on whether an individual reserve is fortunate or unfortunate in the territory allotted to it. Within the reserves the grazing grounds of each *onganda* and *ozonganda* are traditional, and each owner pays a small yearly fee into the Reserve Trust Fund for every beast that he grazes. However, one must remember that a few pennies a head may mean little to an American or a European, but can be a crippling burden to an African.

The total number of livestock on a reserve can be enormous, particularly in a reserve of the Herero, those obsessive herdsmen. Old Chief Kambabezi had owned 25,000 head of cattle, and even today there are between 40,000 and 50,000 cattle on the Waterberg Reserve, not to mention smaller herds of sheep, goats, and upwards of a thousand horses. Grazing these large numbers of stock presents obvious difficulties, in a land deficient in minerals and water, and strict measures have to be enforced to prevent over-grazing. Among the difficulties is the fact that cattle represent wealth and status to the Herero, who are therefore reluctant to part with them. A man with thirty cattle is a king in Waterberg. Nevertheless, in recent years the Herero

The Land God Made in Anger

built a schoolhouse, attended in due time by seventy Herero, including Chief Kambabezi, and had introduced his pupils to

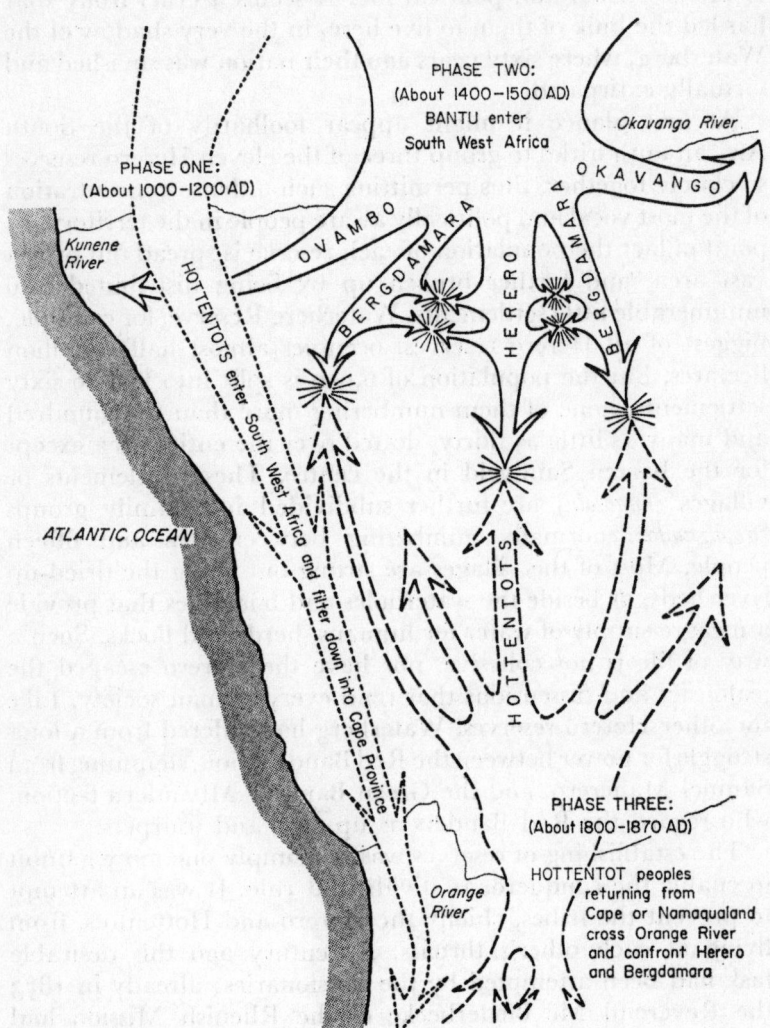

TRIBAL INCURSIONS INTO SOUTH WEST AFRICA IN HISTORIC TIMES

Okahandja: but it is from the reserves that they come, and to the reserves that they return. The three reserves are the foci of Herero tribal and political life. It seems a cruel irony that has led the bulk of them to live here, in the very shadow of the Waterberg, where sixty years ago their nation was smashed and virtually extirpated.

At first glance it might appear foolhardy of the South African authorities to group three of the eleven Herero reserves so closely together, thus permitting such a dense concentration of the most vocal and politically aware people in the territory. In point of fact the population of each reserve is spread out over a vast area, and further broken up by being distributed into innumerable little settlements. Waterberg Reserve, for example, biggest of all Herero reserves, occupies almost half a million hectares, but the population of 6,000 is split into fifty to sixty settlements, none of them numbering more than two hundred and many as little as thirty, dotted over the entire area except for the barren Sandveld in the centre. These settlements or villages (*onganda*) are further subdivided into family groups (*ozonganda*), normally numbering between five and fifteen people. Most of the villages are strung out along the dried-up river beds, or beside the waterholes and boreholes that provide a meagre supply of water for humans, herds and flocks. Such a way of life is not cohesive, nor have the Herero escaped the jealousies and dissensions that rend every human society. Like the other Herero reserves, Waterberg has suffered from a long struggle for power between the Red Band faction, stemming from Samuel Maherero, and the Green Band or Mbanderu faction, who regard the Red Banders as upstarts and usurpers.

The establishing of reserves was not simply one more gambit to enable the conqueror to divide and rule. It was an attempt to prevent the tribes, chiefly the Herero and Hottentots, from flying at each other's throats. A century ago this desirable task had been attempted by the missionaries; already in 1873 the Reverend Mr Biederbecke of the Rhenish Mission had taken up residence within the boundaries of the future reserve at Otjozondjupa, 'The Place of the Gourds'. There he had

of the country south of the Police Zone the proportion is only two to one: so we can see that in the colonial sense South West Africa is very much a 'White Man's Country'. In most of the African countries once ruled by white men the actual size of the white community was diminutive. In Rhodesia at the present time the whites are outnumbered by the blacks by sixteen to one. Therefore the plain truth, whether one likes it or not, is that dislodging the white population from South West Africa would be as formidable an undertaking as dislodging them from South Africa. It could be done, of course; history is filled with examples of such mass ejections and mass evacuations: but the whites in Southern Africa are, as they proved at Majuba, Spion Kop, Delville Wood and in the Western Desert, able and courageous fighters. Therefore one hopes that the politicians of the United Nations, who have stood Clausewitz's dictum on its head and hold that diplomacy is a continuation of war by other means, will bear this in mind before they send men to a very dusty death in the Kaokoveld.

The policeman hitches his hefty shoulders under the khaki tunic and turns with a feeling of relief towards the east. He surveys the wide sweep of veld from south-east to north-east. Across there are the rich, orderly and well-policed towns of Tsumeb and Grootfontein. Grootfontein, forty-five miles from Tsumeb and 160 from Otjiwarongo, is a prosperous market town, centre of a cattle area, where over 3,000 Europeans live and work as a counter-balance to the African work-force of 4,000 Ovambo, 1,500 Damara and 1,000 Herero.

The Herero, of course, are always a problem. There are only a thousand working at Grootfontein, the most remote of all the sizeable towns of South West Africa: but there are no less than ten thousand of them in the important block of Herero reserves almost touching the outskirts of the town. These reserves are three in number: Waterberg (population 6,000), Epikuro (3,000), and Otjituo (1,500). They are more or less contiguous, and represent in effect the homeland of the Herero people. Every year the Herero hold their annual celebrations at

sailors, and their mothers were Hottentot, Malay or Chinese women. There are perhaps two thousand of these coloured or *Kleurling* people in South West Africa, where they came to seek work, principally at Walvis Bay, when they heard that skilled and semi-skilled workers were needed after the Second World War. An off-shoot of the million-and-a-half strong Coloured community in the West Cape, they are intelligent and clever with their hands; but they live unhappily and in isolation, fitting into the society of South West no more successfully than their brothers to the south. Although they speak Afrikaans and possess white blood, the Afrikaners shun them as wholeheartedly as the Africans. They enjoy the economic status of the poorer whites, but apartheid has handed them a particular dirty deal. They have been struck off the Cape electoral roll and have been compelled to lead a kind of non-existence, like the Eurasians in India. But a million-and-a-half people cannot fade away: and there is nowhere for them to fade to. They have been called the most marginal of marginal peoples—'God's step-children'—and it falls to their lot to suffer humiliation and indignity in silence, with no pressure-group, black or white, to speak up for them. Their fate serves to underline the good fortune and sturdy character of the Rehobothers.

The remaining ethnic element, the Caucasoid or European, is also extremely diverse. There are 73,000, split into three distinct groups: 49,000 Afrikaners, 17,000 Germans, 7,000 English. They nourish much the same mutual antagonisms as the Africans, but are more adept in concealing them. In number they are exceeded only by the Ovambo. They outnumber the third largest group, the Bergdama, by almost two to one, and are twice as numerous as the Hottentots and Herero put together. They represent 14 per cent of the total population, giving a proportion of Africans to Europeans of seven to one. If Ovamboland eventually achieves true independence, the proportion of white to black in the remainder of the country would fall to four to one, which is the present proportion of Europeans to non-Europeans in South Africa. Already in the two-thirds

disease. Nevertheless their mutual detestation has not greatly lessened with the years, although it is somewhat muted as they attempt to make common cause against the white man.

The last of the non-white groups, the Basters, are relative newcomers to the country. Known also as the Baasters or Baastards, they were originally a band of men and women of mixed parentage—Dutch fathers and Hottentot mothers. Under the captainship of their leader, Dick Filander, they had congregated in Great Bushman Land, just south of the Orange River. Later, harried by drought and the hostility of the white farmers, with immense heroism and sense of community they crossed the river and trekked north to find a new place to settle. They were led by another redoubtable captain, Hermanus van Wyck, who finally brought them out of the wilderness and into a grassy haven on the temperate uplands near Windhoek. Here, in 1870, they settled at Rehoboth, forty miles south of the future capital. Pastoral people, of a sober and religious caste of mind, they fended off their brother Hottentots and the alien Herero, came to an understanding with the Germans and their successors, and have managed to live for a hundred years at Rehoboth in tolerable peace with themselves and their neighbours. This is a considerable achievement in a country like South West Africa. Their Gebiet or District has enjoyed virtual independence from the beginning. The white settlers at Windhoek have often cast envious eyes at the fertile acres of their reserve, but they have resisted all encroachment. There are 9,000 of them farming in the Gebiet, and another 2,000 in the reserves or working in white areas outside it. Unlike the Nama, who loathe their older name of Hottentot, the Basters are proud of their 'Baastard' descent and do not resent their name. None the less they usually figure in modern literature under the polite designation of 'Rehobothers'.

There are also a certain number of other 'Coloureds' in the country—that is, half-castes of similar racial admixture to the Basters, but hailing more immediately from the Cape. This small group are not Rehobothers, but belong to the people called Cape Coloureds. Their fathers were Boers or passing

The Wa-benz and Others

The four remaining non-white groups are, in order of size, the Bergdama, the Herero, the Nama (Hottentots), and the Basters or Coloureds. As we saw in the opening chapter, the Bergdama, who are also known by the names of Bergdamara, Damara or Dama, are a people whose origin is wrapped in mystery. Although they are Bantu, they speak the language of their long-time masters, the Hottentots. They may have drifted into the country with—or slightly ahead of—the main wave of the Bantu invasion, and have lived in the less coveted areas of the north for several generations before becoming the slaves of the Hottentots. At one time they were so numerous and widespread that the entire country north of Windhoek was known as Damaraland. The 44,000 who have survived the ill-usage of the ages still live mainly in the north of the country, but today they are landless, except for the reserved land granted to them by the bounty of the white men who saved them from annihilation. Peaceable folk, they managed to achieve a *modus vivendi* with the Bushmen: but they could not withstand the onslaught of their fellow-Herero and the Hottentots. Most were enslaved; many fled to Ovamboland and were there accorded shelter and succour. These amiable and ill-used people are still despised as servile and cowardly by the Hottentots and Herero. If and when the Africans rule South West, the Bergdama know they will once more be in for a thin time.

Neither Hottentots nor Herero are now as numerous as the Damara, whom they used to term their 'black bondsmen'. Today both number about 35,000. Originally they were the two largest, most aggressive and powerful peoples in South West. They disputed the whole country, save Ovamboland, between them. The battle swayed backwards and forwards across the enormous savage landscape as with immense relish and not a little success they strove to wipe one another off the face of the earth. The nineteenth century in South West is a monotonous record of their encounters, ambushes, outrages, massacres and treacheries. Then, having paved the way for their own downfall, they were smashed by the *Schutztruppe,* and after their military defeat they fell prey to disintegration and

of the country. Once lords of creation, their status has now shrunk to that of court dwarfs or domestic pets. Only about 3,000 to 4,000 remain to continue the ancient rôle of hunters in the Kalahari, and to remind us of what our own lives were like at the beginning of our history.

Side by side with the Bushmen, on the borders of the Kalahari and the more habitable portion of the Namib Desert to the west of it, can be found the Kaukauvelders. The Kaukau Veld, or 'The Place of Silence', is the name given to the broken country in the north which, though largely barren, is still not quite desert. The Kaukauvelders are the poor relations of the tribe that constituted the third prong of the Bantu invasion, the Herero. While the Herero spearheaded down towards the Orange River, the Kaukauvelders were a rump of the main body left behind in the barren north. They thus occupy the uninviting territory which was the principal property of the Herero as recently as 150 or even 100 years ago. There are between 9,000 and 12,000 of them, and they belong almost entirely to a tribe called the Ovatjimba, with a small admixture of Ovahimba and true Herero.

All these five African peoples—Ovambo, Okavango, East Caprivians, Bushmen and Kaukauvelders—are confined to reserves or tribal areas in what is designated the 'Police Zone'. The Zone is rigidly defined. It is the preserve of a lonely band of government administrators and Finnish missionaries, whose total is less than four hundred. Though vast by absolute standards, the extent of the Zone amounts to little more than one quarter of the area of the country: yet it is here that the great majority of the African population can be found. Even in the south of the country the remainder of the African population is not free to range widely, but is restricted to a tribal area. There are eighteen such areas or tribal reserves in the south: and of the 460,000 natives and coloured people in South West Africa, no less than 287,000 live in the reserves, 109,000 in the so-called 'rural areas', and only 64,000 in the towns. Towns, however, can scarcely be said to exist. Of the twenty four 'towns' in the country, only nine possess a thousand vehicles of all types.

tribes, they are substantially smaller in number than their neighbours, and comprise about 28,000 in all. The tribes are the Kuangari (7,000), the Diriko (5,000), the Hambukushu (4,700), the Bunja (4,700) and the Sambio (4,200). Excessively shy in temperament, they follow pursuits as primitive hunters and simple fisherfolk, poling their dug-out canoes up and down the steaming river, and never travel southwards outside the Okavango Native Territory to seek employment in the south.

In this they resemble the four tribes, again to the east, congregated into another Bantu people called the East Caprivians. There are between 16,000 and 17,000 of them, and they are even more withdrawn in character than the Okavango. They owe their quaint name to the fact that they live in the Caprivi Strip or Caprivi Zipfel. The Strip is one of those artificial tongues of territory that cause endless international trouble: 'Two thousand souls and twenty thousand ducats / Will not debate the question of this straw.' The Strip is modern Africa's Danzig Corridor. Called after Count Caprivi di Montecuccoli, a Prussian with an unlikely name who became chancellor of the Reich, it was given to Germany in 1890, during the era of the European scramble for colonies. Germany was anxious to link up South West Africa with German East Africa, just as Portugal was striving to link up Angola with Mozambique. And Cecil Rhodes, eager to thwart both of them, came driving up through the Rhodesias to hammer a wedge between them. The modern South Africans regard the Strip as an essential strategic safeguard. It is an arm embracing the new black state of Botswana (Bechuanaland), and it links South West Africa with Rhodesia to form a vital segment of South Africa's northern boundary. The East Caprivi tribes who live in the Strip are the Mafue (8,000), the Basubie (6,300), the Boyoy (1,500), and a small contingent of the Hambukushu (650).

Also in the extreme north of the country live two more ethnic groups. The first place must be given to the Bushmen—or what is left of them. Only a handful of them now survive in their original wild state. Of the 14,000 listed in the latest returns, 10,000 earn a wretched pittance as farm-workers in the south

10 Aus: a town in a river bed

9 Lüderitz Bay

Hahn, administrator in Ovamboland for many years. When Hahn wrote an essay on them in 1926, for a symposium called *The Native Tribes of South-West Africa*, they numbered about 150,000; today they number over twice that figure, and are still thriving. Hahn persuaded them to take two revolutionary steps: to give up their *onganga*, or witch-doctors, and to store their grain. Today they follow their traditional way of life in compact, well-organized kraals enclosed by high stockades of sharpened stakes. The headman and his people occupy beehive huts on raised mounds in an inner compound; and in the outer compound stand the kraals that house the cattle and the reserves of grain, contained in oval baskets perched on stilts. They grow their corn and millet on raised ridges on the flooded plains, and in addition to their rich herds obtain a plentiful supply of fish from the nearby rivers.

To an altogether exceptional degree the Ovambo have kept intact their social cohesion and their spiritual pride. Change has now come to the banks of the Cunene, for in April, 1967, the South African Government gave partial self-government to the 16,000 square miles of Ovamboland, designating it the Republic's second 'Bantustan', or semi-autonomous native region, after the Transkei. A five-year development plan, costing £$15\frac{1}{2}$ million, was announced, and in time the 'homeland' will become totally independent. The capital of the new state is Ondangua. As an off-shoot of the Odendaal plan, the creation of Ovamboland was at once repudiated by the United Nations; but it may be that, with the dual strength of their character and their unimpaired tribal structure, the new national framework may enable the Ovambo ultimately to emerge into the modern world free from some at least of the despair and demoralization which have overtaken so many new African states in recent years.

Immediately to the east of the Ovambo are another Bantu people, their first cousins, who came out of central Africa at the same time. These are the Okavango, who live along the Okavango River, also on the Angolan border. Divided into five

servant. But, in fact, the distinctions of rank and wealth are nowhere more sharply defined than among savages. Pauperism is as common in Africa as it is in Europe, and it is a great credit to the Ovambo that it is not found among them.'

The Ovambo are grouped in eight tribes, the largest of which, the Ukuanyama, numbers 74,000. The other tribes, in order of size, are the Ondonga (58,500), the Ukuambi (24,000), the Ongandjera (15,500), the Ombalantu (15,000), the Ukualuthi (10,000) and the Onkolonkathi and Eunda (5,500). The Ovambo settled in South West Africa about six or seven hundred years ago. They were one of a number of central African peoples who at that time grew restless, and for some reason departed southwards in a great *Völkerwanderung*. They constituted one of the three prongs of the first advance of the Bantu peoples into the territory. The Bantu are Negroes proper—tall, excessively dark-skinned people, with everted lips and fine physique. In South West the Ovambo stayed in the north, and kept themselves to themselves, while their fellow-Bantu continued south until they clashed with the two peoples who were already in occupation: the Bushmen, who were the country's original owners, and who had possessed it from time immemorial, and the Hottentots (today called the Nama), who entered it only two or three hundred years before the Bantu.

Bushman, Hottentots and Bantu fought each other continuously and mercilessly. The Hottentots and the Bantu were cattle-drovers, wandering from one water-hole and patch of grazing to the next. They disputed these scanty necessities with each other, while the Bushman shot both them and their cattle impartially with poisoned arrows, in an attempt to ensure the survival of the wild animals on which they themselves also depended.

The Ovambo, remaining in a single, solid, isolated unit, were never seriously molested. In many ways they have had a more fortunate history than almost every other tribe in Africa. Negley Farson described them a quarter of a century ago as the happiest people he had met in the whole continent. At that time they were still under the tutelage of the legendary Major

At the present time the Ovambo appear to be living in reasonable contentment, tending their wide-horned Ankole cattle and cultivating their millet on the ridges between the *oshanas*, the water-courses that grow turbid with water in the rainy season. The eight tribes seem happy under the guidance of their headmen and their three principal chieftains. They appear to need only the minimum of tactful control from their handful of white administrators, doctors, and missionaries. Nevertheless it is always the nightmare of colonial authorities that their charges will suddenly and inexplicably turn against them. Colonial rule teaches the ruled how to mask their murderous intentions.

The Ovambo number 240,000, or more than 45 per cent of the total population. They are an exceptionally alert and vigorous people, and although 90 per cent of them are to be found at any one time living in Ovamboland, they are much sought after as contract labour at the diamond-mines in the Forbidden Area. Most of the men travel to Oranjemund at some time in their lives to work for De Beers, or hire themselves out to the mines at Tsumeb, to the farms in the south, or to the canning-factories at Walvis Bay. Their qualities of stability and good-humour, allied to their keen intelligence and physical strength, are highly valued.

The Ovambo have always received praise from outside observers. Thus J. G. Wood, in his invaluable *Natural History of Man* (1874), records that already, a hundred years ago, they were called 'the Merry People', and speaks of the 'real superiority of this remarkable tribe'. The traveller Andersson told Wood of their extraordinary honesty, which was so strong that 'they would not touch any of his property without permission, much less steal it.' Wood also noted that they were 'kind and attentive to their old, sick and aged, which one fact alone is sufficient to place them immeasurably above the neighbouring tribes'. He related that 'there is no pauperism among them', adding: 'This may not seem to be an astonishing fact to those who entertain the popular idea of a savage life, namely, that with them there is no distinction of rich or poor, master and

NINE
The Wa-benz and Others

THE South African policeman who stands beside you on the battlements of Namutoni resembles the Roman sentinel on Hadrian's Wall, or the British sentry on the Khyber Pass. He gazes out towards the north, in the direction of Ovamboland, straining his eyes for any hint that the war-drums might be beating or that the tribes might be gathering their strength.

The view from the ramparts runs away to the rim of the horizon. There is a sense of illimitable space. The land looks utterly peaceful. But is it?

True, the Ovambo seem peaceful enough, as you watch them working away for good wages in the south of the country, outside the Police Zone: but up there in the north, between Namutoni and the Cunene River, there is a jam-packed mass of nearly a quarter of a million of them, almost one half of South West's entire population. And from across the Cunene drift rumours of terrorism and secret 'liberation armies', plentifully supplied with Russian and Chinese arms. . . .

The Land God Made in Anger

When I was in the Welsh Guards, I was turned out one morning at four o'clock to welcome a battalion of the Coldstream Guards returning to Victoria Barracks at Windsor from duty abroad. The station-master was on the platform waiting to greet them, and according to custom he was dressed for the occasion in his full regalia, silk hat and cut-away coat. The men of the Coldstream fell in in the station yard. Then they marched through the sleeping streets to the barracks. They marched strictly at attention, arms swinging, rifles on shoulders, packs on backs, eyes front, shoulders square, eighty measured regulation steps to the minute. Up the winding hill beneath the rounded ramparts of the castle they marched, boots clashing on the cobbled stones between the high narrow shops and the ancient houses. The only light came from the dim blue flames of the gas-lamps. There was no one to watch them, no one to wave. There was not a soul in the streets except a solitary policeman (probably an old Guardsman himself) who stood to attention and raised a gloved hand to his helmet as the column went by. Four o'clock in the morning: and they marched as steadily and precisely as if they were trooping the Colour or moving towards the sound of the guns.

They were General Monk's men, raised in Northumberland to help King Charles II regain his throne from a dictator. They had fought all the campaigns of the Empire. The Empire was already dying. But that was through no fault of theirs.

I too, though I did not realize it at the time—being young then, and full of dreams and hope, and wearing a Guardsman's tunic—have watched an Empire marching in the night.

My Guardsmen were marching off the stage of history.

They went with style.

In the Land of Fat Cattle

job men, and hospital orderlies. Led by the heroic lavatory-man, the Magnificent Seven held off the Ovambo for a week: then, when the main force had still not appeared on the seventh night, they crept out of the rear gate and stole away between the enemy watch-fires. It took them another day to reach the main body and give the alarm, and within another twenty-four hours the Ovambo were expelled from the fort and put to flight.

Such excitements were rare. For the most part, life for the garrison of Namutoni was monotonous and grim. The troops were about as far away from the motherland as they could be, and their pleasures were few and tended to be cruel. It is said the officers would make a Herero girl strip and use her naked body as a card-table.

There are the inevitable Lost Legion stories about the place. 'The dead are the dead,' says the rissaldar-major to the subaltern in Kipling's *The Lost Legion*. 'For that reason they walk at night. They march to and fro below there. I saw them in the lightning.' Miss Levinson puts much the same story imaginatively about Namutoni when she relates how: 'The Etosha Bushmen say that on some nights, when the moon is full, casting its light on the pale gleaming walls of the fort, they can hear the sound of sharp commands within and the clarion call of bugles. Then the gates are opened and they see ghostly troops march out in order with German colours flying—out into the silent veld where they disappear into the shadows of the night . . .'

I am not so sunk in illusion as to claim that I have seen phantom armies flickering to and fro. However, the Bushmens' world is very strange and ancient, and there is no doubt that their psychic powers have remained more delicately tuned than ours. I envy them. It must be a bewitching experience to see the gates swing wide and the pallid column stride out, the bleached flag streaming in the windless air. The troops of a vanished empire, marching into oblivion. . . .

I too can claim to have watched a battalion marching silently and to attention in the dead of the night. These were men of flesh-and-blood: but even so the sight was weird.

Is this illusion?

Africa needs Europe. Europe needs Africa. Once there was unity: later came divorce. The Europe of the practical people and the Africa of illusion hunger for one another. Each will wither without the other. Europe and Africa are not merely continents: they are complementary states of mind.

Africa gives one back the necessary feeling that the world is vast, prodigious and noble. In spite of what the pundits say, our planet is neither congested nor contemptible.

If this is an illusion, it is not one that I am anxious to surrender.

The eastern approaches to the Etosha Pan are guarded by Fort Namutoni. This is the most northerly of the old German fortresses, constructed to police the borders of Ovamboland. It is also the most attractive and best preserved.

Namutoni was built between 1901 and 1903, and in 1950 was declared a national monument. When you first see it, glittering white on the flat plain in front of you, it makes you feel like a member of the *bataillon d'Afrique* returning from patrol. The feeling grows as you stroll through its courtyards and along its battlements. The government, hoping to encourage tourists to the Game Reserve, keeps the paint and plaster in faultless condition: and you have the sensation that the garrison has just departed on an exercise and will return at any moment. You realize how the sailors who boarded the *Marie Celeste* must have felt, when they saw the captain's table neatly laid, and smelt the dinner cooking in the galley. . . .

Beside the main gate a marble tablet commemorates the exploit of the seven men whose photograph I had seen in the hotel at Tsumeb. The tablet records that on January 28, 1904, the fort was attacked by 500 Ovambo. They launched their attack at a moment when almost the entire garrison were fifty miles away at a sub-station. The only soldiers left at the fort were *'sieben tapfere deutsche Reiter'*—seven brave German soldiers. They were commanded by Sergeant Bruno Lassmann, a Sanitation Sergeant. Presumably the others were cooks, odd-

In the Land of Fat Cattle

Brandberg. It is thickly ringed with stately huilbooms and apiesdorings, and the green waters below the dolomite bluffs are perfectly clear and calm. Galton was right in his estimate of the depth of the lake, which until his arrival was reputed to be bottomless; his figure was confirmed a century later by an enquiring engineer from Tsumeb. But Galton was wrong by half in his estimate of its width. This is a curious mistake for so scientifically-minded a man, and I would like to think that the lake played a trick on him. He also missed seeing the fish with which the lake swarms, and which belong to two strange genera, *Tilapia guinasana* and *Haplochromis philander*, known as mouth-breeders. Nature did not yield him all its secrets.

At intervals the surface of the lake is pocked by goose-flesh, as if a breeze ruffles it. The fact that the same type of fish are found in Otjikoto and Guinas seems to show that the two lakes are joined by an underground passage. The Ovambo and Ovahimba maintain that the lakes are haunted. I cannot see that simply lowering a plumb-line into them proves that they are not. You can take a man's finger-prints, but you cannot tell what occult processes he harbours in his heart.

Nothing would induce me to swim in those crystalline waters—but then, I do not belong to the bold and imperious generation of Francis Galton. Nor have I any desire to 'dispel illusions from the savage mind'. I have illusions of my own. I value them. I am not sure that our illusions should not be cherished. Perhaps the world's stock of illusions is becoming dangerously run down.

In South West Africa I felt that the land around me was informed with a spirit and character of its own. The mountains and the vleis, the desert and veld, seemed to possess their own existence, in a dimension I could barely apprehend and which scarcely touched my own. There were moments when I felt that the mountains were not inert lumps of matter, that the deserts were not dead and sterile, but that they were all pervaded with some immanent, breathing personality. They came together and had meaning at some level and according to some pattern which I could glimpse but not understand.

herd of 16,000 head of cattle he collected a private army of 3,000 Herero and thrashed Jan Jonker and his Hottentots in a pitched battle. In 1866 his passion for exploration and collecting specimens returned, and he set out on one more push towards the Cunene, whose waters had never been seen by a white man. He succeeded in reaching the great river, but on its banks he died. He was thirty-nine.

Galton's attitude to exploration and Africans was engagingly Victorian. He, too, had trouble with Jan Jonker, who had just emerged from the blood-bath at Okahandja which was described in Chapter Two. He would have liked to punish Jan Jonker, but was restrained by the fact that, as he put it, 'I had no idea of undertaking a piece of Quixotism on behalf of a people who are themselves a nation of thieves and cut-throats.' His solution was to don hunting-pink and a pair of polished riding-boots, mount an ox, and ride alone not only into Jan Jonker's camp but right into Jan Jonker's hut. There he laid down the law with typical Victorian assurance, drawing up a combined peace treaty and constitution for Jan Jonker's benefit, and showing him how to run the country.

I particularly like Galton's entry in his diary for May 26. 'Without the least warning,' he says, 'we came suddenly upon that remarkable tarn, Otchikoto. It is a deep bucket-shaped hole, 400 feet across; deep below us lay a placid sheet of water, which I plumbed leaning over the cliff above, to the enormous depth of 180 feet. The water could be reached by a couple of broken foot-paths. There were infinite superstitions about Otchikoto, the chief of which was, that no living thing which ever got into it could come out again. However, Andersson and myself dispelled that illusion from the savage mind, by stripping and swimming all about it.'

I have visited Otjikoto, which is fifteen miles north of Tsumeb on the road to Etosha. It is the crater of an extinct volcano, like the similar lake of Guinas a further nine miles away. As Galton said, you come upon the tarn without warning. The sight of it in the middle of the lonely veld is totally unexpected and very startling. The place is uncanny: a Presence, like the

In the Land of Fat Cattle

wild life. The packs of lions that come down each evening to drink at the spring called Leobrunn are the most numerous and impressive in Africa. The Pan was discovered in 1851 by Francis Galton, Charles Andersson, and the Danish baggage-master they had brought with them from Walvis Bay.

According to Galton's diary, published in his highly entertaining *Narrative of an Explorer in Tropical South Africa* (1853), they first set eyes on it on May 30. During this epic journey to Ovamboland, undertaken purely in a spirit of adventure, Galton and Andersson were both young men in their twenties. Galton, a cousin of Charles Darwin, had devoted his early years to sport, but then threw himself with characteristic energy into the business of exploration. After travelling in Egypt and the Levant, he set out from London with the young Swedish naturalist Charles Andersson to explore Damaraland. In later years this lively and remarkable man became one of the leading scientists of his age. He was a pioneer in the fields of psychology, statistics and meteorology, and was the originator of finger-printing. Freud was impressed by his ingenious method of superimposing family photographs on one another in order to demonstrate a definite resemblance. The invention of finger-printing is often wrongly credited to the Frenchman, Bertillon: but the Bertillon System was a method of registering convicted criminals by recording their individual measurements, and was anthropometrical. It was Galton who showed that finger-prints were a unique index of identity. He persuaded Scotland Yard to adopt finger-printing as a means of detection, and devised the technical terms 'whorl', 'loop' and 'arch' which are still in use today. As for Charles Andersson, South West Africa laid a spell upon him, and he settled down there as a trader. He, too, was a remarkable man. His dream was to reach Lake Ngami, a dream which he ultimately realized, and he was also the first white man to reach the Okavango River. His two books, *Lake Ngami* and *The Okavango*, make good reading, and testify to his genius as a naturalist. Eventually he acquired a farm at Otjimbingwe, which became the first official capital of South West; and when Jan Jonker Afrikaner seized his immense

what was happening until a volunteer squad roped it and brought it out. Unlike the eland, which now exists only in the north, the kudu roams freely over the whole of South West, wherever there is a bit of coarse shrub to nibble. It is sometimes a nuisance when it gets into a poor African's mealie patch, but by and large the people of South West are devoted to it. There is a magnificent statue of a kudu at the southern end of Kaiserstrasse in Windhoek, where Kaiserstrasse joins Lüderitzstrasse. It is the work of the Münich sculptor, Behn. The animal stands high on its stone plinth. The noble horns, the mane and the dewlap have been gilded, and ripple in the sunlight. The bronze head is raised to snuff the breeze, the back legs are braced to kick off into a searing gallop. '*Tiene casta*,' a Spaniard would say: 'It has breeding.' The figure recalls the verdict of Captain Harris: 'The Kudu is absolutely regal. Majestic in its carriage, and brilliant in its colour, it may with propriety be styled the king of the antelopes.' I was told that sometimes a pair of male kudus will die of starvation after locking their horns inextricably in combat, and that when this happens no other animal will touch the dead bodies. There is something so tragic and mysterious about this happening, something so royal about the kudu, even in death, that even the scavengers are impressed by it.

The people of South West have shown imagination in choosing the kudu as their emblem. In the final analysis, most animals seem to be fearful, perplexed, somewhat dim-witted. The kudu on the other hand is spirited, confident, curious, brimming with life. It has electricity. You can see it in those lustrous eyes and tingling flanks.

The Etosha Pan is one of the largest salt pans in the world. It occupies no less than 2,300 square miles, and a million years ago was a gigantic lake or inland sea, fed by the Cunene. With the retreat of the parent river, the lake evaporated to form the salt pan. The pan is not a solid crust, but consists of a linked series of sheets of shallow water where millions of birds nest among the reeds. In the rainy season it turns into a regular marsh. It would be desolate if it were not for its multitudinous

In the Land of Fat Cattle

Herds of other animals usually considered wild might also be established. The wart-hog, for example, is not difficult to domesticate, and its flesh when cooked is reputed to be a delicious combination of the flavours of roast beef and roast turkey. Only fads and prejudices prevent us from eating such exotic meats. If people will pay fancy prices for snails, squid, fungi, kangaroo tails, and bird's nest soup, they would hardly baulk at eland or warthog. During the war the English ate whale-meat—and liked it; and as Burchell remarked, after eating a hippopotamus steak, 'If our English lovers of good eating could but once taste such a steak, they would not rest till they had caused hippopotamus meat to be an article of regular importation.' In the world food shortage that lies ahead, any method of supplementing the food supply, however unorthodox, is surely to be welcomed.

The gemsbok and the eland are very fine beasts. But for me the animal that takes the prize is the kudu. In contrast to the slightly cobby gemsbok and the somewhat bovine eland, the kudu is all grace. To quote Selous again: 'The kudu is one of the most beautiful animals in the whole world.' It is worth travelling across a dozen deserts to see a group of young kudu males staring at you at almost point-blank range. The kudu is slender, stands five foot at the shoulder, and its colour is a lively French grey. Its horns are three to four foot long—two splendid spiky arabesques, curving and widely set and carried with the airy pride of a stag. The ears are alert as a fawn's, the muzzle sensitive and tapering. The kudu is a thoroughbred. It has all the thoroughbred's nerve and mettle. It is intensely curious, and when it rushes away from you it cannot resist pulling up short to turn round and have another look at you. It can heave those trim, maculate flanks eight feet in the air, and is always frisking, leaping, darting about. It will often cannon into a vehicle travelling at night: and one evening when I was at Windhoek one of them jumped a high wire fence and landed with a mighty splash in a big swimming pool off the Gartenstrasse. I heard a tremendous commotion and heard its curious loud sharp deep bark or bell, and was entirely mystified as to

The eland is equally imposing, for although it is somewhat thick and cumbersome it stands over six feet at the withers and weighs 2,000 pounds. It has a body which resembles a light breed of ox, to which is attached a very delicate head. The eyes are large and jewel-like, and the straight horns are between two and three feet long, solid and elegantly twisted. The pelt of the Etosha specimens is extremely subtle in colour, varying from an extraordinary ashen blue tinged with ochre to a pale sandy grey. At one time it was widely distributed throughout south and central Africa, but the Boers gradually shot it out until its only refuge now in South West is in the Etosha Reserve. Its skin was coveted for its remarkable strength, stronger even than a buffalo's, and the harness and reins of the huge eight-span trek-wagons were cut from eland hide. It was also first-rate eating. Captain Cornwallis Harris, writing in the 1880s, recorded that: 'The flesh is esteemed by all classes in Africa above that of any other animal; in grain and colour it resembles beef, but is better tasting and more delicate, possessing a pure game flavour, and the quantity of fat with which it is interlarded is surprising, greatly exceeding that of any other game quadruped with which I am acquainted.'

In point of fact the eland, which goes crashing coyly away from you when you startle it, resembles the ox in more than a superficial fashion, for like the ox it can be easily domesticated. It is interesting to learn that in 1892, twelve years before a German furrier introduced the karakul sheep into South West Africa from Russia, the Russians had imported from Africa four pairs of eland. From these animals the Russians gradually acclimatized and built up over the years a regular herd of eland in the steppes of central Asia, and today it is said to number 400. The herd has been milked since 1950, and its milk is said to be outstandingly rich in protein. An International Biological Programme has been studying the possibilities of creating additional herds of eland, which have the advantage of being able to browse on parched veld that is useless for ordinary cattle; and a careful system of rotation would ensure that the scanty grazing was conserved.

In the Land of Fat Cattle

Africa used to be one of the zebra's principal habitats, and herds of more than a hundred strong were common. Today at Etosha you can still see sizeable platoons of them. Like other animals, they have no fear of a moving car. Only if you stop and get out will they turn tail and bolt, alarmed by the sight of the strange forked animal stalking towards them as we ourselves would be by the appearance of Venusians or Martians. These zebra belong to the species known as Burchell's Zebra, so named as a result of the specimens brought back by William Burchell from the great collecting trip he made across the Orange and Vaal Rivers in 1811–12; they have black and yellow stripes instead of the black and white stripes of the common zebra. Their vivid markings make them stand out conspicuously against the deep brown soil and dark green shrubs of the veld.

The blue wildebeest, the zebra's constant companion, also grazes in large packs, forty or fifty at a time. It is an awkward looking animal, with a black shaggy outline: but a herd of wildebeest streaming over the plain gives an impression of tremendous speed and power. Its relative, the Cape hartebeest, or *tsesebe*, shares its large, clumsy appearance, lacking the grace that is normally associated with the tribe of antelopes. But it too can streak away with a sense of bulk and thrust when it takes to its heels.

The most memorable animals at Etosha are the three giant antelopes: the oryx or gemsbok, the eland, and the kudu. To catch sight of these princely creatures in their wild state gives you an instant of sudden, stinging joy. The gemsbok stands four to five feet high, and has a splendid pair of straight long slender horns ringed at the base. The horns, together with its general build, pale grey flanks, white face and sweeping black tail, have caused it in times past to be taken for the unicorn. It is exceptionally handsome, and for the famous Victorian traveller and hunter, Frederick Selous, it was 'the most vivid and gamey-looking of all open-country antelope'. It runs effortlessly and compactly, skimming over the plain, and Selous compared a herd of gemsbok in flight to a regiment of soldiers—though perhaps a squadron of lancers would be a better comparison.

practiced here is to turn out your cattle under the supervision of native herdsmen and let the beasts roam where they will until the time eventually arrives to call them in. There is plenty of room for them to roam in, for the average farm is at least thirty miles in extent and may be as much as 150 miles.

It is sixty miles from Tsumeb to Namutoni. Long before you reach your destination the noble animals for which the region is celebrated begin to appear. Until you arrive in the north, the country seems to be as sparingly endowed with animals as humans. Now you are entering one of Africa's finest game reserves. Covering an area of 26,000 square miles, it is in fact the largest game reserve in the world.

There is a restriction on hunting game in two-thirds of the Kaokoveld, but the ban seems almost unnecessary, because hardly any animals seem to exist there. All you will have seen in the major portion of the namib is an occasional klipspringer, 'pronking' in heraldic style as it fleets away from you. Or you may have caught sight of a tiny, fragile steinbok, or the diminutive dik-dik, one of the smallest antelopes in existence, a mere fifteen inches at the shoulder and with horns only four inches long. The hoofs of these delicate little creatures are the size of human fingernails and seem to whisper over the stones when they run. They are marvellously adapted to life in the desert, and are said to be able to survive for weeks without water.

The more luxuriant veld around Etosha Pan and the fort at Namutoni is capable of supporting the larger fauna. There are lions here, together with rhinos and leopards. The limitations on killing in the Etosha reserve are severely applied. If the game-wardens catch you with a dead animal, they will confiscate your vehicle, take your guns, fine you, and probably throw you in prison into the bargain. It must be hard for a keen huntsman, presented with so many mouth-watering targets, to abstain. Klaas and Sarel cast longing glances on the battalions of splendid animals that passed within easy range of the Land Rover.

The breeds that are most numerous and continually catch the eye are the zebras, wildebeests and hartebeests. South West

yard beneath a shady palm tree, eating the local pawpaw and drinking good cold Windhoek lager. The Herero servant-women swam through the splashes of sunlight like jewelled fish, brilliant in their flowing dresses and Minerva caps. The place was an oasis within an oasis; an agreeable spot to idle away a placid hour.

I left Tsumeb for Namutoni without a pang. It was not so much that the town itself had made me ill at ease: it was simply that I had not journeyed thousands of miles in order to hang around one more mine-shaft. Tsumeb stood in its rough-and-ready way for my own industrialized civilization: and when I was within its boundaries I was squeezed by the problems and pressures of being 'civilized'. There was also the additional pressure of the conflict between my civilization and the African's. And this pressure was uncomfortable because that conflict seemed insoluble. On the long drive across the Namib I had enjoyed a temporary release from it: but my first glimpse of a gang of Ovambo digging drains as I drove into Tsumeb had brought it flooding back.

It was therefore with downright relief that I escaped again into the Namib. The dunes of the Namib and the vacant stretches of the Skeleton Coast and the Kaokoveld know nothing of apartheid, or winds of change, or nationalism, or capitalism, or socialism, or man's fecklessness and cruelty. The desert doesn't care a damn. Probably it doesn't even care a damn about all that grubbing and burrowing at Tsumeb. It is a healing thought. The great boulders lie about the desert like props on a stage where the play has not yet even begun. They represent the incurable untidiness and indifference of nature, its neglectful power. Man has made no appreciable impact on the Namib. It seems safe to suppose he never will. I found that comforting.

The country north of Tsumeb is not so much desert as savannah. It consists of scorified grass, sprinkled with dusty bushes and straggly trees. This is farming country, but there are few marks to be seen of human activity. The method of farming

in from abroad. Wales, like South West, used to be run by a hierarchy of 'reliable' outsiders, sent in to keep the natives in their place: coal-owners, shipping-barons, steelmasters, landlords—right down to the foremen and the gamekeepers.

Xenophobia is obnoxious: but the roots of xenophobia do not grow without feeding. I can sympathize with the resentment of the Africans.

Paradoxically, this sprawling mining town, with its tangle of railway sidings, its spider's web of transporters and conveyors, its gigantic aluminium ore-bins, is the greenest and leafiest town in the whole of South West. It is a man-made oasis in the drouth of the Namib. Its workaday character is, of course, impossible to camouflage: but the angular outlines have been softened by the creation of parks and avenues lined with trees.

This miracle has been brought about by the surfeit of water created by the daily pumping-out of hundreds of thousands of gallons of water from the mine. Indeed, the irony of South West is that there appears to be more than enough water deep down to turn the country into a Garden of Eden. Unfortunately it can only be reached by large-scale outfits like the Tsumeb Corporation, and remains inaccessible to the puny rigs which are all that even the richest cattle-farmer can afford. You will see bougainvillaea in profusion here for the first time since you let Windhoek; you will see poinsettias, flame-trees and jacarandas. There are fat glossy oleanders, acacias smothered with cones of white and yellow blossom. The vinegary reek of the mines is counterbalanced by the perfumes of a hundred different trees and flowering shrubs.

A sprinkling of old German shops and houses helps to mellow the utilitarian tone of the rest of the town. My own favourite building was a German hostelry in the main street, its ancient façade contrasting strongly with the down-to-earth modern shops on either side of it. On its walls hung portraits of Kaiser Wilhelm II and Hindenburg, with an old sepia photograph of seven German riflemen who had performed a notable feat of arms up at Fort Namutoni. It was pleasant to sit in the court-

In the Land of Fat Cattle

Mining is calculated destruction. Its function is to tear the lights and liver out of nature. It represents the rape and murder of our mother earth. What the Tsumeb Corporation takes out it cannot put back. And what it takes out it takes with an obscene haste. The present calculation is that the resources of the pipe will last until 1980. But we can be certain that, if there is any likelihood that South Africa will have to surrender the mandate and abandon South West, then the copper, zinc and lead will have disappeared a long time before 1980. The rate of extraction will be stepped up. It is the same, as we shall see, with the diamond mining at Oranjemund. At Oranjemund the diamond beds are expected to be stripped bare by roughly the same date as the veins of ore at Tsumeb. But if Consolidated Diamond Mines see any chance that they may be ordered to pack up and leave, we can be sure there will be precious few pickings for its successors.

The people who regard themselves as the natural owners of the territory's resources, in this case the Nama and Herero, cannot be expected to be pleased. As I have already said, the Nama and Herero have no more claim to be the legitimate owners of South West than the whites. They are all usurpers. The real proprietors are the Bushmen, whose title to South West, indeed to most of Africa, goes back two hundred thousand years. But the Bushmen have no more chance of regaining their patrimony than other victims of history, the Australian aborigine, or the North American Indian. As Sarah Gertrude Millin observes: 'They will not compete for the title; they are all dead.'

None the less, I can understand the anger of a Nama or Herero as he watches the activity at Tsumeb. It is hard to stand by while what you regard as *your* wealth, *your* property, is filched from you by foreigners. Those efficient foreign engineers at Tsumeb are the counterparts of the foreign engineers the English sent to the Rhondda to bring out the coal. In such circumstances the situation of the resident population is humiliating. The interlopers treat them as a pool of ignorant unskilled labour. They are dragooned by drill-masters drafted

part of the entire process—sold. Newmont and Metal Climax have metallurgical interests in South Africa, Rhodesia, Texas, Mexico: but they still have rivals, face difficulties with the fluctuations of world prices, and are required to cope with a hundred other commercial complications.

When I began to write fiction, I used to publish novels about a heroic breed of steely-eyed and two-fisted engineers. These titans struggled against the forces of nature and against boardroom intrigue, bulldozing their way towards triumph or disaster. Since those youthful days my enthusiasm for technocrats has somewhat lessened—and in any case Tsumeb is dedicated to mining, and I have never had much affection for mining. It has always seemed to me to be one of the more dismal forms of industrial activity. Mining always comes down in the end to a gang of men crawling around on their bellies in the bowels of the earth, in semi-darkness, in muck and slime. It is a dispiriting business. I grew up with the sooty valleys of the Rhondda outside my back door, and had a ringside view of what mining had done to Wales. It had turned the country of Dafydd ap Gwilym into the land of Dai Lossin. Together, the English conquest and the mining industry had pulverized the old high culture of Wales. In place of *cynghanedd*, court-life and the French connection, Welsh culture had degenerated into an exaggerated worship of beer, bad singing and rugby football. Its ultimate expression has become *Under Milk Wood*. Welsh Toy Town. Welsh Uncle Tom.

No. I am uneasy in the neighbourhood of a mine. It brings back afternoons in the bracken on the hills above the Parc and Dare Colliery. A Miltonic vision of hell. Coal-mining is a dying industry in Wales—and the quicker it dies the better. It has poisoned Welsh skies, poisoned Welsh streams, poisoned Welsh bodies. When I was in my early teens the famous Pneumoconiosis Reports of the 1930s influenced me almost as deeply as *Portrait of the Artist* or *Les Illuminations*. They explained why as a child I had seen so many men in Cardiff and Swansea stopping in the street to hang on to the nearest railings and cough their lungs out.

In the Land of Fat Cattle

Africa Company of London secured from the German Government the three million acre Damaraland Concession, which included the mines at Tsumeb and Otavi. The mines were later exploited by a subsidiary of the S.W.A. Company known as the Otavi Minen und Eisenbahn Gesellschaft (OMEG). The early operations were interrupted by the Herero and Witbooi wars, and were not made easier by the remoteness of the sites. The railway was not built to Swakopmund until 1906, and the first ores were not shipped until the following year. Mining closed down between 1914 and 1921, and again during the Depression between 1929 and 1937. So until the Tsumeb Corporation took over in 1947 industrial activity had been sporadic, to say the least.

The outstanding efficiency and determination of the Corporation is not the least of the reproaches against it. It employs 3,000 white technicians and 3,000 Ovambo labourers. The Afrikaners call all the technicians 'Americans', and all the ore trains 'copper trains'. They are wrong on both counts. Most of the technicians are Canadians, Scotsmen, Englishmen—highly skilled men of every nationality. There are also many different fingers in the Corporation's financial pie. Two-thirds of the shares are controlled by two American giants, Newmont Mining Corporation and American Metal Climax; while smaller slices are owned by Selection Trust, De Beers, and the South West Africa Company—still clinging to 3,000 square miles of the original Damaraland Concession. Kingdoms rise and fall, regimes come and go: but financiers possess a knack of staying put.

The Corporation is stupendously successful, in a field where success is never assured and never painless. The critics of such enterprises always assume that they maintain themselves and grow without exercising any effort whatsoever. In the past twenty years an impressive amount of brain and sweat have been invested in Tsumeb. The raw material has got to be scooped out of the ground, crushed, concentrated, dried, then carried almost four hundred miles across the desert to Walvis Bay. It must then be shipped, and—a not entirely negligible

a tarred road to link up with its southern subsidiary at Otavi.

The Tsumeb mines were put up for sale by the South African government in 1947. The highest bid by a South African company was under half a million pounds, and the South Africans laughed their heads off when an American consortium, with what they took to be typical transatlantic bravura, offered a round million. They were hopping mad when the Americans recovered their purchase price in the first year alone—and not even by doing any actual mining, but simply by sifting the remaining minerals out of the tailings left by the previous owners. Within twelve years the value of the concentrates from the mines rose to £10 million ($24 million) a year. There have since been heartrending laments from the South African Nationalists about the way in which the Americans are 'stealing' their minerals.

Tsumeb was traditionally a copper mine, but it has turned out to be the largest source of lead and zinc in Africa. It is the world's second largest supplier of germanium. Well over fifty distinct rocks and ores have been found within the enormous subterranean reef into which the shafts have been sunk. They exist in the form of a horizontal oval pipe, like the pipes which yield diamonds. At the top of the pipe, a thousand feet down, come the oxides, below the oxides are the sulphides, and at two thousand feet there is another treasure-house of oxides. Before the Tsumeb Corporation began its operations virtually no attempt had been made at underground investigation. Most of the mining was of the opencast type, and had gone on sporadically for generations. It was principally for copper, which now accounts for only a third of the mine's total output.

The copper wealth of Tsumeb had been known for a century. The English explorer, Sir Francis Galton, described the rich blue-green surface outcrops of almost pure copper in 1851; and it was known that the Ovambo used to make expeditions to Tsumeb to collect ore for smelting into bracelets and spearheads. The copper boom in the second half of the century drew the copper prospectors north from their camps in Namaqualand, south of the Orange river; and in 1892 the South West

polished locally. The jewellery business is highly organized in South West. Every visitor leaves with at least one necklace, brooch, or bracelet. In every town there is an excellent jeweller's shop, in whose back room one or more young women in white overalls are bent over a vice or wheel working on a fine stone. The floor of our Land Rover was always cluttered with interesting rocks and pebbles. You would find it hard to discover a diamond: but semi-precious stones are scattered about for the taking. The difficulty is girding yourself for the trip into the desert to get them. It is no uncommon sight in the Kaokoveld to see whole rifts and veins of glittering stones in the eiselbergs, or even entire kopjes composed of rose-quartz. The drawback is the time and trouble needed for hacking them out and transporting them, and usually it does not pay a prospector, who is probably after bigger game, to make the effort.

The second shop-window that caught my eye contained something very bizarre. Standing in a row, among sacks of fertilizer and cement, was a platoon of those little plaster gnomes you see in the front gardens of English suburban homes—little gnomes with pointed ears, white whiskers and red jackets, with little picks and shovels on their shoulders, or fishing with little rods. I was staggered. I would have thought the African countryside would have furnished plenty of goblins and mischievous spirits of its own, without the need of importing new ones. The salesman who sold the burghers of Otjiwarongo that particular line of goods was a genius, the brother of the man who sold the sand to the Arabs and the ice to the Eskimos.

Rotarianism, parking-signs—and plaster gnomes. Western culture has reached the outposts of South West Africa with a vengeance.

While you go rummaging around in the Namib for a few trinkets, the professionals are gouging the really valuable minerals out of the ground at Tsumeb.

Tsumeb is 110 miles along the dirt highway to the northeast of Otjiwarongo, although the last forty miles are easy motoring because the Tsumeb Corporation has now built itself

The Land God Made in Anger

nalia of the jeweller's craft. The taste and skill with which the display was presented would have done credit to Cartier's or Garrard's. The shop was admirably run, and from it I bought two magnificently cut and polished pieces of the semi-precious stone called *Tigeraugen*, Tiger's Eyes, one blue and one brown—a veiled, mutable stone of which there are many lovely varieties in South West. The whole country abounds in stones of every description: aquamarines, agates, chrysoprases, heliodores,

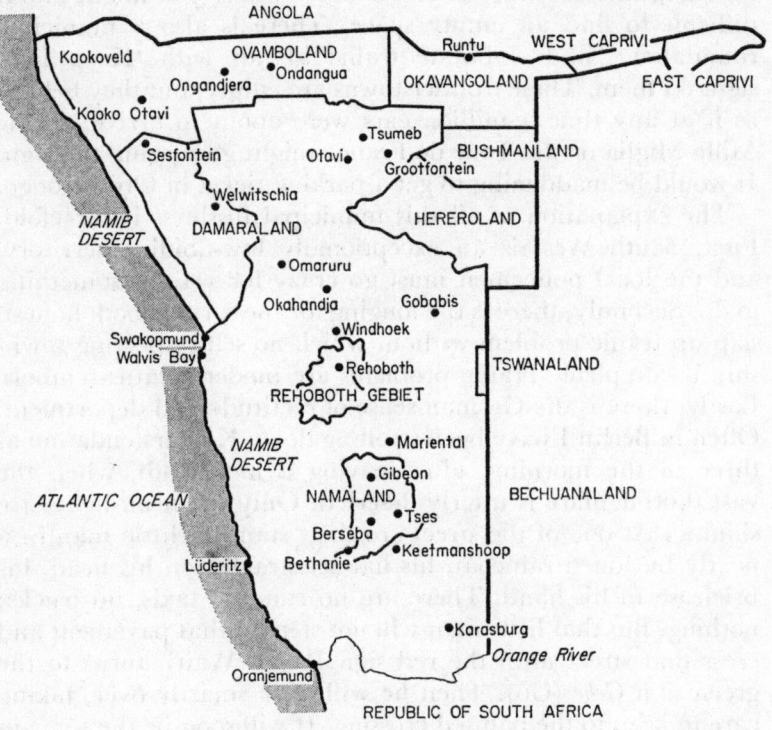

THE PROPOSED HOMELANDS OF THE AFRICAN PEOPLES
UNDER THE ODENDAAL SCHEME

garnets, sards, beryls, tourmalines, peridots, topazes—stones of every conceivable colour and variety. Many are sent for cutting and polishing to Germany, but a large proportion are

place is crawling with them. You drive past the neat little shingle that tells you that you are in Bahnhof Strasse, and come face to face with a slick metal panel embellished with an arrow and the legend 'Waterberg, Outjo, Omaruru, Windhoek'. You could hardly have missed the Windhoek road in the first place, of course: there is no other road to take. And beside this splendid direction-sign is a sign with the letter 'P'. 'P' for 'Parking'. This is to help you, if you had been led to believe that Otjiwarongo was the sort of place where you might find it difficult to find an empty space. There is also a municipal roundabout, and elaborate traffic islands with 'Keep Left' signs on them. These frontier towns are empty, but they behave as if at any time a million cars were about to arrive, or the Mille Miglia or the Tour de France might go surging through. It would be maddening to get a parking ticket in Otjiwarongo.

The explanation of all this municipal fussiness is threefold. First, South West is an exceptionally law-abiding territory, and the local policemen must go crazy for want of something to do. Secondly, there is the longing for the sort of good, honest, slap-up traffic problem without which no self-respecting township is complete. Traffic problems are modern status-symbols. Lastly, there is the German sense of rectitude and deportment. Often in Berlin I have been strolling down Kurfürstendamm at three in the morning, after leaving a night-club, when the vast thoroughfare is utterly deserted. Only the neon-lights are shining. At one of the street-crossings stands a little man in a neatly buttoned raincoat, his hat set straight on his head, his briefcase in his hand. There are no cars, no taxis, no trucks: nothing. But that little man will not step off that pavement and cross that street until the red sign *Warte* (Wait), turns to the green sign *Gehe* (Go). Then he will walk smartly over, taking care to keep to the painted crossing. It will soon be the same in Otjiwarongo. Roundabouts and 'keep-left' signs are the marks of progress and civilization.

At Otjiwarongo I saw two very remarkable shops. One was a jeweller's, a small establishment set back on its own. In its windows were laid out a selection of the tools and parapher-

technology, to set the pace. Interestingly enough, the Germans in South West do not appear on the whole to be unduly aggressive. They have lost their battle in the territory. They lost it, like Germany itself, in 1945, even though I was assured that there are rabid ex-Nazis who refuse to believe that Hitler is dead—and I heard several hints to the effect that Martin Bormann is living incognito in South West. But the Germans are no longer the masters there. Since 1945 the South African government has stimulated a constant flow of Afrikaner settlers to make sure that the former German preponderance will be forever destroyed. The Germans are now a minority. True, they early threw in their lot with the Nationalist Party of South Africa, which had the merit of being authoritarian, anti-British and pro-Nazi; they hated Smuts, who had smashed the Nazi organization in South West, had interned its leaders, and who, while he was only deputy premier, had brought South Africa (by 97 votes to 85) into the war on the side of the Allies. The Germans helped the Nationalists to rout the United Party in South West, and in return have received many favours from the Nationalists. But their eyes are no longer turned towards Germany, even though they are assiduous in visiting it and sending their children whenever possible to be educated there. Significantly, the death of the imperial dream has made them more co-operative and easier to live with. They inspire by example instead of threat; their great virtues flourish more freely and amiably. The sinister outburst of two world wars has drained off the evil humours.

The Hamburger Hof is not the only attractive modern building in Otjiwarongo. The station near by is also trim and serviceable in appearance: and if the buildings in the main street are utilitarian rather than beautiful, they compare favourably with the shabby tin-shack farming-towns to the south. The streets are immaculately tarred, with broad pavements, smartly painted lamp-standards, and fresh white lines to indicate parking spaces. Above the names of the shop hang the familiar brand signs: *Shell, Opel, Mercedes, Bosch, Agfa*.

As in all these one-street towns, signs are everywhere. The

nothing more than a group of the local Rotarians, indulging in their annual Christmas bun-fight and ceremonial junketings. The knowledge did not lessen my respect for them. It needs courage and a lot of dotty optimism to keep up your standards and try to lead the good life in a place called Otjiwarongo.

Otjiwarongo means, in fact, the 'Place of Fat Cattle'. It is the centre of the richest farming country of South West—though in terms of more fortunate lands it is not outstandingly rich. Farming has always been tough and chancy in South West, with two farmers being wiped out for every one who succeeds. Farming is the poor relation of mining and fishing, as far as the revenue figures are concerned. South West exports annually over a quarter of a million cattle and 2 million karakul pelts, each to the value of about £5 million: and these are impressive figures, until you compare them with a mining industry yielding upwards of £100 million and a fishing industry upwards of £20 million. If it was dependent on its profits from farming, the economy of the country would be almost on a par with that of Mali or Morocco. Nevertheless there are almost 3,000 white people at Otjiwarongo, constituting a large bloc of the total white population. Only Windhoek, Walvis Bay and Keetmanshoop have more white citizens, and there are more whites here than at Swakopmund, Lüderitz or Oranjemund.

The lead in building up the area has been taken by the Germans. There are a thousand cars in the district, and every second one appears to be a Volkswagen. The Germans have become the cultural fugelmen of South West. The Afrikaners and the British are aesthetically matter-of-fact; they are still not convinced by the correlation which the Germans established long ago between smartness and efficiency. Even in a world dedicated increasingly to sales-drives and productivity, the traditional values of the Afrikaner and the Briton are still not the values of the German; they are still not entirely sold on the doctrine of work. Left to themselves, they like to bumble along, keeping their main energies in reserve for moments of great national crisis. It therefore falls to the Germans, with their abundant vitality, discipline, love of business, and delight in

We walked slowly towards the entrance as though the place might suddenly disappear. The feeling of illusion was heightened as we dumped our airline bags beside the reception-desk and saw that the hotel was full of ladies in long evening dresses and men in white tie and tails. So much for *ongandas* and *okuruuos*, leather aprons and *ekoris*. Through a pair of wide glass doors I glimpsed a crowd of dancers togged up in full evening fig, whirling and gyrating in time to the music. I had heard of Englishmen changing for dinner in the middle of the jungle: but this was incredible.

The dancers were confident and cheerful. They stepped out vigorously. I noticed that they danced in an old-fashioned style, a style that went out thirty years ago. The music changed from a fox-trot to the waltz from the *Merry Widow*. *ONE-two-three. ONE-two-three.* They swung each other around with the energy of actors in a ball-room scene in a Max Ophuls or René Claire picture. They swept across the floor, hands held exaggeratedly high, the ladies leaning well back in the male arms clamped firmly around their broad silk-clad backs. Staring through the glass doors, as I wrestled with the process of registering my sense of wonder and unreality increased. I felt like the watcher whom Ravel describes in the preamble to *La Valse*, caught up in 'the idea of a fantastic whirl of destiny'. This was the ball on the eve of Waterloo, or in Marie Antoinette's Versailles. Whatever else they were, these people believed in themselves and their way of life. They were hurling defiance at the bogies of drought and pestilence, the threat of nationalism and international anathema. They danced. It was impressive. It made me marvel once more at the stubbornness and tenacity of human beings. It takes a bit of doing, to deck yourself up to the eyebrows and waltz and fox-trot in a town stuck out at the end of the world, in the bush, with the African night pressing down all round you.

I would have liked to have kept the vision of the dancers at the end of the world intact by remaining in ignorance about them—just as I had kept the mystery of the Brandberg intact by not seeing the White Lady. Alas, the girl at the reception-desk told me that this extraordinary band of revellers was

In the Land of Fat Cattle

shirted, felt-hatted Africans of Windhoek and the coast. They would be the real tribal Africans, the two middle teeth of their lower jaw knocked out, the two middle teeth of their upper jaw notched and sharpened. They would wear simple aprons of cloth or goatskin, sandals, a necklace, a head-wrapping of soft lambskin. The women would be clad equally simply in a long leather skirt, a beaded belt and anklets, and would be covered with multiple copper bracelets. On their heads they would wear the *ekori*, the distinctive leather headdress with a stiff coif or crest, the lappets falling on to the small drooping triangular paps.

A pleasant, pastoral scene.

I was wrong about Walvis Bay. I was wrong about Otjiwarongo.

In the 'thirties in England there was a famous dance-band conducted by a man called Henry Hall. His band was like Guy Lombardo's, the King of Corn, and it played several times a week on the old steam-radio. Its signature-tune was a number called *Here's to the Next Time*. I don't suppose I had heard that tune for thirty years, since I was a boy. So it was pretty startling to ease myself out of the Land Rover and hear that superannuated number booming out of the hotel's well-lighted windows, ricochetting down the darkened main street, and rolling away over the deserted veld.

The hotel, too, was unexpected. The Hotel Hamburger Hof was of modern and imaginative design. Its glass and concrete façade was set off by the row of young acacias sedulously planted in front of it. Through the glass wall of the lounge I could see the guests circulating from one room to the other, or sitting at small tables talking and drinking. An inviting spectacle after a hot dusty drive, through what was virtually the back of beyond. There is a German saying to the effect that wherever you go you will find a Saxon has got there ahead of you. There must be a lot of Saxons in the hotel business in South West. Probably if you travel in Spitzbergen or Yucatán your weary eyes will spy a Hamburger Hof in front of you, spick and span, complete with brisk and imperturbable German staff.

EIGHT
In the Land of Fat Cattle

IF you were travelling towards a town called Otjiwarongo, what would you expect it to be like?

For me, the name conjured up a picture of an African *onganda*. There would be a little community living in the usual beehive-shaped huts made of sticks plastered with mud and dung. The huts would be grouped in a circle around the cattle kraal, and beside the chief's hut would be the *okuruuo* or sacred hearth. The men of the village would be squatting round it, chatting, tending the holy flame, passing from one to another a bowl brimming with *omaere*—curdled milk—the favourite drink of the African herdsman. They would resemble the bands of Himba and Tjimba I had seen on the Kaokoveld, relations of the lordly Herero, wandering with their scrawny herds from one rancid patch of grazing to the next.

Because the town was 150 miles north of Windhoek, in the neighbourhood of the Police Zone, European influence would be negligible. The men of the *onganda* would not be the khaki-

sounded like the voice of a sea-serpent, and the Portuguese fishermen quarrelled and went outside to fight, and the diamond detective and I picked the best teams ever to play for Wales and for the Springboks. . . .

Evenings in the open, sitting at a table at the Strandbad, breathing the astringent air off the Atlantic, knocking back schooners of beer with chasers of Steinhäger, listening to the waves and looking up at the stars in the cold clear African sky. . . .

. . . Stars. Always so brilliant in Africa, dense and close above you. Unlike any stars you see in the Northern Hemisphere. Strange to swallow your drink and reflect that the stars too are nothing more than enormous gems. Masses of flaming, flaring carbon, reducing themselves to diamond. . . .

There are riches up there, waiting for a new race of prospectors and entrepreneurs to gouge them out of the universe. *See how the floor of heaven is thick inlaid with patines of bright gold*. We belong to a greedy and acquisitive breed.

Man has not yet hit on a way to turn the stars into coin.

He is working at it.

I passed an hour luxuriating in thoughts of melancholy and mortality among the flaking, flame-red ruins.

> ... Round behind the gashouse
> Musing upon the king my brother's wreck
> And on the king my father's death before him ...

Down among the rocks I came across an enormous seal. It was helpless and dying. One eye was blind, a mere milky circle. The other was bloodshot, damaged, its sight fading. The creature had been wounded in a fight, either with one of its own kind or with some other creature of the sea. Now that it was useless and disfigured it had been cast out from the pack. It lay stranded on the shore, several yards from the sea which it would never enter again. Around it lay its young, gnawed and bitten by the jackals that came slinking along the beach at night. I picked up one of them. It was rigid, its fur staring. It was like a small cocoon or papoose, or one of the mummified ibises you can pick up by the thousand on the plateau at Sakkara, where they are clearing the galleries in a search for the tomb of Imhotep.

There was a fearful stench of decay. The huge creature flailed its unwieldy, deliquescent grey carcase this way and that, opening and closing its cavernous mouth with the broken yellow molars and the blubbery lips ringed with stiff white hairs. It reared and writhed, swinging its great blunt head from side to side towards any strange sound, impotent to attack me, baffled by the heartless ocean that boomed and crashed behind it. Blind, it was still dangerous, defending its dead.

Tonight the jackals would pluck up enough courage to set upon it. They would tear bloody gobbets of flesh from its flanks.

Not yet. Now it could still fight. It was angry, unreconciled, keeping the darkness at bay with its last ounce of strength.

Lüderitz.
Evenings in the warmly-lit, brass-and-mahogany bar at Kapps Hotel, when the fog came rolling in, and the fog-horn

and bedrooms where the original paint and paper were still intact. The people might have walked out four months and not forty years ago. The sensation was akin to the sensation you feel when you walk around the temples of the upper Nile—Kom Ombo, Edfu, Esna—and realize that the normal processes of time have been compacted and crushed together. The smooth and regular flow of time has been disrupted. Does a smooth and regular flow really exist? ...

There is time—and Time ... Elizabeth Bay was disconcerting. Forty years had passed: the buildings were scarcely touched. The same sun. The same sea. *La mer, la mer, toujours recommencée.* The time-scale of the sun and sea is not our time-scale. We can scarcely believe those brilliant, chilling waters are not immortal: though the sun, we know, is dying and consuming itself, steadily reducing itself to dark dead ash. Each time we stare at our warm fire in winter we watch a rehearsal of the death of the universe.

My customary perspective was restored by the sight of the machinery. Wrecked, twisted, tangled, deliberately cracked by its owners into useless bits, it lay strewn over a dozen acres, jumbled up among broken orthogonals of concrete. The crazy geometry was heightened by the sharp bright traceries of rust. It was as if a family of giants had been playing with the metal puzzles you give to children and thrown them away in pique. The hundred-foot high girders of the huge pulsator, which used to rock and clatter as it shook and sorted the precious gravels, resembled an abandoned swing in an ogre's garden, or a big dipper in a deserted fair-ground.

Again the abstract quality of the South Western landscape—its gaunt, spare, sculptured lines—had imposed its character on the men who had sought to dominate it. The mounds of scrap posed one more South Western enigma. Here in a country which had only just begun to industrialize itself were the relics of a great industry that had long ago flowered and declined. South West is certainly the place to visit if you are entertained by the feeling that some agency is playing tricks with your sense of time.

8 The Brandberg

7 Namib Desert above Lüderitz

A kokerboom in the Schwarzrand

morning for giants. Their necks and shoulders were humped like Bohórquez bulls. Their skins were so black they shone grape-purple in the sunshine. I could see the clubs that were stuck down their trouserlegs on the outside of the right thigh.

It will be a bad day for the rest of us when the Ovambo take up rugby football.

The detective went into the hut and came out with a register. He brought it across to my window. I signed it. He signed it himself, carefully noting the time, snapped it shut, and handed it to one of the Ovambo, who tucked it under his arm. The detective got in and slammed the door, smacked in his first gear, and we were off again. The Ovambo, still at attention, saluted and remained at the salute until the jeep was out of sight. It was my first glimpse of the fact that the diamonds of South West are guarded, after all, with the vigilance of a well-disciplined army. . . .

The track was the old road to Elizabeth Bay. Sixty years ago many men and mules had trudged along it with food, liquor and mining gear. It had been a long and sweaty journey. Now we covered the distance in an hour. As with so much in South West, I had no idea of what I was going to see until I actually saw it. My companion was not the man to enlighten me. I expected Elizabeth Bay to look like the trenches, pits, mounds and hollows in the ground I had seen in the Namib, north of Swakopmund, though on a greatly enlarged scale.

Not for the first or the last time, my expectations were confounded. The road emerged with unexpected abruptness on the coast, and I was confronted with what appeared to be a complete and extensive township. The only unusual feature was that it seemed to be empty of inhabitants.

Coming closer, it became clear that Elizabeth bay was a well-preserved ghost-town. It was built by the Germans before the First World War, and abandoned in the mid 1920s: but if the diggings were reactivated tomorrow the employees would be able to move in and make the place habitable again without much trouble. What destroys abandoned houses is rain and frost. Here there was neither. I wandered through living rooms

of an elephant's trunk. The massive, weathered, Roman head was thatched with thick bleached hair cropped in the murderous fashion of the Afrikaner farmer. He had received instructions from Windhoek to show me round, but his manner was deeply suspicious. He thawed out when we found we had a topic in common: rugby football. This made me respectable. He thawed further when he learned that I had played against the first South African international team to tour Britain after the war. It was the grimmest match I ever played in. I still have the marks to prove it. Most of the Springbok forwards were as big as he was. That day neither side took any prisoners.

He drove that jeep up hill and down dale with tremendous brio. I have a friend in London, a famous horseman and writer of books on horsemanship, who drives cars like that. He treats them as if they were nappy hunters and have to be shown who is master. There is a lot of spirited mounting of the pavement and cornering on the short rein, with muffled grunts of 'Come up, damn it! . . . Steady! . . . Whoa! . . . Easy now, blast you! . . .' The diamond detective drove in the same way. Like my friend in London, he was a first-rate driver but a brutal one. He had no respect for machinery. When he changed gear he thudded the lever in without delicacy or finesse, as if he intended to stand no nonsense from the gear-box. On a later occasion I was with him in much rougher country far to the south, and we got into trouble in a very tricky stretch of sand. I was interested to see how well his methods paid off in such circumstances. He went at those dunes like a dragoon in a cavalry charge. He never stopped or faltered. Slithering, heaving, grating, growling, he got us through.

Suddenly he slammed on the brakes without warning and slid out of the driving-seat in one powerful movement. I saw that we had reached a check-point: a wooden hut beside the track, situated in the middle of nowhere. Beside the hut two Ovambo clad in white singlets were standing at quivering attention, fists clenched, thumbs rigidly aligned down the seams of their denims. They were two of the most massive men I had ever seen, bigger even than the detective. This was a

passport to the *lekker lewe*, the sweet life. An unwavering, impossible vision.

Probably it was wrong to do it, but I hung around with the old man after everyone else eventually left the bar and went up to bed. Then I gave him fifty rand.

He was delighted, knocked endways. He had obviously not seriously expected to be able to touch me for cash. He subjected me to a bone-bruising handshake. I thought he might despise me as a sucker, a simpleton. Not so. In all sincerity he called me a partner, and promised me a share of the profits.

Thus he bestowed upon me a piece of the great dream.

I often think of old Martiens sitting down there in Africa, alert under the night sky, a blanket around his shoulders, his .22 across his knees. I don't think of him wiping up greasy plates in a smelly kitchen: I think of him out there in the desert. My partner. My two partners: Martiens and the donkey.

All the same, I worry about it. I hope the old man is really as strong and smart as he thinks he is, and that he manages to stay out of Windhoek gaol. . . .

I went down to Elizabeth Bay, twenty miles south of Lüderitz, where one of the strikes was made sixty years ago, and spent a day there.

One of the diamond detectives picked me up at Kapp's Hotel in a government vehicle—a big, high-sided, solid affair, with a spartan interior, much more like a recce-car than a jeep. We drove out of the town uphill along the twisting road, blotched with shade from the overhanging boulders.

We reached the plateau at Kolmanskop and took a track across the veld. Except for the dry clarity of the air, and the intensity of the sunshine, we might have been bumping our way across the Cornish or Yorkshire moors. My companion was no great conversationalist, so we kept silent. I am not a small man myself, but he was enormous. He was built on the scale of the landscape. He was huge, his features seemingly sand-blasted, the hands gripping the wheel the size of dinnerplates. His neck had the thickness and texture of the upper part

He was evasive about the jackpot he himself had claimed to have found; evidently the stones had turned out to be tiny, little larger than the diminutive stones known as *boart* that can only be used as industrial grit, individual stones cracked up by the action of the current into a whirl of dust like the rings round Venus. But nothing could take away from him—or ever dim or efface—the extraordinary emotion of that second when his shovel first uncovered the little hole in the bedrock, no bigger than the opening of a beehive. In that moment he thought he had become a millionaire. But more than that— more than the money—was the thought that nature had blessed him, had shown him a miracle, had justified the mad, blind optimism of thirty years, had redeemed a life of sweat and waste....

As the session went on farther and farther into the night he told us other amusing and fascinating things. For example, he claimed that once, when he was leaving the *Sperrgebiet* after one of his illegal forays, he saw the spiral of dust that meant that the jeep of the diamond detectives was approaching. Whereupon he took off the noseband of old Lord Roberts (the donkey was twenty-eight years old at the time) and hid all his own gear in a gully. He then wrapped his diamonds in a rag, inserted the rag deep in Lord Roberts' floppy ear, gave him a smack on the rump, and told him to make his own way back home. At that time Martiens was living on a half-hearted apology for a farm at Aus, sixty miles away. The donkey trotted off. When the detectives searched Martiens he was clean. They gave him a lift home. Lord Roberts turned up at the farm at dusk two days later. He was thirsty, and brayed for his beer.

But the glowing image of the jackpot lingered in the old man's eye. He also maintained his brisk determination, extraordinary in a man of seventy (he was touchy about his age, and never admitted to more than fifty-seven), to extract enough money from us to provide the sinews of one last expedition. He stuck to the tale of the jam-jar, buried by Floors Grobler, his dead friend. What he was after, though, what he was willing to die for, was another jackpot: *Pay Day, the Big One*. It was his

knotting his brown fingers together. He surveyed us with a little grin of perfectly good-humoured contempt.

'I dare say,' he said, 'it all seems a tremendous hard lot to put up with, just on the chance of coming across a pocketful of diamonds?'

None of us contradicted him.

Again he twitched his bony shanks forward, until he was perched once more right forward on the edge of his seat. The pale eyes gleamed at us out of the razor-sharp planes of the temples and cheekbones. A cracked, veiled note entered his voice.

'That's because you ain't none of you had a pile of diamonds right here in your hand.'

He held up a claw-like hand, palm outwards. The skin was calloused, stretched tight, seamed with a close craquelure like the lines on an old brown teapot. We could almost see the diamonds.

'You ain't never hit the jackpot,' he said. '*I have.*' Again the death's-head grin. 'Know what "hitting the jackpot" means? A jackpot's a real thing: it ain't just words. A jackpot's a hole in the solid rock at the bed of an old river, made by a mass of diamonds grinding round and round in an eddy. Grinding round in the current. Grinding, grinding, grinding away. Boring into the rock like a damn drill on a metal plate. And thousands and thousands of years later, when that old river has ceased to flow, that parcel of diamonds is still there, snug in its little nest—waiting for someone like *me* to come along and dig it out.' His eyes burned. 'Man, I tell you that's the most tremendous exciting sight in the world. Even van der Heever and Paul Boussouw, the jackpot they found down to Rust-myn-ziel'—the two arms came out in front of him like ramrods—'you couldn't have got your two hands round it. It was valued at quarter-million pounds. Quarter-million pounds, for what Eben brought back to Upington wrapped up in a pocket-handkerchief. And the one Hendrik van Taak got, between the farms called Glencoe and Altona . . .'

He was off on a long catalogue of notable triumphs. Like Fred Cornell, none of the great discoveries had fallen to his lot.

across a few little pools with a yellow crust or yellow scum on top. Don't drink from that. It's saltpetre. An hour after your guts'll drop out and you'll get a raging thirst.'

'What about gourds and squashes?'

'The kaffir gourd's all right, in small doses. Don't touch the yellow or green one, mind. The one what you want's the one with the brown skin and the white band round it.' He chuckled. 'How your old donkey loves them kaffir gourds. Can't drag him away from a patch of them. I always carry a little box of sugar with me. Lump of sugar's the only thing to pull him away from them gourds.'

He rubbed his chin and glanced at me thoughtfully, as though reluctant to give away any more professional secrets. Then, as though the knowledge might someday save my life, he said:

'I'll give you a couple of wheezes what'll be useful. First, take a rubber groundsheet. When you camp for the night, dig a hole in the sand with shallow sides, then line it with the groundsheet. Put a stone in the middle of the groundsheet and use more stones to anchor the sides. During the night, when the temperature drops, the dew will collect on the sheet and trickle down to the bottom. At the very worst, you've got the stone to lick in the morning. Man, every drop counts.' He paused. 'There's another dodge I've seen, though I ain't used it myself. It's a gadget a pal of mine heard of in Canada, and what he got made up for him in Johannesburg. He brought it out to South West and took it on a trip he made up around Bogenfels. He said it worked marvellous: and he brought back some fine diamonds, too. Biggest was 14 carats. Got £3,000 for them from Chris Swanepoel—he's dead now—down in Garies. Well, this contraption which he used was two plates of glass, a foot square, set a inch apart in a wooden frame, with a carrying handle on the top. Like a little tashie-case. He carried the damn thing cross the Namib with him, and the condensation inside the glass ran down to the bottom, where he'd got a little tap. Neat, eh?'

At this point he broke off and leaned back in his chair,

be out in the desert, anyway. You come with me, you won't get into no trouble like that.'

Like the Ancient Mariner, he fixed me with a glittering eye, and hitched his lean body forward in his seat.

'Ever seen men dying of thirst? Know what happens to them? They walk round and round in circles, choking. They've got tongues sticking out of them like big cracked lumps of leather, hanging down as far as their chins, thick and swollen so they look like big grey dried-up beaks of parrots. Well, when they reach that stage it's a hundred to one they're going to cash in. Best thing to do with a man in that state's just to trickle a few drops on his tongue. Don't give him too much, or you'll kill him.' His long face grew grave. 'That's what you've got to train yourself to do on your own account—never touch more than a few drops of water at a time. Just a sip. Enough to wet your lips. You'll be tempted to take huge big swallows. Don't. A few minutes later you'll feel worse—real bad.'

'You mean, you feel thirsty all the time?'

'All the time. Least, I do—and I'm used to it. I reckon a man can't last ten hours in there without water before he pegs out. You got to take it easy on your water supply. Some people like to chew tobacco—keeps the saliva going. Me, I suck a pebble—carry a special bag of them.'

'Special bag?'

'That's it, a bag of pebbles we call *bantahms*. They're brown and sort of soapy. You can collect them from the Orange, or where there's been diamonds. They're round, flat, all shapes, with white rings round them. I choose twelve or fifteen and keep them in a bag. When I get fed up with sucking one, I put it back and pick out another.'

'And what happens when you get fed up with sucking the *bantahms*?'

'Suck something else. Bullets are good.'

'Any other ways of getting water?'

'There are springs of course.' The smile became sly. 'Not many—but I know where they are. Which is why I can travel wherever I like in there.' He grew serious again. 'You'll run when you're on your way out. Many a man has died which couldn't recognize the same hills and rocks what he'd passed only three or four days previous.'

He paused and took a small mouthful of light ale, then went on:

'Of course, if there's a fog rolling in, or a sandstorm, then there ain't a damn thing you can do about it. You just got to find a snug spot to hole up and pray for it to pass—soon as possible, because if it lasts two, three days then you're going to run low on water and you'll have to turn back. I've spent some pretty miserable days squeezed up in a crack in the rocks with a blanket over my head.'

He frowned for a moment, then brightened again.

'Otherwise,' he said, 'just keep that old koppie steady in view and shuffle, shuffle, shuffle away. That's what they call us sometimes—"Sandshufflers".' (I remembered the stiff, wading gait with which he had crossed the bar of the hotel towards me, steely fingers extended.) He smiled. 'That old donkey, he'll shuffle, shuffle, shuffle along too, right beside you. Ever seen the feet of a sand donkey? You don't clip its hoofs, but let them grow long. Sometimes they grow out a whole foot in length, and make a huge big curve up at the ends. Helps them get along.'

'But what about food and water?' I asked. 'You've got to carry them for the donkey, haven't you?'

'Him don't drink half as much as what a truck would. And you don't need fodder. Him'll browse all day on that burnt-up scrub. God knows what he finds to nourish him in it—but he tucks it away like it was cabbage. What's more, if you get in a tight spot him'll often find you water—and what damn truck can do that? Him's got a wonderful sharp nose for water. Can smell it miles away. Takes you right to it. Scrapes away with his paws like a dog. Don't matter if it's five foot down—him'll find it.'

'And what if he doesn't?'

'If he don't, and your canteen's empty, and you've buried your last tyre thirty miles back—then, man, you're in trouble. But if you get into that kind of trouble, you got no business to

stick to your block of biltong. But pick one that ain't too hot and spicey.'

'All the same, you try and hunt if you can?'

'Yes—but you've got to save your energy, remember. You can't go running around in the heat, in the open. And you'll have to be a terrible good shot—.'

'Why?'

'Because you'll only have taken a small gun. A .22. You can't risk using a big noisy gun. Sound carries miles in the desert. Pity to spend ten years in gaol for missing a duiker. Ever tried to shoot a duiker with a .22?'

'If you travel at night, how do you find your way?'

'By the stars, or your map and compass. You've also got to learn to use landmarks.'

'It sounds tricky.'

'It is. The great thing's to take your time. Stay calm and don't rush. Don't even think fast. It's not a race. If you've got enough water, you can take all the time in the world. Don't try to dash in and out quickly. It ain't a raid: it's a battle of nerves. It's the man what keeps thinking and uses his brains what comes through.'

'Yes, but what happens if you get lost?'

'You'll find that's a fear which stays with you most of the time. You can't shake it off. Man, it's a hell of a feeling.'

'So what do you do about it?'

'You've got to fight down your panic. Remind yourself all the time that this ain't just a huge big fight with the desert: it's a huge big fight with yourself. You get scared, you're done for. You'll just go roaming around in a great big circle and come back to where you started from. It's a horrible thing, when you look down and recognize your own footsteps in the sand.'

'It must be!'

'Take your bearing with your compass, nice and comfortable. Then go ahead, nice and slow. Stop every now and again and look behind you at where you've come from—kind of glance back over your shoulder. Memorize the features of the landscape you just crossed. You may be glad you took the trouble

and water him. He'll be happy. Marvellous happy animals, donkeys. Best one I had was called Lord Roberts. Liked his wad of chewing-tobacco and his drop of beer. Very fond of music too. Loved a tune on the mouth-organ.'

'What sort of gear and provisions do you carry?'

'Well, first off you'll need five blankets.'

'Five?'

He nodded.

'Thick ones. In the day you get temperatures of 110 or 120. At night it falls below zero. Man, you can't tell if the rocks in there are split by the hot or by the cold.'

'Blankets. What else?'

'Next off, your water. Your best thing is to get three inner tubes from motor-car tyres. Fill them with water and sling them round the donkey's neck. Mark three places on your map between where you start off from and where you want to end up. Prominent places. Landmarks. Then unship one of your tyres whenever you reach a landmark and bury it. Bury it deep. Keeps it out of sight and keeps it cool.'

'I see. What do you take to eat?'

'Me, I take plenty of dried stuff. A little goes a long way, and it's easy to carry. Dried apricots and plums, plenty of dried raisins. Ten or twelve big boer rusks. Sometimes I bake bread. Keep the dough a day, then bake it in a dead or dried-up anthill, stopping up the ant-eater's hole with clay.'

'What about fresh meat?'

'It's nice if you can get it, but strictly speaking you won't need it. Maybe you can shoot a fat little buck, round about sundown. You cook it—'

'How?'

'On the blade of your shovel. Wrap the heart and liver in the stomach-fat and fry them. Oh, and cut out the bladder before you start, so you can drink the fluid in it. You can't drink the blood, because it turns to jelly. Now and then you'll get a snake. A python's particular good. Bake it, so the meat falls away from the bone and muscle. Tastes like white fish. Most of the time, though, if you've a tooth for meat, you'll have to

He showed no reluctance in revealing the details of how to organize a trip to the Forbidden Area. He wanted to demonstrate how experienced and tough he was, how capable of recovering the miraculous jam-jar. But he was also caught up in the recital of his own exploits. He was a professional discussing the minutiae of his trade. He enjoyed an audience.

The first thing he told me was that it was useless to try to make the trip in any kind of car or truck. What you wanted, he said, was a donkey.

'Man, that's a huge big country in there,' he said, in his quick, creaky voice. 'How are you going to carry all that fuel? What are you going to do when you break down? Where are you going to get all that water for your radiator? Two and a half pints a day, that's what you'll need—minimum. You won't have none to spare for topping up any boiling radiators.

'Take a pack animal. And of all the animals which is on the veld, the best is the donkey. Lassoo a wild donkey from a car, break him in, and you'll find he'll do marvellous for you. Some of the way in you'll be able to ride him, at least as far as the soft sand. You can ride him further than you could ride a truck. And he's wonderful clever at picking up the hard ridges. What's more, if you was in a truck your tyre tracks would show up to the air patrols, or give you away to the detectives in the jeeps. But a donkey, they can't tell his prints from a zebra's, and for some reason the bloodhounds can't smell him, neither.'

Someone asked: 'What about your own footprints, then?'

'Man, what you want to do is make sheepskin muffles. Wipes out your tracks at the same time you're making them. Or cut a pair of foot covers out of the feet of an ostrich. Ostriches walk the same way a man does.'

'What's the best season to set out?'

'June, July. Winter months. Less wind and heat.'

'You just walk over the line?'

'Just walk over the line. What's to stop you? You'll be travelling by night, anyway. You can't travel at all by day. Daytime you'll sit up or sleep in the shade, with your gun. But first take everything off your donkey's back. Tether him. Feed

spot, he insisted, deep inside the *Sperrgebiet*, where there was a jam-jar full of choice diamonds left by a friend of his who had died in the mountains before he could bring them out.

Nobody wanted to give him any money. It was like giving a drink to a dipso, they told me. But they would have staked him soon enough, I realized, if they thought that at his time of life there was any chance of his getting in and out of the Namib alive. I could see that they were inclined to believe the tale about the jam-jar: it was his ability to reach it and bring it back that they doubted. And he was not fool enough to give any of them exact details about its location.

I was interested to note that no one thought any the less of him for his poverty. He was working for a few cents a day as a washer-up in the kitchen of a hotel down the road: but when he came into the bar to meet me he was treated like a king. He had glamour and authority; he was listened to with profound respect; he was an old man who had seen and done things which no one present, perhaps very few living South Africans, had seen and done. He was that very rare creature: his own man.

To look at he had something of the imposing but slightly dotty air of Don Quixote, or Captain Ahab, or the Ancient Mariner. He certainly had the Ancient Mariner's skinny hand and glittering eye: he was 'long, and lank, and brown, as is the ribb'd sea sand'. He was so slender as to be almost emaciated: a tall streak of human biltong. The desert sands had permanently dried the juices out of him. His toothless cheeks had been sucked in, making his jaw look as wide and flat as a shovel. He was tall, and his cropped, sandy hair rose abruptly from a forehead burnt to the colour of bitter chocolate. His fingers when we shook hands cut into mine like strong thin wires. He was unaware of the instinctive force of his grip. All his movements crackled with a jerky, incessant, faintly lunatic energy. I noticed, however, that he would accept nothing more potent than a glass of light beer, and that he sipped at it in a delicate and perfunctory way, making it last four or five times as long as the drinks of the people around him.

possessed by the *trek-gees* or wanderlust, a man of the old straightforward virtues who could not adapt to the new commercial society. Needless to say, it was not difficult for the politicians to fool him. The farmers at Alexander Bay got no compensation or *ex gratia* payment, and had no option but to hitch up and move on. During the course of the abortive rebellion, one of Maritz's sharpshooters ensconced himself in the pile of boulders in the middle of Springbok. He made the entire population keep its collective head down. He shot at anyone who appeared at a window, and sniped all the bottles off the hotel bar. An exhilarating scene. I wish I could have found out what happened to him.

Martiens had been a citizen of Springbok for three years, ever since he had emerged from his last spell in prison. Everyone knew that sooner or later the urge to go back to South West in search of diamonds would prove too strong for him, and that one night he would slip back over the line again. What stopped him was lack of funds. Like most obsessive diamond-hunters, he was broke. He had made some sizeable strikes in his day, but the money had all gone on financing more ambitious and abortive expeditions, or buying expensive digging equipment. And also like most of his kind, he was curiously unlucky. He had blazed trails and opened up fields that were later exploited by cooler and cannier characters, without reaping any of the benefit himself. He had stumbled on likely places where the stuff might be found, but had always wandered on before fully investigating them. He gave the impression, like fishermen or mountaineers, that the pursuit was more important than the quarry. Finding the diamonds somehow spoiled the fun.

Fred Cornell, too, had been broke for most of his career. Ironically, after all his fantastic feats and bouts of endurance in South West, Cornell died of a haemorrhage caused by a trivial traffic accident in Piccadilly—Theodore Powys's son in reverse. Martiens, on the other hand, had every intention of laying down his bones in South West. As soon as he had scraped together a stake, he would be off. His object in talking to me was to induce me to put up money for a wild-cat scheme. He knew a

Diggers and Donkeys

I was lucky enough to meet one of the most famous of the pioneer diamond prospectors of South West. I will call him Martiens. He was of the generation of Fred Cornell, one of the last representatives of a dying breed. His conversation, couched in the bubbling anfractuosities of his thick Afrikaans accent, gave me a piercing insight into the conditions that men like Stauch, Scheibe and Cornell had faced. He also provided the answers to many of the problems which I had put to myself on the journey through the *Sperrgebeit*, concerning ways in which a man could get in among those deadly wastes in search of diamonds and live to tell the tale.

Martiens was acknowledged to be the greatest authority alive on the geography of the Namib and the Skeleton Coast. Nevertheless he had been banned from South West, and the next time he crossed the Orange River and was caught by the diamond detectives it would mean life-imprisonment. In effect it would be a death sentence, for he was now seventy years old, and if he went to gaol he would certainly die there.

We met in Springbok, in a hotel opposite the big mound of boulders in the middle of the main crossroads. This pyramid of boulders is a famous landmark. The legendary General Maritz, 'Mannie' Maritz, had fought in this area against the English during the Boer War, a companion-in-arms of Smuts and Denys Reitz, whose famous mounted irregulars—the original 'Commandos'—were operating in Namaqualand. Later Maritz reappeared to lead another revolt, when the South African government played a despicable trick on the *trekkboer* community who had settled down to the life of poor farmers at Alexander Bay, a few miles south of present-day Orangemund. After the war, the government sold the land to the *trekkboers* at 4d a plot. Then diamonds were found there, and the authorities humbugged these simple folk into selling the land back for 5s a plot. The farmers were delighted. Their delight vanished when the government sealed off Alexander Bay with barbed-wire and began to bring out diamonds by the cartload. Mannie Maritz arrived to put himself at their head. He was himself by nature a *trekkboer*, unreconstructed, stubborn, loyal, romantic,

German authorities in South West to co-operate in maintaining an agreed price for diamonds.

Nevertheless, in 1914 De Beers sent a brilliant thirty-four year old businessman, together with one of their best young geologists, to take an informed look at Lüderitz. The businessman was Ernest Oppenheimer; the geologist was Alpheus Williams, son of the famous Gardner Williams, the American engineer from Saginaw, Michigan, who was De Beer's first general manager.

Oppenheimer judged that Lüderitz was indeed becoming played out. But he also had a hunch that the last had not been heard of diamonds on the coast of South West. For the moment he was unable to do anything about it: and in the war-years that followed he had a bad time. He was ostracized because of his German and Jewish origins; he was torpedoed at sea; and he went through one of those periods of indecision and self-doubt that often afflict exceptional men in their thirties. But in 1917, when still a long way short of forty, he launched the first of his giant enterprises, the Anglo-American Corporation of South Africa.

South West Africa had never been far from his thoughts. The war was scarcely over before he was on his way to the Netherlands with the head of the Mines Office at Lüderitz and one of the directors of Anglo-American, who later became the Finance Minister of South Africa. A meeting had been arranged with the leaders of the German firms in South West Africa, now in difficulties because British and South African concerns were able to compete with them in the ex-German colony. All the German companies except one sold out to Oppenheimer. In February 1920 Consolidated Diamond Mines of South West Africa was incorporated with a capital of eight-and-a-half million pounds.

For anyone other than Oppenheimer, the venture would have seemed a gamble. The mines of the old German Regié were clearly faltering. Yet Oppenheimer's instinct about that enigmatic coastline, reinforced by the opinion of Alpheus Williams, was sound. How very, very sound it was will become evident in a later chapter.

put the rest, even began stuffing them into his mouth. It is related that they lay as thick "as plums under a plum tree". Dr Scheibe, staring in amazement at the scene, kept on crying *"Ein Märchen . . . ein Märchen . . ."* (a fairy tale . . . a fairy tale). It was a fairy tale indeed. Stauch had become a millionaire overnight.'

The search duly spread out and intensified along the coast to north and south of Lüderitz. A strike was made at Elizabeth Bay, twenty miles south of the town, between Kolmanskop and Pomona; and twenty miles south of Pomona, at Bogenfels, another lucrative area was discovered. To the north, prospectors pegged claims in Spencer Bay and Conception Bay; while a few hardy souls struggled as far as Meob Bay, 150 miles north of Lüderitz, and only a hundred from Walvis Bay. Eventually, after the private diggers had been brought out, or driven off by such strong-arm methods as hijacking their supplies and selling them water at an exorbitant price, eleven companies were left holding concessions from the D.K.G. In the five years that remained before the outbreak of war stopped mining, the companies squeezed 5 million carats of diamonds out of the ground to the value of nearly £10 million ($24 million). Their methods were thorough and not gentle. The characteristic trait of diamond-mining in South West at this date was that most of the diamonds actually lay on the surface of the ground, or lodged in small hard runnels in the sand. I have seen a photograph in the Windhoek museum of a long line of natives, with German overseers behind them, crawling along a beach on their hands and knees, examining every millimetre of it.

Five million carats was an impressive yield. However, much to the relief of the giant producers at Kimberley, by 1914 the diamond-fields at Lüderitz already appeared to be petering out. Furthermore, the stones were small. The leading diamond companies usually indulged in a joint nervous breakdown when any new source of diamonds was discovered. The mid-1900s were years of severe depression in the diamond-industry, and the depression had not been alleviated by the reluctance of the

betting-men ("brokers" they usually styled themselves) and sharpers of all sorts, on the lookout for prey in the shape of lucky diggers or discoverers. Then, too, there were a number of self-styled "prospectors", runaway ship's cooks, stewards, stokers, and seamen, the bulk of whom had never seen a rough diamond in their lives, and of course, a modicum of genuine men of past experience—principally ex-"river diggers"—men whose small capital was running away like water for bare necessities in this miserable dust-hole of creation.'

The weird appearance of this odd crew, as they toiled and sweated in the stink and glare of the diggings, was enhanced by the monstrous sun-goggles they wore—a tip picked up from the German *Schutztruppe*. The goggles were made from bits of bottle-glass, smoked in the fire, fixed in wire-frames and provided with thick metal rims to protect the eyes from the flying sand and grit.

As usual, the freelance diggers were quickly frozen out by the big battalions. The Deutsche Kolonial Gesellschaft almost immediately refused to issue further licences and reserved the Kolmanskop region for itself. Parcels of land were then leased out to major industrial combines. It is pleasant to record that Adolf Stauch kept a jump ahead of the D.K.G. Having created the fuss at Kolmanskop, he stole unobtrusively away into the Namib, well provided with wagons, mules, food and water and prospecting equipment. He was accompanied by Dr. Scheibe, a German geologist who was sufficiently impressed by Stauch to throw up his job with a diamond-company working at Gibeon, and go trekking off down the coast with the ex-railway inspector.

Scheibe was a good judge of character. At Pomona, ninety miles south of Lüderitz, Stauch struck it rich again—richer than at Kolmanskop. Once more Miss Levinson tells the story:

'On New Year's Eve Stauch had set off on horseback with a sea-chart to try and plot their position; on returning to camp he told his Herero servant, who had been gathering wood, to look for diamonds. The boy was scarcely on his knees when he began filling both hands with diamonds, and not knowing where to

Diggers and Donkeys

nubbled with giant boulders, and in its coarse sand you can still see the scooped-out hollows of the original diggings. You will also see a wind-sock, a hangar, and a light aircraft or two, for today Kolmanskop serves as the town's airstrip.

It says much for Stauch's discretion, and for the minimal expectation that such a place would yield diamonds, that there was no immediate stampede from South Africa to Lüderitz. Only in June 1908, when Stauch's findings were verified and the German government hurriedly despatched a high official from Berlin, did the rush begin. But when it came, like all the early diamond rushes, this one was rough. The scenes at Lüderitz resembled those in Nevada described by Mark Twain in *Roughing It*, or those at Ballarat described by Henry Handel Richardson. I am not sure whether the authorities at Lüderitz allotted claims by the classic nineteenth-century method of a literal 'rush', as employed in the Transvaal, in North America, and Australia. This was the method whereby the claimants were lined up on a mark carrying their pegs, mallets and markers, and the presiding official fired a pistol. That must have been something to see: a thousand men hurling themselves forward in a mad steeple-chase—cursing, yelling, barging, tripping, ankle-tapping. The racket must have been tremendous, with the professional sprinters who had been craftily imported by the syndicates gaining on the rest of the field. Whether or not this method was used, it must have been exciting to have been a resident of Kapps Hotel in the summer of 1908.

Fred Cornell, the most famous and unfortunate of all the prospectors of his generation, was at Lüderitz then, and left us a description of the fortune-hunters in his *Rip Van Winkle of the Kalahari*, published seven years later. He was no Twain or Richardson, but his book is a valuable and entertaining first-hand account:

'What a lot they were! Only a small minority were genuine prospectors, engineers, or mining men with a legitimate interest in diamond discovering; the majority were shady "company promoters", bucket-shop experts, warned-off bookmakers and

soon as he was appointed overseer of the railway line between Lüderitz and Aus, he paid the Deutsche Kolonial Gesellschaft a few marks and acquired a licence to prospect. No one took him seriously; he did not take the matter very seriously himself. De Beers, Rhodes's old company, had been prospecting in South West Africa for four years; but this was far inland, 200 miles to the north-east, in the country around Gibeon. There was 'blue ground' there: the distinctive soil that had once formed the interior of volcanic pipes and escape-flues, and from which diamonds had been extracted at Kimberley for forty years. The 'blue ground' was classically the best milieu for finding diamonds, and De Beers had searched at Gibeon without result. It was known, of course, that diamonds could be washed away by ancient rivers from the vicinity of the pipes: the earliest diamond diggings had been on the banks of the Vaal. But although the Orange River and the shores to north and south of it had been systematically surveyed, no diamonds had yet been discovered.

Stauch's main task was to keep the railway line clear of the walking dunes of sand that tirelessly obliterated it. For this purpose he employed gangs of Cape Coloured workmen. He told them to keep their eyes open for diamonds. In a half-hearted way they did. And within a matter of weeks Zacharias Lewala, one of Stauch's 'boys', came up to his master and handed him what he called 'a pretty stone'. Stauch, excited, scraped it on the glass of his wristwatch, and realized that the 'pretty stone' was a diamond.

Like a good Pomeranian, he kept his head. Miss Levinson describes what happened next. 'Quietly and calmly Stauch took the necessary measures to peg out his claims. He applied for a discharge from his job, obtained some capital from two directors of his company, then pitched a tent on one of his claims and began serious prospecting operations. He soon was rewarded with further discoveries of "pretty stones".'

The site of Stauch's strike was Kolmanskop, up in the hills three or four miles above Lüderitz. You pass it as you drive into Lüderitz on the road from Aus. It is a wind-whipped plateau,

SEVEN
Diggers and Donkeys

IN May 1907 a new railway inspector arrived at Lüderitz from Germany. August Stauch was an employee of the Deutschen Kolonial-Eisenbahnbau und Betriebsgesellschaft of Stettin, and he had been working in Pomerania. He had a weak chest, and on his doctor's advice he asked his company to transfer him to Südwest Afrika, where it was engaged on the railway-construction programme. He must have felt that his fortunes were at a low ebb when he landed and took up the post assigned to him in this forbidding land. His job was a minor one and paid poorly, and he had been compelled to leave his wife and two children behind him in Germany. Within a year he was to perform the equivalent of breaking the bank at Monte Carlo, or winning a fortune for sixpence on the football pools. He pulled off the diamond digger's dream.

It was luck: but like many lucky people, he deserved it. That is to say, he used his brains to put himself in a position to exploit a lucky break if it ever happened to come his way. As

at the attainment of full citizenship rights by people of all races, and that by supporting it they were giving the non-white a chance of real development in the future'.

As with most politicians and reformers, the trouble with Dr Malan and his Nationalist colleagues was not that they lacked principles, but that they had too many. Heaven deliver us from all such 'men of impeccable moral standing'. They are every bit as bad as the 'professors of energy'. Neither of them will let us poor people breathe.

Smuts, had been used by the National Socialists 'as a base for intrigue, and for undermining our liberties and seducing our citizens'.

Smuts had called Hirskorn's bluff: and shortly afterwards, beating down the opposition of Herzog and Malan, he embarked on the more formidable task of helping Churchill to call Hitler's bluff. In South West the Nazi leaders were arrested and interned. The National Socialist movement collapsed. The Germans gave little trouble thereafter, and contented themselves with listening to Goebbel's bloodthirsty broadcasts from Zeesen. They prayed for the Japanese to land at Walvis Bay.

Their opportunity to hit at the British did not come until 1949, when the South West Africa Affairs Amendment Act gave the white South Westers the right to send six representatives to the South African parliament. The German community voted for the Nationalist Party, under Dr Malan. In the previous year Malan had defeated the government of Jan Smuts; now he created the six South West African seats to increase his majority. The Germans obliged. It was a petty, belated revenge, but it was the only one open to them.

What happened to their former allies, the members of the *Ossewa Brandwag*? Smuts, of course, dealt with them in a masterful way—and with the assistance, be it noted, of no less a person than Dr Malan. Dr Malan was a Nationalist, and he was unrelentingly anti-British. But the *Ossewa Brandwag* had committed the unpardonable sins of being godless and pagan, and of splitting the Afrikaner nation into factions. Dr Malan was single-minded, and he was a Christian; one of his colleagues at the Sunday school in the little up-country town of Piketberg had been Jan Smuts.

It will come as a surprise to many readers that Dr Malan, the architect of apartheid, was an opponent of Nazism. In fact many of the early proponents of apartheid were, in the words of Z. J. de Beer, author of *Multi-Racial South Africa*, and a founder of the Progressive Party, 'men of impeccable moral standing, who believed that the idea of apartheid, or separateness, aimed

Sea and the Chad Sea, which in turn would be used to irrigate the Sahara.

Like many of Hitler's plans, it is impossible not to be astonished by its breath-taking scale and audacity. However, too many of his other plans were realized in cold-blooded reality for us to be over-enthusiastic about Allantropa. It may be, as I suggested earlier, that smaller, gradualistic solutions to our problems invariably prove more human and less harmful. The solutions of the 'professors of energy', as Barrès called Napoleon, occasionally give humanity a useful jolt, but they also inflict wounds that take generations to heal. Döblin's most celebrated pre-war novel was *Berlin, Alexanderplatz*. Marxist though he was, I doubt if he would like what technocracy and political ideology, as represented by Gottwald and Ulbricht, have done to Berlin in later years. Alexanderplatz today is a drab, dispirited mess.

Hitler and Hirskorn were defeated because one man had the courage to stand up to them. The man was Smuts, one of the noblest, most intelligent, and most steadfast men of our century. On the eve of the Second World War he was in his late sixties, and was generally regarded as a superannuated elder statesman. He was serving as Minister of Justice in the cabinet of General Herzog. Herzog was a moody, taciturn, but in many ways admirable and sympathetic man, who all his life had been pro-German and anti-British. It was the Germans, after all, who had given his country moral and material support in the Boer War, and he had never subscribed to the British-engineered South Africa Act of 1909. Unlike Smuts and Botha, he had never become reconciled with the old enemy. Now he gave his support to the German alliance and the *Ossewa Brandwag*. He connived with the *Deutsche Südwest Bund*'s bid for a take-over in South West.

Smuts was not deterred. Nor was he intimidated when the *Ossewa Brandwag* threatened to kill him. Four months before the outbreak of the Second World War he took over the South West African police and sent a force of 300 troops armed with machine-guns to Windhoek. On April 18, 1939, they occupied all the public buildings. South West Africa, charged

adventurous English geographer, Sir Halford Mackinder. And no dreams that any German—even Hitler himself—ever dreamed were as extravagant as those of Cecil Rhodes, the poor boy from Bishop's Stortford. Painting the map red from the Cape to Cairo was only the first phase of Rhodes's master-plan. His aim was to 'bring the whole of the civilized world under British rule'. The United States was to apply for readmission to the British Empire, and Africa, South America and most of Asia were to be thickly colonized by English-speaking settlers. Only then, according to Rhodes, would the permanent peace and prosperity of the world be assured.

The Germans worked out an early blue-print for Africa that caused Rhodes much heartburn. They envisaged an entity to be called Mittel-Afrika, a deep belt of German territory joining the South Atlantic to the Indian Ocean. Its flanking bastions were to be South West Africa and East Africa, and it would be linked to Mittel-Europa by means of alliances with the Arab countries and with Turkey. This was the heyday of the Berlin-Baghdad railway, when German pashas, following the example of von Moltke in Egypt, held sway throughout the Levant.

Hitler was the legatee of these heady schemes for a German world-order. A man who had spent his youth fiddling about with motor-bike engines, he had the temperament of a demented garage-mechanic; his imagination had been fed, like many members of his generation, by the technolatrous fantasies of Jules Verne, H. G. Wells and Alfred Döblin. Döblin wrote a memorable novel called *Mountains, Seas and Men* in which an engineering genius employs flame-throwers to melt the polar icecaps, using the water released to generate electric power. Hitler nourished equally grandiose designs for Africa. He intended to create a new continent, to be called Allantropa, formed by the merging of Europe with Africa by damming up both ends of the Mediterranean. Roads and railways could then run on dry land from the heart of Europe into the heart of Africa, while a second system of dams would control the lakes and rivers of Africa and create two vast inland seas, the Congo

the Germans and their Italian allies would make a concerted effort to seize the Suez Canal. If South Africa went Nazi, the route via the Cape to India and Australia would also be cut. A hostile navy would be free to operate in the South Atlantic and the Indian Ocean. Simonstown would become an operational base for German U-boat packs. Africa, with her wealth and her man-power, could be written off.

South West Africa, then, served as a Trojan horse outside the South African gates, and Dr Hirskorn was the leader of the troops concealed inside it. Hitler took a close personal interest in the course of events. Whatever else he was, Hitler was supersensitive to the possibilities latent in the most improbable situations, and he was quick to appreciate the tremendous prize that might fall into his lap in southern Africa. He poured money and specialists into South West. Nor was he merely an opportunist: even at this date he was in the thrall of those cloudy all-embracing geopolitical theories that four years later were to impel him to send his armies eastwards into Russia to capture the world's 'Heartland'.

Such romantic theories had a special appeal for Germans. Fichte was mesmerized by what he took to be the global aspirations of Napoleon; and a line could be traced from such respectable geographers and ethnologists as Bastian, Ratzel and Max Müller, through Wagner and the ridiculous Houston Stewart Chamberlain, to sinister degenerates like Alfred Rosenberg and Walther Darré. Distinguished members of the General Staff, like von Seeckt, who rebuilt the Wehrmacht after the First World War, also toyed with geopolitical ideas. The notions of the British and French were much more stolid and pragmatic. After all, they already possessed large tracts of the earth's surface, and were absorbed in the day-to-day business of administering them. The Germans had few actual responsibilities to interfere with their dreams of what they would do with the world when they had conquered it. However, it is worth noting that the fascinating, splendidly elaborated and utterly wrong-headed theories of Haushofer, the principal exponent of geopolitics, were anticipated by the writings of an

that number. They put on uniforms, waved swastika banners, and staged torchlight processions. At Lüderitz they even managed to organize the martial but rather obviously non-Aryan Herero into a well-drilled Fifth Column. By no means the whole of the German community were pro-Nazi, but Hirskorn booted them mercilessly into line. Their sons and daughters were sent to Germany for education and indoctrination, and became hostages for their parents. After the First World War, the South Africans had treated the Germans in South West generously, and in 1924 offered them South African citizenship. Hirskorn now warned his flock that any of them who failed to renounce sole South African citizenship and claim dual German–South African nationality would be considered a traitor, and would get short shift when The Day arrived.

The troubles in South West appeared insignificant when set beside the uproar in Europe. This was not entirely the case. They were serious enough for Smuts to declare that he was uncertain whether the incident that would set off the Second World War would occur in Poland or South West Africa. This distant, desolate, underpopulated, disregarded patch of land was the focus of a crisis even more dangerous than the crisis which is taking place there today. Dr Hirskorn had powerful and numerous allies inside South Africa. He was no small-time agitator: he was a leading light in a plot to bring South Africa, with her gold, diamonds, mineral resources, and efficient and well-equipped army, over to the side of the Third Reich. On the eve of the war, a party existed in South Africa which was dedicated to the Nazi cause and ideology. It came into existence in 1938, and called itself the *Ossewa Brandwag*—the 'Sentinels of the Ox-Wagon'. At its peak it was reckoned to have enrolled 350,000 members—nearly 15 per cent of the population. It represented the most vociferous, fanatical and violent element in South African politics, and by 1940 it was the second most powerful party in the state, and virtually constituted the parliamentary opposition. The threat to Britain and her allies was immense. It was already obvious that in the event of war

stantial areas of territory, he had also concluded trade agreements with Hottentot and Herero chiefs, and had induced a number of them to ask for the protection of the Reich. Dr Nachtigall, the new Consul General, together with Doctors Goering and Beuttner, were immediately despatched to clinch these agreements. With the subsequent landmarks of German rule in South West I have dealt briefly in a previous chapter: How, in 1889, Kurt von François arrived to deal with the latest outbreak of the Hottentot–Herero war, and founded Windhoek the following year; how, after fourteen years of German rule, General von Trotha, an S.S. general born before his time, broke the back of the Herero nation at the Waterberg, and of the Hottentot nation at Warmbad and Keetmanshoop; and how, in July 1915, the exiguous German forces surrendered to the South African Army, and signed the Peace of Korab.

Throughout these thirty stormy years Lüderitz throve in a modest way. It was the original depot of the *Deutsche-Gesellschaft für Südwest-Afrika*, which took over Adolf Lüderitz's assets on his death; and until the construction of Swakopmund it was the colony's only port.

It has retained its German character. In Lüderitz you can talk to German commercial-travellers, German schoolteachers on contract, and young men and women newly returned from university in Germany. During the 1930s it was 200 per cent Nazi, and only a fraction of a point behind Swakopmund where loutishness and fanaticism were concerned.

That must have been a particularly unpleasant time to have lived in South West. The nastiness in Central Europe percolated even as far as this remote part of Africa. Those were the days when the *Swakopmunder Zeitung* changed its name to the *Deutsche Beobachter*, in honour of Streicher's rag, and when a cunning bully called Dr Hans Hirskorn was sent from Berlin to take charge of a Nazi front-organization, the *Deutsche Südwest Bund*. He brought with him Nazi propagandists and sabotage experts.

There were only 6,000 Germans in South West at this time, but they made as much racket as if there had been ten times

no further than to authorize Cape Province to annex Walvis Bay and its immediate environs. The renewal of the strife between Herero and Hottentots provided it with its excuse. In the meantime Adolf Lüderitz had bought, through a young intermediary named Heinrich Vogelsang, a twenty-mile stretch of the coastal area in and around Angra Pequeña. The Hottentot chief from whom he bought it, who lived 160 miles inland at Bethanie, was delighted to part with it. In this the chief resembled the legendary Redskin who sold Manhattan to the Dutch for $24 and a string of beads.

Lüderitz went at once to Berlin and began lobbying energetically. He argued that as the British would not stir from Walvis Bay, Germany must step in to protect German lives and property in 'Lüderitz-Land'. The German government realized that by now prestige and commerce were alike involved. At the last moment, the British woke up and sent the gunboat *Boadicea* to proclaim Angra Pequeña well and truly British. *Boadicea* found the German gunboat *Nautilus* blocking the mouth of the harbour.

The British did not press the point. They had recently engorged themselves on too many of the choicest cuts of Africa to begrudge the Germans this derisory morsel. At this epoch the British attitude to the continent was lofty in the extreme. When Queen Victoria was seeking a suitable little knick-knack as a wedding present for her grandson, Kaiser Wilhelm II, she gave him Mount Kilimanjaro: surely one of the grandest and most useless presents on record.

'Lüderitz-Land' was German at last: but the author of the astutely managed coup did not live long to enjoy its fruits. Adolf Lüderitz was no chair-bound financial manipulator. Like Rhodes, if he wanted to name a country after himself, at least he was willing to go out and grab it with his own hands. He made arduous trips in an effort to enlarge the boundaries of his kingdom; and in 1886, only two years after he had persuaded his fellow countrymen to annexe 'Lüderitz-Land', he was drowned exploring the Orange in a twelve-foot canvas boat.

He had done his work well. Not only had he purchased sub-

to death and defeat at the Falkland Islands; and it was the final halt made by the Russian fleet in 1906, circumnavigating the world on its way to annihilation at the hands of the Japanese at Port Arthur.

In 1856 the trading company of De Pass and Spence set up a ship repair yard at what was then called Angra Pequeña. But it was a man from Bremen who saw the wider possibilities of Namaqualand, and used Angra Pequeña as his point of ingress. Adolf Lüderitz, whom we have already met in Chapter Three in connection with Walvis Bay, was the son of a prosperous tobacco merchant. He was a shrewd and sophisticated young entrepreneur who had made a considerable fortune in the United States and Mexico. At this time he specialized in setting up factories and warehouses in African ports; and had done so well at Lagos in Nigeria that he was looking around for outlets farther south. The European powers were moving into Africa speedily when he arrived in South West, and he saw that Germany would have to act quickly if she was to pick up any of the slices of territory that were still available. He was familiar with the inertia of the British with regard to Namaqualand and Damaraland, which they could have incorporated in Cape Province at any time during the past eighty years: but he realized that in Dr William Coates Palgrave, whom the Cape government had sent to South West in 1876 with the title of special commissioner, he was confronted with a British rival of uncommon insight and ability. Palgrave's task was to investigate the unrest caused on Cape Province's northern frontier by the Hottentot-Herero wars, and if possible to act as mediator. The authorities at the Cape were trying to induce their superiors in London to annex South West, and Palgrave's mission was so successful that the Cape Parliament was able to report to England that the country was in a fit condition to be taken over. Palgrave signed an agreement with the Herero chiefs at Okahandja in 1876, and in 1880 returned to South West as magistrate at Walvis Bay. It looked as if the British were getting ready to add South West to their other possessions.

But London still hesitated. The home government would go

rough stones on to his palm, poked them about for a while, then poured them back on the cloth. He gave a brief shake of the head. One of the other men took the cloth, looked as if he was going to say something, then changed his mind and turned on his heel and walked away. He and his companion got into the Pontiac and drove off. Not a word was spoken. The transaction was over in two minutes.

'*Schlenters*,' explained my friend as we made our way back to Springbok.

Schlenters, or *slenters*, are fake diamonds. The best *Schlenters* in South West are made from the marbles in the necks of the lemonade or mineral-water bottles that can be found in dozens at the old German diggings.

I have sometimes wondered what I would have done if my friend had decided to nod his head at the olive grove, instead of shaking it . . . ?

Lüderitz Bay had not been entirely uninhabited before the German trader Adolf Lüderitz arrived there in the early 1880s. Bartolomeu Dias, of course, had done no more when he landed in 1487 than erect his cross or *padrão*. Later there were sporadic visits from Dutch and British men-o'-war to stake out territorial claims for their respective countries. These claims were more speculative than real. The British sloop *Nautilus* touched at Lüderitz in 1786; the Dutch sloop *Meermin* in 1793; and the British sloop *Star* after the British had annexed the Cape in 1795.

From the early 1840s there was a guano-rush, and coastal captains by the score sailed for the off-shore islands of Namaqualand and fought bloody battles with one another to fetch their squalid and evil-smelling cargoes home. Possession Island, Ichabod, Pomona, Plum Pudding, and Halifax Islands, all south of Lüderitz, were the scenes of skirmishes in which crews of ruffians dished out plentiful helpings of belaying-pin soup to one another. It is worth recording that, in later years, Lüderitz was a last port of call for two great doomed naval squadrons. Admiral von Spee refuelled there in World War I, on his way

court a few steps from the DDD office, and is on his way in handcuffs to gaol in Windhoek. As the notice at the edge of the *Sperrgebiet* warns you, the penalties are steep. For a first offence you may be let off with a fine of £200 and six months imprisonment: but a second offence draws you £500 and a year in gaol, and a third £1,000, two years in gaol, and banishment from South West. If diamond-fever still tempts you back, and you are convicted a fourth time, the punishment is five years in gaol, a heavier fine, and so on *pro rata*. The diamond detectives are armed: and need to be. They are not loved, and diamond-smugglers are playing for high stakes. In Springbok, a few years ago, Captain Erasmus, the local head of the DDD, shot a smuggler in the thigh, and the man bled to death. Captain Erasmus himself was later found shot, his face smashed, and his chest kicked in. Feelings run high over those insignificant-looking little stones.

It is a little outside the scope of this book, but when I was at Springbok, a sizeable town in South Africa, seventy-five miles south of the Orange River and a notorious centre for smuggling, I was offered a package of uncut diamonds. The transaction was an elaborate pantomime. With a companion, I left the hotel and drove around for an hour to make sure we had thrown off the local DDs, before going to the place set up for a meeting in a thick grove of wild olives off the main road to Pofadder. I only agreed to go because I was unable to resist finding out what such an experience felt like: and my South African companion (not Klaas or Sarel) was nervous that the whole affair was actually a put-up job by the DDD. At the olive grove we both came forward and met the two would-be sellers—stringy, thin-faced men who got out of a battered Pontiac. It is the only time I have been to a meeting where the plenipotentiaries were armed. My friend had a gun, and I am certain one or both of the others had. Without any preliminaries, I was handed a dirty scrap of cloth in which were wrapped the alleged diamonds. I took a look at them, trying to hide my ignorance, then passed it to my friend. The two other men watched carefully. My friend poured the eight or nine little

Forbidden Area

After all, the town is 485 miles north of Cape Town, 250 miles south of Walvis Bay, and 550 miles west of Windhoek. Air travel, of course, could solve the problem: but the cheapest and still the main means of access is the railway, which reaches the town only after a penitential ride across the Namib. The citizens of Lüderitz make large claims for their town, and love it. They possess the same kind of local patriotism as my Uncle Jack, who sees no reason to visit Rome, or Rio, or Rangoon, because it is so well-known that Cardiff has the finest climate, finest buildings, finest people, and finest Rugby Union football club in the whole of the world.

Unfortunately, the only source of amusement at Lüderitz is the arrival of that same railway-train. There are four arrivals and departures a week: and when a train is due the whole town seems to turn out to welcome it. At first I was puzzled when I saw a stream of people, the men in white shirts, the women in bright cotton dresses, strolling past Kapps Hotel and converging on the railway-station. I went out and joined them. They milled around the platform, greeting acquaintances, waiting for the train to bring them parcels, friends or relatives, or simply a flicker of activity to lighten the long day. That first afternoon, I remember, the train was on time, and it came clattering in with a prolonged arrogant toot of its whistle. On occasions when it was late, on the otherhand, I noticed that it slunk in as meekly and silently as possible. Standing well back on the platform, one at one end and one at the other, scrutinizing the passengers as they got stiffly down from the chocolate-coloured carriages, were two large men in brown suits. The diamond detectives. They too were wondering if they would see any familiar faces. ...

The Diamond Detection Department is represented at Lüderitz, as in every other town throughout South West, by beefy, efficient, sun-burned men who operate from a little office, strategically placed in the centre of the town, with an unobtrusive plate on the door. They have summary powers. Within a few hours of arrest, a diamond-thief or illicit diamond-buyer has been tried and sentenced in the poky little magistrate's

6 Dunes at Swakopmund

5 Swakopmund: south-western baroque

Swakopmund: African shanties or pondoks

Southampton: but Lüderitz has exactly the right atmosphere. I shall always think of *Youth*, *Almayer's Folly* and *The Arrow of Gold* with the sharp light off the water darting across the pages. I have always had a special veneration for Conrad, not only because of a boyhood piety for my old seafaring uncles, but because he finished the final pages of the *Nigger of the Narcissus*, his first major book, a few doors away from the house where I lived as a boy in Cathedral Road in Cardiff.

I felt close to him at Lüderitz.

Conrad's Marlowe would have appreciated the hotel where I stayed. There are three hotels in the town: Reummler's Hotel, the Café Maurer, and Kapps Hotel. I stayed at the latter. Behind it was a new courtyard with comfortable bedrooms, but the hotel itself was all dark mahogany, ground glass, and old brass polished to the sheen and texture of satin. It was a perfectly preserved period-piece, a relic of the 1870s and 1880s. On one wall hung steel engravings of Kaiser Wilhelm II's father and mother. Heaven knows how many hundreds of seamen had sat drinking at the big solid tables in that magnificent bar. It was a bar that reminded you that drinking had once been a solemn and weighty occupation. I have always thought the Windsor Hotel on the Pier Head in Cardiff, looking out on the Bristol Channel, near the Windsor Esplanade, where my grandparents and my great-grandparents lived and my father was born, was a splendid example of an old-time seaman's hotel. It is—but I think it is shaded by Kapps. There was a disturbing rumour that Kapps was to be demolished. I could hardly believe it. But if it disappears, then at least I shall have had the satisfaction of sleeping and drinking in such a unique and evocative old-time sailors' hotel.

The local publicity board beats the big drum for Lüderitz, attempting to build it up into a second Swakopmund. Some first-class two- and four-room bungalows have been built, and also some one-room buildings with the piquant name of 'rondavels'. But I cannot help feeling that the board has got its work cut out: another example of South West African optimism.

twenty million tons a year are processed in the canning-factories along the shore. Separate factories deal with the other fish, such as snoek, kingklip, steenbras, and the meaty and mouthwatering kabeljaauw. It is interesting to note that the multi-million-pound crawfish-tail industry is less than half a century old. It began as recently as 1921, and it started at Lüderitz, thanks to the enterprise of a free-lance Italian skipper called Napoli, who came cruising down the coast in his cutter with a crew of six men. Lüderitz owes a particular debt to Napoli, in that the town at that time was economically at its last gasp. The fantastic diamond strikes of the previous decade had petered out, and it looked as if there was no future for Lüderitz, a shallow harbour where every mouthful of food and drop of water had to be brought in from Cape Town or Walvis Bay. Then Lüderitz suddenly scored a first with crawfish, as thirteen years earlier it had scored a first with diamonds. Like every other town in South West—like the country itself—it bears a charmed life, prosperous yet precarious.

Near the 500-foot concrete jetty outside the canning-factories, with their cranes and overhead lights, is a pier running out a hundred yards into the harbour. Again, when we first arrived, Klaas and Sarel played a trick on me. Hot and tired after the drive from Aus, I changed quickly, ran out along the jetty, and plunged headlong into those crystalline and too-inviting waters. The temperature of the sea at Lüderitz cannot be far off freezing. I almost passed out.

Subsequently, except for a few dips taken with the squeals and shudders of Mack Sennett bathing-beauties, we confined our seaside activities to the small Strand Café at the beach end of the pier. This had all the appeal of a North Sea *plage* or *strandbad*—Le Touquet or Scheveningen—without the trippers. Here, beneath a gaily-striped umbrella, I spent hours staring at the sea in a mood of Germanic contentment, sipping a glass of beer and chatting with the local people. In these Conradian surroundings I read the three novels in the handy little Essex edition I had brought with me in my airline bag. Nowadays there is little left to remind you of Conrad in Liverpool or

dreary, like Walvis Bay: but Lüderitz supplied me with the picturesque old German atmosphere I had missed at Walvis. There were Gothic turrets, pinnacles, half-timbering and ironwork in plenty, and the buildings were painted in the rich and idiosyncratic colours characteristic of old-fashioned German buildings: pale limes and turquoises, warm plums and apricots. The architecture of Lüderitz takes you back three generations, to the picture-postcards our grandparents used to send from the Kingdom of Bavaria and the Grand-Duchy of Baden-Würtemberg. But it also boasts some up-to-date features, carried out with a taste that is absent in utilitarian towns like Walvis or Keetmanshoop. Lüderitz is rather like Swakopmund with additions of modern Windhoek. I would say that it was a very well-run little town.

What gives it originality is not so much the buildings themselves, as their setting. Everywhere you look there are huge smooth grey boulders, rearing up between the houses or from the centre of the roadway. The big Wagnerian villas on the hill rise from a foundation of twisted rocks like a miniature Venusberg. The effect is of a town where the architecture is interspersed with abstract, elemental shapes, or with pieces of sculpture—like living with a Moore or a Hepworth outside your front door.

The situation is striking. The town is built on the cliffs that surround the small harbour, on whose waters of vivid blue bob dozens of small fishing-boats drawn up in neat flotillas. The horns of the harbour are formed by two islands, Shark Island and Seal Island, the former of which is joined to the mainland by a causeway and contains a number of buildings, including a hospital. The channel into the inner harbour is not deep enough to take ships over 250 tons, and larger vessels have to anchor outside; and the absence of big ships adds to the compact, pocket-size atmosphere of the harbour where the rocks with their guano deposits glare white in the sun.

Not that the little fishing-boats should be regarded as toys. They bring back impressive hauls from the waters off that dangerous coast. The bulk of the catch is crawfish, of which

would have disappeared at Keetmanshoop, 250 miles back. . . .

Ah yes, but your disappearance would have been noticed. The diamond detectives are not green. And although there are no regular air patrols, light aircraft carrying passengers cross the area several times a day, and the crews are instructed to keep their eyes open. Ten to one they will spot your wheel-tracks across the desert. Ten to one, too, that your car will sink in over its hubcaps in the sand, or you will break an axle on one of those blasted boulders. . . .

I worked out several fancy schemes and outlined them to Klaas and Sarel. They simply smiled, and kept their own counsel. I looked at the blistered landscape, stunned by the sun, and reflected that it was lucky, after all, that I had no knowledge of a pot of diamonds that might lure me, like a host of dead men before me, into the Namib. . . .

And now, as I was revolving these hypothetical plans, we came over the last of a thousand ridges and caught sight of the sea. I cannot say I felt quite the leaping of the heart which Gert Alberts, the scout for the Thirstland Trekkers, felt when he emerged on the sea-coast below the Cunene River. He and his companions, as I shall describe later, were Transvaal farmers, and had never before in their lives set eyes upon the ocean. . . .

But after the gritty plains and fallow mountains, it raised my spirits to be returning to the coast and to gaze, once more, on the translucent cobalt of the South Atlantic. . . .

I had been warned that Lüderitz was the end of the world. It is: but it delighted me.

Although it was the first town, after Walvis Bay, to be established in South West, Lüderitz is tiny. It has about 4,000 inhabitants: 1,500 whites; just over 1,000 Ovambo, who work in the canning-factories; and just under 1,000 Cape Coloureds, who also work in the factories or serve as kanakas aboard the trawling-fleet. There is an insignificant scattering of Nama, Bergdama and Herero, in that order.

The appeal of Lüderitz is its individuality. It is like no other town I have ever visited. I had expected something bleak and

If not, they will have seen your name on the register of the hotel you stayed at in Keetmanshoop or Aus. A strange car, in a part of the world where strange cars are seldom seen, is hardly likely to go unnoticed. A note of the times of your arrival and departure will have been made in that unobtrusive police station opposite the garage at Aus. Better drive steadily once you are inside the area and obey the rule that forbids you to stop on the road. Another detective will be noting down the time you take to reach Lüderitz, and making a few simple calculations.

In any case, you know enough by now to realize that it is futile to go rooting about the countryside like a pig after truffles, in spite of the fact that travelling over ground containing diamonds produces such an extraordinary heightening of the senses. Finding diamonds does not occur like that. You need a lot of time and equipment. Much more sensible to keep your eyes straight ahead, and your foot pressed down on the throttle. Not that there is any temptation to loiter unnecessarily in this savage desert. The veld has given way to the sand and stone-chip surface of the Namib, strewn with its gigantic walking dunes, and alternating with increasing outcrops of boulders.

However, as the Namib grows more rocky and brutal, and the rays of the sun more insufferable, I begin to speculate about the ways a man might challenge this awful desert and survive. Say you knew that a cache of diamonds existed at a certain place—how would you deal with the problem of reaching it? How would you go about it? How would you beat the desert and the diamond detectives?

Could you sneak away from Keetmanshoop, as soon as it was dark, and drive the 170 miles to the *Sperrgebiet* in, say, four or five hours? Then leave the road—drive across the desert to the rough location of the cache—and before dawn hide your car among a cleft in the rocks, covering it with a camouflage-net? Could you lie up until the next night, living on the food and drink in the boot of the car, then start looking around for the cache? You could stay there—prospecting only at night—as long as your stores held out. To all intents and purposes you

the tales which, with perfectly straight faces, Klaas and Sarel told me about the defences of the diamond area. I listened wide-eyed as they described the electrified fence running for hundreds of miles across the desert; the watchtowers with searchlights and machine-guns, placed at strategic intervals; the patrols by armed police in jeeps, with savage dogs; the regular flights by helicopters and light planes; the watch on the coast maintained by fast motor-launches. If you are digging up a quarter of a million dollars' worth of diamonds a day, you can afford to run a private army.

My heart was thumping as we drove across the plain towards another, higher range of mountains. My map told me that we were nearing the Prohibited Area. I strained my eyes to catch sight of the watchtowers, poised above the glittering spiderwork of the famous fence. I expected at any moment to see the spurt of dust as the uniformed police kicked their motor-cycles into life and came roaring down the road to intercept us. It was exciting and romantic: the secret empire of CDM, a country within a country, a commercial kingdom as jealously guarded as Cape Kennedy.

And what was the reality? There was nothing. Nothing but a small black metal notice with white lettering standing beside the road. Klaas and Sarel were grinning at me. It was a miserable anti-climax.

Nevertheless, you would be foolish to venture beyond that modest notice into the mountainous terrain ahead of you. It is truly Thirstland in there. Those mountains are like the Mountains of the Moon. There is no need for the watchtowers and the wire because the Namib will discourage you quite as effectively: and if you still insist on entering, the desert will kill you just as surely as bullets or guard-dogs. The deeper you manage to get in, the slimmer your chances of getting out.

Nor should you assume that the special force of diamond detectives, even though they wear nothing more conspicuous than slacks and sportscoats, have not been busy. They will already have noticed your arrival. Windhoek will have warned them that you are on your way, and that you have permits.

year—that is, a few drops of moisture for less than five minutes—but there are years when it does not rain at all. In 1959, for example, 0.2 millimetres of rain were recorded at Swakopmund. None the less the rainless town of Aus, with its small square houses standing blindingly white in the sunshine, like the Arab houses of north Africa, can boast a fine collection of acacia and eucalyptus trees.

The eucalyptus, as any Australian will tell you, is a magnificent tree. Unfortunately it is almost unknown in Britain, though it will grow well there. This may be because the British associate it with a particularly nasty and evil-smelling oil that was rubbed on their chests when they were children. In South Africa the eucalyptus, with the unforgettable dark green of its foliage, is often grown as a windbreak around the Dutch colonial farm-houses of the Cape. The saplings are planted close together, and their central stems are eventually cut out ten feet from the ground, leaving the delicate subsidiary branches to shoot up in a feathery corona. The tree is quick growing. Soon the farmhouse is surrounded by a tall and handsome screen of foliage, rippling in the breeze like a linked row of gently agitated ostrich fans.

Take a good long look at the trees at Aus. The desert across which you will now travel is bare even of the plucky kokerboom. And except for a few dogged palms, the town to which you are going is as devoid of vegetation as Hell itself.

My companions pulled my leg about what I would find on the frontier of the diamond zone.

PROHIBITED AREA. RESTRICTED AREA. FORBIDDEN AREA. The words were formidable. In Afrikaans they sounded equally sinister: VERBODE GEBIED, or SPERRGEBIET.

I knew that diamonds to the value of £75,000 to £100,000 a day ($181,000–$240,000) were extracted from the shore terraces of South West Africa by Consolidated Diamond Mines, who owned the concessions inside the *Sperrgebiet*. It seemed obvious that CDM would take considerable precautions to safeguard such an impressive investment. I therefore swallowed

flaccid bunches of grass between the graves. On the graves were empty jampots and rows of white seashells, emblems of a resurrection which suddenly seemed in this desolate place to be chillingly unlikely. . . .

The wind made me shiver. And yet—there was a rough nobility here. The wind blowing hard forever. The tarnished gold of the veld. The sooty burnt-out ridges of the volcanoes. There are worse places to be laid to rest than in the light warm soil of Africa. On this spot the first children of man had grown up, played, hunted, loved, died. There was continuity in that. Who would want to rot in one of the crammed and sodden cemeteries of the north, when he could lie on this hill-top beneath a saxe-blue sky, with a pair of kestrels wheeling overhead?

John Cowper Powys told me that his brother, Theodore, had had a brilliant son who was killed by a lion in Kenya. Theodore told John the news, and the two men were silent for a long time.

Then Theodore roused himself and lifted his head.

'Well, John,' he said. 'I suppose he could have been run over by a bus—in Piccadilly. . . .'

His eyes shone.

. . . *'But a LION . . . ! In AFRICA . . . !'*

To reach the border of the diamond area you drive through the little town of Aus. It will be your last sign of civilization for many sweltering miles ahead. You are on the edge of the Namib now—a stretch of it as immitigably malevolent as the Skeleton Coast.

Aus is built around a wide dried-up river-bed. Its location is another of those instances of the triumph of hope over experience which is part of the character of South West.

The town receives on the average about one hundred millimetres of rain a year (about four inches), and it is doing well, at that, compared to Lüderitz, which is lucky if it gets twenty millimetres. Rain is virtually unknown in the Namib. Walvis Bay and Swakopmund might receive 5 millimetres in a good

about seven foot tall and broad to match, his blonde hair cut *en brosse*. In physical appearance he resembles a sergeant-major in a regiment of the Potsdam Grenadiers, and I gathered that his father was in fact one of the original *Schutztruppe*. In addition to keeping this small haven of rest (who, I wondered, could be his regular customers in this wild place?), he is also the custodian of the little cemetery on a nearby hilltop, which contains the graves of a number of his father's old comrades in arms. As the Land Rover climbed the hill I had noticed weapon-pits and gun-emplacements, and stopped to have a closer look at them. I guessed that they were part of a defensive system devised by the Germans in 1914 to protect Lüderitz from attack from the east; now I learned that this conveniently isolated outpost had been chosen as a transit camp for prisoners of war when the Germans surrendered the following year. General Mackenzie had succeeded in landing Union troops at Lüderitz in September, 1914, so the defenders of this gap in the mountains had been caught between two fires. Through the camp also passed the people of Lüderitz on their way to deportation from South West. Some of them succumbed to the rigours of the journey, casualties of one more of Africa's everlasting treks.

The graves of the soldiers had rusty iron crosses above them. It is always moving to stumble on the burial-places of soldiers in foreign lands: graves of fallen Guardsmen in the Libyan desert, in Crete, above Rimini, beside the lake at Bolsena; or of British sailors in the Baltic, the Tyrrhenian Sea, the Arabian Gulf... The German graves on the road to Lüderitz reminded me of the epitaph in *The Iliad*: 'They perished in Troy, far away from their dear native land...'

I am no necrophile. I loathe cemeteries. I have friends who love a Sunday-afternoon stroll around the tombs in Pére Lachaise or Kensal Green. Not me. I was mournful, standing on that hilltop, with its neglected oval mounds. The sight was symbolic of much of Africa: of loneliness, poverty, anonymity, insignificance, the sense of defeat by massive and indifferent powers. A harsh wind blew across the plateau, punishing the

Forbidden Area

It is 227 miles from Keetmanshoop to Lüderitz, 171 to the boundary of the prohibited area. You drive through open country with volcanic ranges in the distance, their tops sawn flat millions of years ago, then the plain around them worn down in turn to leave rows of granitic cones stitched across the landscape. They are the vents and blowholes of what were once a skein of fiery underground rivers.

For much of the distance a little narrow-gauge railway with toy water-towers keeps the road company. The single-track railway was laid out in German times, and as elsewhere was sited for military purposes along the line of the road. Most of the locomotives were brought out in parts from England and assembled in South West. Even today the English cannot bring themselves to subscribe to the notion of planned obsolescence, and in the old days when the English built a locomotive they built it to last. Outside the railway station at Windhoek stand two little English engines that were assembled at Swakopmund in 1903 and withdrawn from service in 1940: and even then they had plenty of life in them.

The road passes between the mountain systems of the Schwarzrand to the north and the Hunsberge to the south, and at one stage begins to twist and turn among desiccated hills. Only the deformed and indomitable kokerboom crowns the heights. The sun hammers down on the roof of the Land Rover, making it hot to the touch. The seat-backs become sticky; big patches of sweat break out on your bush-jackets. It is stifling in these shale-strewn passes.

A totally unexpected respite occurs as you emerge from the hills and begin to thread your way down to the plain. It takes the form of a sturdy brick-built bar and restaurant, complete with forecourt and petrol pump. It is not a luxurious supermotel, but it is neat and spotless, and the beer is ice cold. 'KROEG: BAR' reads the notice outside, in lettering that was fashionable in Germany at the turn of the century; and an accompanying sign reads: 'F. ACKERMAN, JNR. GELISENLEER OM DRANK BY DIE KLEIN MAAT TE VERKOOP'.

Herr Ackermann is a cheerful, good-natured man, seemingly

SIX
Forbidden Area

THE notice reads: 'WARNING. PENALTY £500 OR ONE YEAR'S IMPRISONMENT. THE PUBLIC IS WARNED AGAINST ENTERING THE PROHIBITED DIAMOND AREA WITHOUT PERMITS.'

'WAARSKUWING.' 'WARNUNG.' The words are repeated in Afrikaans and German to make sure the message gets home.

There is only one road into the prohibited diamond area. It starts at Keetmanshoop, 321 miles south of Windhoek and 208 from the Orange River. 'Keetmans', with a European population of nearly 3,500, is a Nama or Hottentot stronghold, and is the third largest town in the South West. It is a hot, dusty, nondescript place, the centre of a hard-working sheep-farming community, and has little time for amenities and graces. Farming in South West, particularly in the southern half of the country, is an unremitting business, not productive of social polish. Keetmanshoop is the kind of town which the traveller is glad to reach at the end of a long day's drive, but is equally glad to leave the following morning, after a good dinner and a sound night's rest.

Kokerboom and Kaokoveld

for ever. Perhaps the pharaohs would be safer in their rock-cut tombs, deep below the earth. . . .

I craned my body round and gazed out of the rear window and watched the Brandberg fading in the lilac dusk.

It was the time of day the Bushmen call 'The Hour when Everything is Beautiful'.

I had not rifled the sanctuary. I had left something for the gods.

accident, missing it after keeping a careful look-out for it. You feel a fool. You feel cheated. When night came down, when we had to give up and grope our way back to the Land Rover, I could have cried with vexation. I lay flat on the back seat and stuck my aching feet out of the window. I did not utter a word during the 150 miles that lay between the Brandberg and Otjiwarango. Very few white men had looked at that famous frieze. I had wanted badly to see it. I had seen many Bushman paintings—in the Erongo mountains, the Gamsberg, the Spitzkoppe, the Naukluft. But I had not seen the White Lady. . . .

Yet wasn't there, perhaps, a compensation for my failure? Wasn't it better, after all, not to have disturbed the gods? Not to have intruded into the innermost shrine? The mystery of the mountain had remained intact for me. With the best intentions in the world, sight-seers and scientific investigators violate the spirit of a holy place. They offend the *genius loci*. I always feel this very strongly, for example, in the north of Africa, in Egypt. If I had my way, I would remove the royal mummies from the Cairo Museum and replace them in their former sepulchres in the Valley of the Kings. I always feel ashamed in that grisly mummy-room, the first and often the only port of call of tourists, when I view the pitiful relics of the powerful pharaohs who once ruled the greatest nation on earth: Amenophis III, Tuthmosis III, Rameses II. Staring at their remains is degrading and insulting. It gives me a perverse comfort to know that in the Valley of the Kings there may still be other pharaohs lying in their proper resting places, in the eternal darkness. This knowledge lends the Valley its potency and fascination, its dignity, its *mana*. The presence of Tutankhamen, whose body has been allowed to remain in its original tomb beneath the shadow of the sacred mountain, adds immeasurably to the character and atmosphere of the Valley. The reinstatement of his predecessors and successors would strengthen this sensation.

Too risky, you say? Remember the perennial outrages of the tomb robbers? Perhaps. But remember also that one stray Israeli bomb on the Cairo Museum—and Ancient Egypt dies

and engravings of huntsmen and animals in these out-of-the-way places. I was as moved as I was when, as an archaeology student, I first saw the cave-art of France and Spain: or when, later, I saw the pictographs of the Apaches and Comanches on the rocks and boulders of West Texas and New Mexico.

Once the hunting-grounds of the Kaokoveld teemed with animals, and with the men who tracked them with spear and arrow. A Carbon-14 test for one of the rock shelters gave a date of 1400 B.C. This is the date suggested by Breuil for the Brandberg paintings, though it is perfectly possible that these and other paintings may have been executed many hundreds or perhaps thousands of years earlier. In that dry air they would have been preserved as perfectly as the wall-art of Egypt. But such primitive art is notoriously hard to date, and from what is known of the movements of peoples and animals in the Kaokoveld it is not unlikely that many of the paintings in the area may be no more than three or four centuries old.

And now I have a very painful—almost an agonizing—confession to make. I have not seen the White Lady with my own eyes. The three of us searched diligently, heaven knows. I had a rough sketch-map, and I forged ahead up what I honestly took to be the so-called Tsisab Valley, in what I was sure was the direction of the cave. The Brandberg proves on close acquaintance to be surrounded by a sprawling and complicated nexus of peaks and hollows, bearing the name of the Twelve Apostles, extending over many miles. We scrambled along a long, rocky gorge; we stumbled down a dried-up river-bed; we climbed and descended, scraping our knees, banging our shins, knocking our ankles, bruising our wrists and fingers. The sun cooked the rocks in the ravine and frazzled us. All for nothing. The cave teased us, eluded us. We never found it.

This was a profound disappointment to me. I had been looking forward eagerly to this particular moment of the trip. Well—these things happen, I suppose, even to the most seasoned and determined of travellers. Everyone knows the mortification of missing some important landmark or monument—missing it by

opinion that she was of Mediterranean origin, and was the work of a band of Cretan sailors who had sailed down the west coast of Africa three thousand years before Diogo Cão. He identified her with Isis and Diana.

The Abbé Breuil was a scholar of world-wide reputation. I remember him well from the days after the last war when I was studying archaeology at Cambridge. Chubby, volatile, a tiny chain-smoking figure in a soutane, torrential in conversation, he was deeply revered; when he appeared at the university he used to be enthusiastically fêted. He was the last surviving representative of the generation of pioneers who had created Old Stone Age studies: and it once fell to my happy lot, as president of the university archaeological society, to welcome him and act as his host. However, where the White Lady is concerned, the redoubtable Abbé was surely at fault. For once his tempestuous enthusiasm carried him away, although it is admittedly difficult to gauge the extent to which Hamito–Semitic ideas and motifs might have been transmitted through Sudanic sources to the far south of the continent. As later writers such as A. R. Willcox have pointed out, Maack's 'White Lady' is almost certainly neither white nor a lady. Indeed Maack's own photograph of the entire frieze on which the 'Lady' occurs shows that she is associated with ten other figures of hunters—and two of these are dressed and decorated in precisely the same manner as the 'Lady' herself. Moreover, three of the remaining figures have also been whitened in the same way.

What is the explanation? These white or demi-white figures were definitely not Europeans, for they show the characteristic steatopygia or fatty backsides of Bushmen or Hottentots. The obvious answer is that they were native huntsmen who followed the widespread African practice of smearing their bodies and lower limbs with ashes or white clay.

It seems a pity to throw doubt on such a colourful legend—though for my part the presumption that the 'White Lady' is a Bushman or Hottentot does not lessen its hold over my imagination. It is profoundly moving to come across these paintings

Kokerboom and Kaokoveld

Klaas stopped the Land Rover in the lee of one of its bronze-coloured bluffs and we got out. I remember that we closed the doors quietly, as if we were afraid to disturb the spirits that kept watch or slumbered there.

A wind blew down towards us through the gullies and ridges of the foothills. All around us were gigantic boulders, spewed out of the bowels of the earth thousands upon thousands of years ago. They bore the brand of the furnace, their surfaces charred and crackled into an angry crimson. They were patterned with blackened whorls and zigzags, the handiwork of flame, looking as if they were covered with runes in a forgotten tongue. They resembled the inscribed fragments of a temple shattered by the force of some divine cataclysm. They revealed why the Brandberg bears its name: the 'Burnt Mountain'.

It was precisely as a temple that the wandering huntsmen regarded the mountain in ancient times. And like other temples, the Brandberg possesses its holy of holies: an inner shrine whose walls were elaborately decorated by the tribes who came to worship there. The shrine was discovered in 1917 by the German geologist, Doctor Reinhard Maack. It was Maack who bestowed the name 'The White Lady' on the central figure of the celebrated frieze, 18 feet long and 7 feet wide, that covers the wall of the principal cave.

The White Lady is an enigma. She has been described as wearing a net of pearls in her hair, with ropes of pearls adorning her breasts and hips. She wears decorated anklets and armlets, her feet are shod, and in her right hand she bears a cup. Many fanciful explanations have been put forward to explain the presence of such a novel figure in this unexpected place. It has been suggested that she derives from Zimbabwe, the deserted walled city situated a thousand miles due eastwards in Rhodesia. A more romantic theory is that she is a European woman who survived shipwreck on the Skeleton Coast, and was adopted by the Bushmen as their white queen. In 1955 the world's leading authority on prehistoric art, Abbé Henri Breuil, published his sumptuous *The White Lady of the Brandberg*, in which he gave his

The Land God Made in Anger

The Brandberg hung in the afternoon sunlight like an object that was supernatural. Its outline scarcely seemed to alter or grow in size. For some time we had all been silent in the Land Rover. This was in accordance with our usual habit of beginning the day with an intensive burst of laughter and conversation, then relapsing after an hour or two into our own thoughts. We were therefore more than a little somnolent—from the heat, from the placidity of the desert, from the unchanging note of the engine. The sight of the Brandberg was ready to induce in us a slightly trance-like state.

It was like something in a dream. My preoccupation with my petty problems drained gently away. My mind was filled by the radiant bulk of the mountain. Its shining image as I saw it at that moment has stayed with me ever afterwards. Sometimes at night, before I go to sleep, I close my eyes and return to that rapt interlude when the Land Rover ran on steadily across the plain towards the glowing reddish mass of the Brandberg.

Such memories and images serve as specifics, as charms against the littleness of life. They provide us with solace and reassurance. I have no hesitation in saying that the experience of that afternoon had an element of magic in it. I felt the mystery of nature in watching the mountain glide towards me:

> Only the earth doth stand forever still:
> Her rocks remove not, nor her mountains meet....

It was easy to understand why, to the Bushmen and prehistoric hunters, the Brandberg had been a Presence, a Personification. It was a palace which the gods had erected for themselves in the middle of the wilderness. It was otherworldly; it existed in another dimension. The sunlight sheathed the mountain with a pearly integument, making it glassy and irridescent, giving the impression that it had been conjured up by the wave of a wand and could as easily be made to vanish. The impression did not disappear when eventually the great seamed sides of the mountain expanded to fill the entire windscreen, blotting out the blue sky. Nor did it disappear when

rises within hailing distance of such famous peaks as Mount Fuji and Mount Olympus. And what it lacks in vulgar stature it more than gains by virtue of its dominating situation. It rears up from the flat veld, already visible when it is still more than sixty miles away. For sheer solitary grandeur the Brandberg is unmatchable.

My first sight of it is stamped deeply on my mind. While the Land Rover was cruising eastwards over the parched and featureless plain I had been sunk in the passenger seat, lost in my own thoughts. One of the conventions of travel books is that the writer represents himself as being wholly and utterly absorbed by the sights and sounds of the country he is describing; he pretends that he has absolutely no room in his mind for anything else. Such a degree of concentration is impossible. Travellers, like lovers, find that irrelevant thoughts keep breaking in at what ought to be the most solemn moments. Even when you are contemplating the front of Chartres, you cannot stop yourself wondering what you are going to eat for dinner, or whether that important letter has been forwarded from London. The human mind is an unruly organ. In the interval before I became aware of the Brandberg I had been brooding about my work, my family, my taxes, my future plans—all the things that writers of travel books pretend to leave behind, but never do.

I say 'became aware' deliberately. The mountain swims gradually into view. You seem to have been staring at it for a long time before you actually become conscious of it. Thereafter you move towards it for what feels like many hours without ever coming any closer to it. It hovers there in front of you—aloof, uncanny. Distances are oddly deceptive on the African veld; an object can be half a mile away or ten miles. What you take to be a stunted bush a few hundred yards away swells into an immense baobab, capable of sheltering a herd of cattle. The veld plays the same tricks on you as the sea. You can watch a flock of ostrich loping along with their undulating gait without being able to make up your mind whether they are running towards you or away from you.

The Land God Made in Anger

As you drive eastwards, leaving the coast farther and farther behind, the number of scraps and tatters of vegetation increases. The desert is still a stone desert, but there are presages of the grassy uplands that lie ahead, running in a wedge from the northern borders down to Windhoek. Among the stones crouch cacti and tufts of reed, and finally a yellow grass begins to clothe the flinty plain. Then come the trees. There are camelthorns, with their spreading umbrella-heads; the tall tambuti, mopani, and marula. These were the trees beloved by the giraffe and the elephant, in the far-off days when the great herds wandered here. It may be that at one time, less than 500 years ago, the deeply-cut bed of the dried-up Ugab was linked to the freely-flowing Cunene and Okavango. Today the Namib and Kaokoveld are destitute of the giraffe, elephant, rhinoceros, kudu and other big game that used to roam there. The animals have retreated two hundred miles to the north, to Etosha Pan. Human beings are equally scarce. The Namib and Kaokoveld comprise 23,000 square miles, much of it unexplored and unmapped. In this vast area, according to the 1960 census, less than three thousand people live, over a thousand of them in the shelter of the Sesfontein reserve. A few dozen strandloopers on the Skeleton Coast; a few families of Himba and Herero around the waterholes. Nobody else.

Sesfontein. Six Fountains. A sudden little patch of lushness north of Fransfontein, barred behind chains of mountains. A group of Nama-Hottentots dwell there in picturesque isolation, grouped around the date palms and crumbling white walls of the old German fort. They cultivate wheat, maize and tobacco, which they send southward, and which provide them with a sufficient and satisfying income.

But if the Kaokoveld is empty, it holds a Presence. The Presence is the holy mountain of the Brandberg, the highest peak in South West Africa.

The Brandberg is 8,550 feet high. This is not a tremendous elevation when one considers that there are forty mountains in the world over 20,000 feet. The Brandberg is less than half the height of Mount Kenya or Kilimanjaro. On the other hand, it

look somewhat the worse for wear. It has a tortured, blackened appearance; its leaves, only one pair of which manages to grow every century, are usually ripped to shreds by the south-westerly gales. It grows in the most barren section of the northern Namib, near the coast. However, this seemingly deadly location actually provides it with its means of survival, for it is thought to exist by absorbing the moisture from the sea-fogs that roll in over the land, produced by the cold air from the Benguela Current meeting the baked air from the desert. As a secondary source of supply, it also grows a sixty-foot tap-root.

I was lucky enough to see a specimen of the plant. It was large, standing four foot high at the centre, with dark stringy green leaves that were torn and charred-looking at the edges. In the middle was a kind of porous grey ring, like crumbled pumice-stone. A few shrivelled brown spikelets stuck out between the inner ring and the leaves. These were the remains, I was told, of the orange flowers and yellow berries put out by the male, which are seldom seen; the female puts out an occasional deep red cone, shaped like a fat carrot or the head of a tulip.

Like the kokerboom, the Welwitschia is protected by law. Also protected, to the extent of being mainly fenced in by the authorities, is the petrified forest at Fransfontein, twenty miles north of the little settlement of Welwitschia. There were various bits and pieces of the 'forest' scattered about outside the fence, enabling the casual visitor to examine them. The trees were blown down by a seismic cataclysm a hundred million years ago, and silicified by the layers of sand that formed on top of them. This process took many millions of years, and many more millions of years passed before the sand wore away again and the fossil trees were uncovered. Some of the fallen trunks are almost perfectly preserved, and run up to sixty feet in length and ten feet in diameter. For the most part, however, they lie about in broken segments, like chopped-up logs. They look as if a race of giants had been hewing wood, and had suddenly hefted their axes and marched away.

centurions of a forgotten legion, inured to wind, sun, thirst, and freezing nights. From a distance they seem immensely sturdy: but when you come close you see how feeble and fragile they are, scarcely able to cling to the rock. Their trunks are peeling away in scabrous patches, and the ground around them is strewn with their snapped-off branches, like fallen weapons. They are sustained in their proud stance not by stout roots, but by nothing more than a stringy mass of weak fibres. You could knock them over with ease. Several times I saw one that had been blown down on its side, its clubbed foot ripped out of the sand, or one which had simply collapsed and died at its post. The sight always made me melancholy. Birds love the kokerboom's branches, and the bees swarm brightly around it to feast on its blossoms: and now there would be one place the less for the birds of the desert to rest, and for the bees to suck their nectar.

The kokerboom has always exercised a fascination over the minds of travellers. Its botanical name is *Aloe dichotoma*, but it is a monocotyledon, and therefore belongs to the same family as the lilies. A very odd-looking lily. It was given its name by Francis Masson in 1776, but had already been examined and described by sturdy old Simon van der Stel almost a century earlier, when he made his great expedition to the Copper Mountains. According to legend, the kokerboom lives to be more than two centuries old—which makes its death, after such a span of austere endurance, even more sad and touching.

The Namib can boast a second unique plant, to be found only in a restricted area of the northern Namib, between Swakopmund and the border of the Police Zone. This plant, first described by the Austrian botanist Friedrich Welwitsch, is named the *Welwitschia mirabilis* or 'Wonderful Welwitschia'. It manages to survive to an age which has been reliably reckoned at upwards of two thousand years. The leaf of one of the less mature specimens has been subjected to the Carbon-14 test, which is used to determine the age of prehistoric pottery and other archaeological artifacts. The test yielded a date of about A.D. 600. It is not surprising that such a venerable object should

Kokerboom and Kaokoveld

pumpkin, or naras, known as the 'Wonder of the Wilderness', pokes itself out of the sand in the shape of a half-buried coil of barbed wire. It has no leaves, but wicked two-inch thorns. From it sprouts a green fruit, the size of a man's fist, which is kept alive by a tap-root going down forty or fifty feet into the subsoil. Nomads collect the fruit, make a hole in it, and mash up the inside into a pulp. The foul watery liquid can then be drunk—again, unless you are a Bushman, preferably boiled. Afterwards the pulp can be extracted and baked into a primitive bread; the husk is dried and used to make flasks, cooking pots or musical instruments; and the pips are roasted and eaten, or sold to confectioners in the small towns who grind them into a flavouring for cakes and puddings. In the desert, nothing goes to waste.

The tsama melon, often found growing in groups of ten or twenty alongside the naras, is used by nomads in the same way. It is the size of a small football, and its appearance as it squats on the naked sand is beguilingly plump and shiny. It resembles a larger version of the coyote melon—sometimes called the buffalo gourd or *calabazilla*—of Arizona and California, or one of those palpitating fruits which René Magritte liked to make the centre of one of his nightmare canvases. Its taste is filthy: and Klaas and I, when we wanted to stretch our legs, used to play soccer with them. Unless you are a Bushman, that is about all they are good for.

For me, the king of this tribe of gnarled and heroic growths is the Kokerboom or Quiver Tree. It derives its name from the fact that the Bushmen and Hottentots cut off its branches to make containers for their arrows. The kokerboom flourishes— or rather, maintains a precarious grip on life—in the southern part of the Namib. It is unique to South West Africa—a strange symbol for a strange country. With its grey bark streaked with white, its short branches tufted with dabs of dusty olive and crowned with yellow panicles, it stands erect on the ribs of the mountains, stark and dignified.

I developed a strong affection for the kokerbooms, with their unforgettable outline and brave blossoms. They are like the

Deserts are not nature's cemeteries, her failures. They are the scene of a ceaseless secret activity. Strange animals are burrowing beneath the crust, strange insects scurry about, strange plants battle up towards the sun. The germs of life are irrepressible. In the cluttered landscapes of industrialized countries you forget to use your eyes; you take your surroundings for granted. In the desert, where the frailest thing is thrown into vivid relief, your sense of wonder is heightened and renewed.

In the more obdurate stretches of the Namib the main forms of life are the succulents. Prominent and widespread are the mesembryanthemums. These are small bipartite plants, their bodies actually consisting of a pair of leaves swollen with the moisture they contain. They grow among stones, which they imitate perfectly in shape and colouring. For half the year they exist entirely without water: but when they tap some hidden source of moisture they put out a magnificent coloured flower, often larger than themselves. There are dozens of genera of mesembryanthemums in South and South West Africa, and the genus which is most commonly met with in the northern Namib is *Lithops*, known to the Afrikaners as 'Bushman's Bottom'. After rain these little stone-like plants shoot forth a brilliant white or yellow star. When picked and squeezed, the leaves yield a smear of brackish water, enough to assuage the tongue. The first question the Bushman or the traveller asks of any growing thing in the desert is: *Does it give water, or mark a spot where water can be found?*

On the glaring heights of the rocky outcrops grows a remarkable plant which is a veritable reservoir. It looks like a succulent, but is technically a member of the vine family. The *Cissus* is a grotesque white growth resembling an illustration by Arthur Rackham or Mervyn Peake. Its surface is scrofulous—pitted and corky—and the stumpy fingers on its stubby arms scrabble at the sky. The liquid in this monstrous tun can be drained off and drunk. Its taste is abominable, but after being boiled it can be sipped sparingly as a last resort.

More commonly distributed and used as a prime source of water are the wild pumpkins and the wild melons. The wild

there is balm in strolling through a summer garden; there are times when it is beneficial to wander out into a desert. You can think clearly in a desert: there are no distractions. And every now and again you come upon some small feature that intrigues and diverts you. In spite of the impression of sterility which the word conveys, a desert is seldom completely void. Even in the Sahara you will run across an oasis, a few houses on a damp blob of green, even a miniature township laid out on a grid-system, its streets running straight out into yellow eternity like the streets of Swakopmund and Walvis Bay. Even on the Skeleton Coast there are obscure and humble scraps of sentient matter, sucking blindly for a last dribble of moisture. Many so-called deserts, like the Kalahari, or like western Texas beyond the Pecos, or the great Chihuahua and Sonora deserts to the south of it, are not really deserts at all: they are inhospitable and cannot support a population, but they are studded with trees and thickly matted with scrub.

The Namib looks completely barren. Nevertheless it supports an extraordinary flora and fauna. You will have to look for it, as you will not have to look for roses and dahlias in a summer garden; but when you find it you will gain a corresponding reward. The Namib demonstrates that nature is never really dormant; she does not know any dead season. There is always the promise of re-birth and resurrection. Osiris stands in his winding-sheet in his tomb in the necropolis, and his face is green with corruption. But the colour of corruption is the colour of the corn, and Osiris is the core of every seed, looking dessicated when you hold it in your palm, but which will sprout and burgeon when you push it into the soil. Often in Britain, in December, I used to walk around my garden in the grey and muddy end of the year. The boughs would be black with wet, the beds were choked with rotting leaves. But around the pond, the sundial, the vinery, and in the patch at the bottom of the paddock, little fat green waxy spikes were already bristling from the puddled earth. Twelve inches down, the daffodils were working. Soon would flower the snowdrops, the glory of the snows, the narcissi, the grape hyacinth.

man-o'-war. Could it be, I wonder, the wreck of Diogo Cão's ship? There are many such hulks, caught up in those grinding sands. The desert is rolling forward all the time, pushing the ocean back, and many of the wrecks are now situated miles inland. Some authorities think that the whole continent of Africa is tilting eastwards like a platter, heaving its western edge inch by inch out of the South Atlantic. Others believe that the colossal Namib Desert itself is ceaselessly heaving and churning. At times the wrecks are smothered with sand, at others they are uncovered, and a Bushman or a wandering Nama will emerge from the wilderness to give news of them. There are modern wrecks in there, too, in addition to caravels and East Indiamen. In 1942 the *Dunedin Star* hit an uncharted reef north of Cape Fria and ran aground. She was one of the Blue Star line, a refrigerator ship built for the New Zealand run. After she beached, her crew huddled on the dreary shore until she was spotted and supplies were dropped from the air. They were eventually taken off by a South African ship. Now the *Dunedin Star* wallows in the desert, cut off from the sea, her plates and upper works stripped of every vestige of paint by the abrasive winds.

You cannot enter the Skeleton Coast. At Cape Cross you must turn east. The Skeleton Coast lies beyond the Police Zone. The domain of the Police Zone extends over this far northern area of the country: but its boundary has been specially extended southwards at this point to discourage you from setting foot in an area penetrated only by the hardiest Bushman or the most suicidal diamond-prospector. You would do well to copy the police themselves, and keep clear of it. There is no water there. There is no vegetation to attract the rainclouds. A thin drip of moisture might descend on the Skeleton Coast twice in a century. If there are diamonds, let them lie where they are: you will lose your life looking for them. Many men have.

If you are a connoisseur of deserts, there is plenty to interest you in the expanse that lies ahead of you east of Cape Cross. Deserts have a fascination of their own. There are times when

Kokerboom and Kaokoveld

nations of the world to abuse and belittle Portugal. The Portuguese are subjected to continuous denigration. Their contribution to the development of the human spirit, which increases with the performance of every feat of courage and intellect, is disparaged. But the nation that bred kings like Henry the Navigator and John II, and explorers like Cabral and Magellan has made very sure of an honourable and abiding place in history.

Exploration on the scale in which the seamen of Portugal pursued it five hundred years ago cannot be undertaken cheaply. There is a heavy price to pay. Diogo Cão is thought to have perished on the Skeleton Coast of South West Africa; Bartolomeu Dias was drowned at the Cape of Good Hope when four of a little flotilla of thirteen ships went down in a storm. Only six of the thirteen eventually reached Calicut. Vasco da Gama lost almost half his fleet during the course of his immortal voyage; and Camões was aboard the sole survivor of four ships that set out for India from Lisbon in 1553. The leaky little caravels, whose crews existed on salt junk and stagnant water, can be aptly compared, as they beat their way across the empty oceans, to the space capsules of our own century. They too were tiny pellets flipped into the unknown.

Today the surviving fragments of the original *padrão* have come to rest, after strange journeyings, in Lisbon, Berlin and New Zealand. One should gaze at them with the respect with which future generations will gaze at the relics of *Vostok* or *Friendship* 7. The South African government has erected a handsome replica of the *padrão* on the lonely foreshore at Cape Cross, beside the breakers of the coldest of the world's oceans, and a similar replica of Dias's *padrão* has been placed on the rim of the bay at Lüderitz. I sat for half an hour one chilly evening on the latter's massive stone plinth, staring at the splintered coastline as it stretched away towards the north and the distant shores of Portugal.

Out there in the Namib, stranded in the wastes of the Skeleton Coast, strewn thick with the flotsam of a thousand wrecks, are said to be the shattered timbers of a Portuguese

Benguela, before returning to Lisbon. At both places he erected a stone *padrão* or pillar with a cross to mark the advancing frontier of Christendom. John II knighted him, gave him an annuity, and granted him a coat-of-arms which featured the two *padrãos*. Shortly after, probably in 1485, he made a second voyage, and this time touched land at Cape Cross, 750 miles further south.

In 1487 another great Portuguese navigator, Bartolomeu Dias, penetrated a further 450 miles south off the arid coast of the Namib and set up his own *padrão* at Lüderitz Bay. It was a stepping-stone towards his achievement of the following year: the rounding of the Cape of Good Hope, so named by John II because it opened up the Orient to Portuguese missionaries and merchants.

Diogo Cão and Dias were only two of the band of Portuguese mariners whose triumphs between 1415, when John de Trasto discovered the Grand Canary and 1522, when Magellan circumnavigated the globe, represent one of the peaks of human skill and endurance. These men were moved by a mania even more potent than the diamond mania: the mania of ocean voyaging. They were the elder brothers of those Hanseatic seamen who took as their motto the stark words: *Navigare necesse est vivere non necesse.* 'It is a necessity to sail, not a necessity to live.' By 1500, when Pedro Alvares Cabral discovered Brazil, the Congo basin had been investigated, the Cape had been rounded, Vasco da Gama had opened the route to India, and Cabot and others had visited Greenland and Labrador. Overland, pursuing their policy of attempting to outmanoeuvre and encircle the infidel Turks, the Portuguese had penetrated to Timbuctoo and into the heart of Abyssinia. There they found the fabled court of Prester John. In less than twenty years their trading missions would be established in India, China and Japan.

Their greatest national poet, Luis de Camões, was not exaggerating when he boasted in his epic poem *Os Lusíadas* that, 'If there were more lands left to discover, those they would have discovered also.' Today it is fashionable for the

farmer let them lapse. He had been paying £5 a month for each of his options. A few weeks later diamonds were discovered on the land, and the potential was valued by the Government Mining Engineer at £30 million (72 million dollars).

You can now appreciate why, when you drive through a diamond or diamond-prospected area in your Land Rover, you keep twisting your head this way and that, eyeballs popping, scanning the desert on each side of the track. The excitement you feel is ridiculous. Even if a diamond as large as the Cullinan lay within a yard of you, you would miss it and mistake it for an ordinary pebble. Diamonds in their natural state do not twinkle at you obligingly: they hide their light under a drab and mottled crust. And just as Hemingway's big-game hunter told Francis Macomber 'We don't shoot them from cars', so the diamond-prospector would remind us 'We don't spot them by driving past at fifty or sixty miles an hour'. But it is none the less true that merely being in an alleged diamond area is enough to cause you to breathe faster and make you behave in a daft and illogical way. You go veering over the desert, darting and scuffling about like a bird pecking for worms. It is immensely exhilarating. Nor is it simply a sensation of unalloyed greed. You feel somehow that to stumble on a diamond, even a little, flawed diamond, would be a mark of a special providence, a token of a favourable destiny. Diamonds are luck.

The diamond mystique is powerful and obscure. It must be. Otherwise it could hardly keep men grubbing for weeks in the dreadful environs of Cape Cross.

It was at Cape Cross that a European seaman first made a landfall in South West Africa, or in southern Africa itself.

The seaman was the Portuguese navigator Diogo Cão or Diego Cam. In 1482 he had been commissioned by John II to explore the African coast beyond the point previously reached by Fernão Gomes. He was the first European to reach the mouth of the Congo, and thence sailed on to touch Cape Santa Maria in Angola, a hundred miles south of the modern port of

coast of South West Africa, for sixty years: but between 1962–65 there was a regular 'diamond-rush' from Swakopmund right up to the border of the Police Zone, 150 miles to the north. Activity continued as much as fifty miles inland. The rush began when a shop-keeper in the forlorn little community of Henties Bay or Hentisbaai, half-way between Swakopmund and Cape Cross, found five diamonds in a river-bed. News of such finds always spreads like wildfire in the tindery world of the diamond-seekers. Within weeks 3,000 of them had flocked to the area to stake out claims in the desert shale. The glare, the heat, the wind, the scraped and sullen solitude—the victim of diamond-fever takes these things in his stride. The worse the conditions, the bleaker the terrain, the more eagerly he wields his pick and shovel. His inflamed imagination prompts him in some dim and superstitious way to believe that the chances of finding a diamond increase with the rigours of the search. Surely, he reasons, nature will take pity on a man who has had the guts to sally out into a dreadful corner of the desert to seek his fortune. At Hentisbaai blocks of land that had been on offer for years for a few shillings an acre changed hands for hundreds or even thousands of pounds.

A metal marker records the name and number of the claim and its date, and is placed at the centre of the claim, whose corners are marked with angle irons. The number of claims made by an individual or a syndicate are regulated by law, and are rented from the state for a set period, either on a monthly or on an annual basis. The diggers at Swakopmund had been warned by geologists that there was little likelihood of the area turning out to be diamondiferous. But the diggers reminded themselves that the geologists, in spite of their elaborate surveys, had often been wrong before. There was always the remote chance that one of the dried-up rivers of the Namib—the Omaruru or the Ugab—would prove to be one of the 'lost' rivers along which diamonds were washed down to the sea in far-off times. In 1964 a geologist told a farmer at Springbok that the options he held on a number of claims, and which he had kept renewing for eight years, were worthless. The

guins and flamingos perch or nest on the islands. All of them eat several times their own weight in food every day. They are packed on the islands as densely as the seals in their rookeries, and when they die their bodies lend weight and stench to the deposits.

The huge artificial bird-island at Swakopmund is an extraordinary sight. It consists of an enormous wooden platform, 1,700 feet square, standing on metal legs on the sea-bed 1,000 yards from the shore. Here a mass of seabirds can be observed as they squat or strut about—maintaining, as has been pointed out, a natural apartheid: white birds at one end, black at the other. The pelicans wait patiently beside the nests of the gulls and gobble down the young as soon as they hatch out: an excellent example of the Good Old Rule as it functions in Nature. The platform was erected in 1932 by an enterprising German carpenter called Adulf Winter, and at first was nicknamed 'Winter's Folly' because the seabirds refused to roost there. However, after a year or two they began to flock to the platform, and for over thirty years they have covered it with an annual four-inch slab of guano. This can be worth as much as £10,000 a year to its proprietor, rewarding him for the humiliating time when, as he has confessed, he used to sit on the shore opposite his virgin platform and shed bitter tears. In late summer a gang of Cape Coloured workers spends four weeks levering up the hardened and horrible stuff, which crawls with lice and ticks, bagging it, and transferring it in a lighter to Swakopmund. The average yield is a thousand tons: and at a price of about £15 or $36 a ton it is evident that guano is an efficacious and highly sought-after substance.

You will notice that all along the road to Cape Cross the floor of the desert is scratched and scarred with mysterious markings. These are the handiwork of the diamond prospectors. The desert here is not sand, but a coarse grit, consisting of brown stone chips packed together and overlaid with rocks and boulders. In this stony substance the pits and trenches of the prospectors assume a permanent character. The search for diamonds has been going on in this area, as everywhere on the

second, a softer, crystalline type of salt is artificially manufactured in hundreds of narrow neatly-cut trenches, dug at places where the sea floods regularly over the level ground. The seawater evaporates in the trenches, and after a number of tides the salt is ready to be shovelled out of the pits and the process begins again. Saltmining is extremely profitable, particularly in proportion to the modest outlay involved, and production varies between 50,000 and 100,000 tons a year, valued at between £50,000 and £100,000, ($120,000 and $240,000) according to the state of the market.

The second industry centred on the coast is the guano industry. The dignified phrase for this merchandise is 'white wealth'—but guano is, of course, solidified bird droppings. Birdlime has been recognized from ancient times as an incomparable source of fertilizer. It is a concentrated form of phosphate, its nitrogen content higher than farmyard manure. The Peruvian Indians made use of it, and Peru has always been the world's most famous source of guano; regular shipments began in 1810, and in the early 1950s exports amounted to half a million tons annually.

The guano deposits of South West Africa were being exploited by the Cape Dutch in the seventeenth century; and the guano islands dotted up and down the coast were annexed by the British in 1866, eight years before the annexation of Walvis Bay. The islands have picturesque names: Roast Beef, Plum Pudding, Mercury, Ichabod, Pomona, Halifax. Most of them are mere rocks, with the exception of Ichabod, off Lüderitz Bay, which is more than a mile square. The guano collectors were first cousins to the seal-hunters: a gang of lost souls, drunkards, deserters, criminals and misanthropes. Many of them remained on their noisome abodes for twenty or thirty years; some of them died and were buried there. It is said that the ammonia in the air acted as a perfect preservative for their corpses, and turned the dead men's hair a bright red.

When the early guano-seekers began to operate, the deposits were often over a hundred feet thick. It has been estimated that twenty to thirty million cormorants, pelicans, gannets, pen-

FIVE
Kokerboom and Kaokoveld

'WHEN God made this land,' say the Bushmen, 'he must have been very angry.'

It is three hundred miles across the Namib between Swakopmund and Otjiwarongo. For a hundred miles the road skirts the desert, winding up the coastline towards Cape Cross. The dunes suddenly peter out, the landscape becomes flat; and if you have picked a day when the pall of sea-fog has rolled away, then the first part of the journey produces a very mild impression, shielding you from the full impact of the nature of the Namib.

As you drive along, the coastal area seems empty enough: but in fact it is the focal point of two lucrative industries. The existence of salt-mining is apparent from the forty-ton trucks with trailers that occasionally go drumming past you—itself a remarkable occurrence on these untenanted highways.

The big rough dazzling blocks of salt are produced in two ways. In the first, the salt is hacked out of the salt-pans; in the

4 Walvis Bay: the end of a dream

3 The Orange River at Vioolsdrift

garage, at the corner of Brückenstrasse and Bismarkstrasse.

We made sure the tank and reserve-tanks were full. We checked the oil, the tyre pressures, the level of the water in the radiator and the battery. We topped up the water-bags hanging from the bumper.

Four or five Ovambo mechanics in blue overalls helped us with zest, running backwards and forwards with the watering-can, the bottles of oil, the flask of distilled water. Three of them hurled themselves at the windshield with moistened rags. As we drove away they collected in a bunch in the middle of the dirt road, grinning and waving vigorously, shouting the farewell of the South West African garage-hand:

'*Bye-bye, baas! Auf wiedersehen! Come back soon! Alles ist vell, baas! Go vell—Go Shell!*'

The Ovambo are sometimes called 'The Merry People'. I hope one day they find the Great Good Life, up there in the north, in their own land, among the reeds and the water.

usually the slaughter was indiscriminate. The number of seals that escaped was negligible; they were jammed together, impeding each others' tails and flippers; they were unable to wriggle and flop their way seaward quickly enough. The females that got free, it is said, would thresh around frantically offshore, listening to the cries of their young; and the story goes that many of them committed suicide by drowning or by dashing themselves against the reefs.

Sealers were an unsavoury lot. An observer who watched them massacre a herd of Greenland or saddle-back seals recorded that: 'As for their personal appearance, as they labour at the work of slaughter, they look the most ruffianly set of men in existence. They are dressed in the queerest caps and coats of various shapes, with smuggler-looking breeches and long boots; moustaches and beards are covered with a mass of frozen tobacco-juice, hoar-frost, and seal's blood. Their matted hair, gory, greasy, unwashed faces and hands, reek and smell with a strong taint of butchery.'

Kicking and clubbing the seals did not kill them: it only immobilized them. While the creatures lay stunned and quivering, the sealer took out a long sharp knife and made a body-long slash along the pelt. Then, with a practised twist, he dexterously stripped the seal out of its protective coat, threw the valuable fur on a pile, and left the living, palpitating carcass sprawled out blood-red and naked on the sharp and frozen rock.

Homo animali lupus. In our own enlightened times the business of sealing at Cape Cross is subject to strict regulations. Ours, after all, is the era of orderly killing. The sealers are allowed to slaughter the seals once a year, at the breeding season. They are only permitted to kill the baby seals. The under-fur of the babies is more glossy and compact than those of mature seals, and under these circumstances it is not necessary to kill the parents. If it were, there would no doubt be proper regulations for that too.

Before we drove off into the desert we stopped at Stekel's

The Land God Made in Anger

like everyone else, of neglecting his own blood brother. Life for the Boers has always been a matter of struggle and poverty, with death and ruin never far away. A few years before the last war, a committee of the Carnegie Institute was invited by General Smuts to enquire impartially into the living conditions of the white South Africans. The committee found that 56 per cent of the white population were living in conditions that could be described as 'below average', while no fewer than 22 per cent were actually living below the bread-line and could be classed, in the American sense, as 'poor whites'. Affluence is a very recent phenomenon in South Africa, and even today it is spread thin. Like the Africans, the South Africans too possess their scars.

We could weep for Swakopmund. We could weep for much more besides. Perhaps we should try to keep in mind the words of Spinoza: 'Neither to laugh, nor to weep: but to understand'.

Ninety miles north of Swakopmund, at Cape Cross, are extensive seal-colonies. Sixty or seventy years ago, 80,000 to 100,000 skins of the Cape Fur Seal were sent annually to the fur auctions in London. The sealers of Cape Cross, who also plied their trade on the nearby islands of Staple Rock, Eighty-Four and Dumfudgeon, went about their work according to time-honoured methods. They would wait until foggy weather, then paddle softly ashore on the rocks below the rookery or hauling-ground—so called from the action of the seals in hauling themselves out of the water. Hundreds of the creatures lay packed head to tail in a dense mass, each bull surrounded by his harem of a dozen wives with their offspring. The sealers would creep along between the herd and the water: then, at a signal, they would leap forward, yelling and shouting, shepherding the whole herd inland towards a suitable killing-ground. There they would let their prey settle down for a few hours, before ploughing in among them, kicking the smaller seals to death with their heavy sea-boots, attacking the bigger ones with spiked clubs. Some of the less murderous sealers let the females go free in order to protect their own livelihood: but

Pondok and Baroque

clamber on to a peak and gaze out across the troughs and ridges. An endless yellow ocean. The combers swelling up from below me were bigger than the compacted masses of water that surf-boarders call dumpers. Some of them were as solid and as geometrical as pyramids. Loose grains blew off the crests and sifted down the angular surfaces in a thin spume, stinging my cheeks.

Forty-five hundred years ago, block by painful block, Khufu, Chephren and Mycerinus had heaped up their man-made dunes on the plateau at Giza. Two hundred million years before the pharaohs, a more powerful finger had casually stirred the Namib into shape and pinched up the pyramids of sand. . . .

Pascal has a famous sentence describing how frightened he was when he contemplated the 'infinite spaces of the universe'.

I was frightened by the infinite spaces of the Namib.

In the desert on the northern edge of the town are the shanties of the Africans. There are about 1,500 Africans at Swakopmund, 1,300 of them Ovambos. The Africaans slang for shanties is *pondoks* or *pondokkies*. This ugly word is particularly ugly at Swakopmund, where the *pondoks* consist of small single-gauge German railway-trucks, sixty years old. Think of that: a whole community of human beings, housed in disused and dilapidated rolling-stock. The desert sand has stripped the paint off the trucks, and they stand there bone-grey, surrounded by a hopeless wash of rusty cans, automobile tyres, bits of cardboard, torn scraps of newspaper. Well, one can hardly expect people condemned to live in railway-trucks to grow roses. . . .

There is an old tag of Plautus's, taken up and illustrated by Bacon and Hobbes, which says *homo homini lupus*. Man is a wolf to man. The tag was much in my mind at Swakopmund.

Nevertheless, one must try to keep one's sense of proportion. Man is a wolf to man in the slums of Naples, Cairo, Tokyo, Glasgow, Chicago, and Moscow as well as among the *pondoks* of Swakopmund. Even in South Africa there are white men, let alone Africans, who live in depressed and loathsome circumstances. If the Afrikaner neglects the African, he is also capable,

whitewash and crenellation, flanked by neat suburban villas almost as large as itself. And not far away from the barracks was the building that used to house the brothel, where the officers killed some of the time which hung so heavily on their hands. Pretty flowers are all very well for passing the hours—but girls are better. The girls used to come out to South West from the mother country—ample, tow-headed girls—and were accommodated in a roomy three-storey house with its front ornamented with plaster cornucopias and cupids. Above its elaborate doorway is a representation of Atlas staggering under the weight of his ball. Today the building has been converted into a rather stuffy block of apartments, whose occupants flatly deny that it was originally dedicated to more spirited purposes.

In spite of the up-to-date bookshops and chemists' shops in Swakopmund there are abundant touches of the old imperial days. Wherever you look you see Gothic turrets and half-timbering, and some of the shops are still provided with the old Biedermeier fittings and furnishings. In a tea-shop I ate *torte*, sipped (salty) coffee with cream, and stared at a pair of steel engravings on the opposite wall. They showed castles in the moonlight and knights riding through the forest, in the manner of Schnorr von Carolsfeld or Moritz von Schwind.

As I sat there, customers drifted into the shop to buy the fragrant sweets and pastries. Many were Ovambo women—bulky, big-hipped, inextinguishably cheerful. The blonde proprietress, chatting in German to her assistants, served the African women exactly as she would have served her sister Europeans.

There is seldom any apartheid where money is concerned.

The Emperor Vespasian, reproached with accepting tax money from public lavatories, raised one of the offending coins to his nose. *'Sed non olet,'* he remarked. 'It does not smell.' ...

The dunes at Swakopmund are taller than the dunes at Walvis Bay. I used to potter about among them, scrambling up and slithering down, a child again among monstrous sand-castles. The exercise was a cross between surfing and mountaineering. Taking care to keep the roofs of the town in sight, I would

Pondok and Baroque

edge of a terrifying desert, Swakopmund has a certain style. I admired that. The town ought by rights to have looked as woebegone as Walvis Bay, or Karibib: there would have been an equal excuse for it. But it did not. It was a tribute to human pride and self-respect, and to the German aptitude for making a silk purse out of a sow's ear. We drove down Kaiserstrasse, past a white baroque church with a domed roof and a neat white tower crowned with a double-onion pinnacle. It was not one of the masterpieces of Fischer von Erlach. It was not Weingarten, or Zwiefalten, or Steinhausen. It was small and provincial, and had a tin roof: a baroque church with a tin roof! But wasn't it a remarkable thing to set eyes upon a baroque church at all, forty-five miles below the Tropic of Capricorn?

The other public buildings had the same air of ancient breeding. The railway-station was wide and stately; by all accounts much too pretentious for the traffic—principally the morning and evening train to Walvis Bay—that trickled along its narrow-gauge single line. As for the green-roofed gaol, it was the most imposing gaol I have ever seen, anywhere. It would be almost a pleasure to serve a sentence in a gaol like that. However, to prevent prisoners from cluttering it up, and making it dirty, it had a large sign outside with the sensible but superfluous admonition: *Privaat—Keep Out!* ... The post office building near by was equally stately, although I was told that during the heavier sulphur eruptions its spotless façade had a habit of turning black, while the clock adorning it became so tarnished that it was impossible to tell the time. Such are the odds against which the people of Swakopmund struggle so bravely.

Life in Africa demands a dash of dottiness and bravura if it is to become endurable. Swakopmund had unexpectedly satisfied much of the hunger for quaintness which had been raised but not quenched by my trip to Walvis Bay. There was even, I am pleased to say, a hotel called the 'Hansa'.

The two most individual buildings in Swakopmund, however, were military, or had military associations. The first was the old *kaserne* in Bismarkstrasse: a tiny bijou barracks, all

sulphuretted hydrogen was lurking in the air—though I was never, alas, to get a glimpse of those islands heaving themselves like whales out of the deep. On the other hand the sky was a crisp and clear electric blue. Swakopmund is only twenty-three miles north of the town we had just come from, but its climate is a complete contrast to the mephitic atmosphere of Walvis Bay.

Swakopmund, in fact, was the summer residence of the rulers of Deutsch Südwestafrika. It was the cool and gracious spot for which the Governor and his satraps headed when conditions grew sticky in Windhoek. Denied the use of Walvis Bay by the British, the Germans had to build a jetty and landing-facilities at Swakopmund. Soon after its founding, in 1892, at the mouth of the dried-up river-bed of the Swakop, it was recognized that the settlement was refreshing and healthy; and it quickly became a fashionable seaside resort. There is a cluster of excellent hotels and boarding-houses; the famous pier; a lighthouse painted in glittering red and white rings; a problematical golf-course where the greens are sand, and you have to tee up for every shot; and first-rate tennis-courts where the territory's tennis championships are staged each year. The municipal museum has been impeccably arranged, and is a pleasure to visit.

It is also pleasant, after arriving from Walvis Bay, to visit the Namib Gardens, which have been laid out on the rise that is topped by the lighthouse. The gardens, the result of seventy years of loving toil, contain specimens of every rare shrub in South West, and the redeeming effect of greenery can be seen elsewhere in some fine private gardens and in the palm trees set in special irrigation pits in the streets. German civic pride is much in evidence, as one can see from the sidewalks that line some of the main roads. The roads themselves are of the same depressing oil-sprayed materials as at Walvis Bay: but here they are extraordinarily wide and lend the town an atmosphere of spaciousness, producing the illusion that the place is larger and grander than it actually is.

For a town of only 2,500 white inhabitants, stranded on the

Pondok and Baroque

these marine explosions are so violent that vast quantities of mud are thrust to the surface and form temporary islands. The islands last only a few hours and then subside again into the depths; but now and again they remain for three or four days, and hardy spirits like to row out and land on them and have their photographs taken.

The likeliest explanation for these eruptions is that they are caused by the decay of the enormous spongy masses of plankton which float about in the South Atlantic near the shore, and on which the whales come to feed. The decay of the dead diatoms, the micro-organisms of which most plankton is composed, increases the normal amount of sulphate in the sea-water. This exhausts the oxygen supply, which leads in turn to the death of the fish. Pockets of gas are created which are liberated from time to time by the action of undersea currents. The bursting of the bubbles is accompanied by the unpleasant spectacle of a shore-line awash with soggy rafts of dead fish, their flesh so saturated with hydrogen sulphide that even the gannets refuse to touch them. Similar islands appear from time to time in the West Indies, where they are thought to be associated with underwater oil. Oil is the one raw material that the Republic of South Africa lacks, and in her present state of siege psychosis she is engaged in a frantic search for it. Are the sulphur eruptions a sign that oil will be one more of the gifts vouchsafed to her by South West? And is it also possible that the old Celtic legends of Tir-nan-og, St Brendan's Island, the Blessed Islands, and the Disappearing Islands of the West, might owe something of their origins to a similar phenomenon? Perhaps there were once disturbances on the sea-bed in the vicinity of Mayo, Galway, and Cardigan Bay. It would be sad if such poetic and holy legends were grounded in nothing more than some gigantic natural fart.

The salty drinking-water, the Swakopmunders, the eructations with which nature indicates her lazy indifference to the presence of man—these hardly put me in a mood to suppose that Swakopmund would be more inviting than Walvis Bay. And indeed as we drove into town the metallic odour of

FOUR
Pondok and Baroque

ALL I knew about Swakopmund was that the South West African name for an upset stomach is a 'Swakopmunder'.
   This undignified complaint is brought about by the local water. The water is excessively brackish. It lends everything you drink the taint of Epsom salts. Some people develop a taste for it. Like Sarel, they like to add a pinch of salt to their tea and coffee. I have come across the same thing elsewhere. In Ontario, for example, some of the eating-houses in the remoter towns have a big metal shaker on the table. You think it is for the steak and chips: and you get a shock when you see a miner or a lumberjack pick it up and sprinkle salt in his glass of Black Horse beer. It certainly acts as a speedy way of working up a thirst without losing valuable drinking time.
   On the road from Walvis Bay I heard from Klaas of Swakopmund's other claim to distinction: the sulphur eruptions. These occur every summer, between November and April, on the sea-bed a mile or two distant from the town. Occasionally

Where the Whales Make Love

To my surprise he glanced in our direction when he heard the Land Rover. I took my hand off the wheel and lifted it in a tentative salute. Again to my surprise, he gave a recognizable if perfunctory wave back. . . .

community wringing out a livelihood on a strip of land between a lonely ocean and a lonelier desert.

Walvis Bay was hard and ugly. It always was: I saw that at last. So were the lives of my uncles. Yet surely there was an outlandish beauty, all the same, about the lives of men who, as I remembered from my boyhood, took as their own the motto of the old-time whalers, whether from Cardiff, Nantucket, Bergen or Walvis Bay: 'Either a dead whale or a stove boat...'?

I was given one more touch of strange beauty before Walvis Bay was lost to view along the road above the rocky coastline.

We had stopped for a moment to wander among the mountainous sand-dunes on the other side of the road. When we came back, half an hour later, I noticed a Herero woman standing on the tawny stretch of sand below us. She was supervising the paddling of a little white boy. She was tall, stout, middle-aged, her back and arms thick and powerful. She had the marvellous smooth, burnished copper complexion of her people, contrasting with the chubby creamy limbs of the boy whom she hoisted shrieking up and down in the nibbling waves. Her carmine-and-emerald Minerva cap and Victorian bodice and skirt were a startling patch against the sand and rocks and water. It was an engaging glimpse of human trust and tenderness—forever renewed—forever betrayed. It reminded me of some innocent pre-Raphaelite painting brought to life; a Millais, a William Dyce, an Edgar Bundy . . .

A couple of miles further down the road we passed the old Citroën, parked once more bang in the middle of the highway. I had forgotten about the painter. I turned my head and looked around for him. After a moment I saw him, planted half-way up the flank of a dune, his back to the sea, gazing eastwards across the nothingness of the Namib. He stood motionless, arms hanging by his sides, something in his right hand (a sketchbook?), and with the sun gleaming on his fair hair.

no character as individuals, but to express themselves through the collective consciousness of the flock. They wander all together in a compact band, a sunset cloud brushing the ground. If one stops, they all stop; if one scents danger, lifting his head on the long thin neck like a pink periscope, they all lift their heads. If you can get close enough to them, you can hear them clicking softly away in chorus, *tck-tck-tck-tck-tck*. Occasionally one will utter a hollow, lonely, unexpectedly resonant cry, like that of a bittern or a curlew.

The colour of all species of flamingos produces in the spectator a momentary flash of disbelief, a brief visual occlusion. It strikes at the senses, confusing them, making one realize why Keats remarked that when someone uttered the word *flamingo* he felt the taste of copper filings on his tongue. I might have been a little disappointed in my expectations of Walvis Bay: but no one could feel disappointed by the sight of a flamingo: it outsoars reality.

These Walvis Bay specimens are a paler hue than the American or Cuban flamingos, which possess a deep vermilion plumage; and they do not have the contrasting ghostly green of the legs of the Chilean flamingo. Their pallor lent them in my eyes an additional delicacy. Most of all I loved to see them wheeling in the sky above the glittering ocean, flying with a lazy fluttery action that was nevertheless supple and strong. Once I came upon a dead bird that had killed itself by flying into a tangle of telephone wires in the desert behind the oil-depot. It lay crumpled on the sand like a beautiful snapped kite, a bunch of inert pink ruffled feathers. I mourned that bird. I still carry some of its feathers in the side-pocket of my airline bag.

Riding away from Walvis Bay in the Land Rover, I realized that the town had actually given me all that I had sought. It had given me the beauty of the dunes, the flamingos, the chrysanthemums, the white hulls and yellow derricks of the cargo boats, the swing and dip of the dockside cranes. It had presented me with the spectacle of a busy and successful

The Land God Made in Anger

Under no circumstances will Walvis Bay ever become an attractive place. It is a glorified mining-camp. It is hard to beautify a town where you cannot plant a tree. But soon you grow to appreciate the majesty of the setting: the cut-steel of the sea, the burning amber of the dunes with their brilliant violet shadows. And every individual touch of colour, which would be commonplace elsewhere, flames here with a jewel-like fascination. I remember being astonished at seeing on a shop-counter a bunch of fresh chrysanthemums in a vase, with a sad little rhyme printed on a card beneath them:

> Pretty flowers
> To pass the hours

At Walvis Bay there are plenty of hours to spare for staring at pretty flowers. I had never before been so conscious of the supernatural shape, texture and colour of a flower. As for the little rhyme, it almost brought tears to my eyes. To read two lines of doggerel at Walvis Bay is like hearing a couplet by Racine at the Comédie française.

There was, I discovered, one sight of such a breath-catching quality that the journey to Walvis Bay would have been worth making for that reason alone. This was the spectacle of the Walvis Bay flamingos. To approach them, you have to drive out circumspectly towards the farther reaches of the bay, over the mud-flats. At first all you can see is a white line at the edge of the flats: then you realize that the line is flickering and undulating. Leaving the Land Rover, wading through the shallows, you can finally see that the water's rim is packed with thousands upon thousands of flamingos.

I used to stand on the flats for hours, watching these sensational fowls with the naked eye or through binoculars. They stalk about on their long thin legs—looking, as Frank Haythornthwaite puts it in his *All The Way to Abenab*, for all the world like something out of Tenniel's illustrations to Lewis Carroll. They are at the same time impossibly ungainly and impossibly elegant. They scoop and tap with their dreamlike beaks, prodding among the surf for molluscs and fish-fry. They seem to have

chauvinism and exaggerated patriotism of the new colonial settlers, to whose homesickness was added a desire to seek any means of maintaining their identity in a hostile and frightening environment. It is interesting to note, in passing, that the principal impetus behind the 'scramble' of the 1880s may have been prompted not so much by colonial ambitions as local European rivalry. As R. A. Oliver and D. D. Fage put it in their *A Short History of Africa* (1962), 'Recent historical research has tended to show that Germany entered Africa as part of a wider design to deflect French hostility against her in Europe by fomenting rivalries in Africa and by creating a situation in which Germany would be the arbiter between British and French ambitions.'

After Bismarck had instructed the German consul in Cape Town that Lüderitz Land was formally under German protection, the British staging-post or bridge-head at Walvis Bay was, like so many other British bridge-heads down the centuries, well and truly encircled and invested. None the less the port jogged along with the help of whaling and general cargo: and in 1910, under the Act of Union, Walvis Bay was formally made over to South Africa. It remained a back-water until the Second World War, when it became a rendezvous and formation-point for transatlantic convoys; and subsequently it shared in the general prosperity that has gradually begun to transform the territory. It is now the second largest town in South West. Although its population of 13,000 is not to be compared with Windhoek's 47,000, it gives the impression of a community thriving under unpromising circumstances.

The South African government jealously maintains the town's independent status. Walvis Bay is a trump card in the South African hand if trouble comes to South West. In 1962 it was quietly announced in the Odendaal Report that the original 374 square miles had been 're-estimated' at 434 square miles. In these days it is not as easy as it used to be to 're-estimate' territory, and you have to admire the cool way in which the South Africans have awarded themselves an additional 60-mile slice of strategically priceless terrain. . . .

could only be defended by powerful fleets, and Germany's geographical position prevents her from developing into a first-class maritime power.' In the year that Lüderitz stepped ashore at Lüderitz Bay, the Chancellor still held to his eminently sensible opinion: 'So long as I am Imperial Chancellor we shall carry on no colonial policy. We have a navy that cannot sail; and we must have no vulnerable points in other parts of the world which would serve as booty for France as soon as we went to war with her.'

Bismarck tried to resist Lüderitz's importunities as long as he could. In 1883 he gave the British another broad hint to annexe Damaraland, asking them if they would police the Lüderitz Bay region. The reply from Whitehall, which took several weeks to reach Berlin, was to the effect that the British did not know where the Lüderitz Bay region was, adding that it was 'impossible to say whether the British Government could afford this protection, if required'. So Bismarck was forced to send the proverbial gun-boat to hoist the German flag, and the German Empire was at last in being.

What had forced the reluctant Chancellor to take this step? First, Europe had entered its fevered colonial phase, and Germany could no longer afford to stand aside while England, France, Belgium, The Netherlands, Italy, Spain and Portugal snatched up the pick of the spoils. Secondly, as Negley Farson points out, in his *Behind God's Back*, Bismarck was being pushed from behind, as Lüderitz well knew, by the various German Colonial Societies that had sprung up in the late 1870s. These included the societies for the protection of overseas Germans in such places as Texas and Brazil. In 1906 there were 345,000 inhabitants of German birth or descent in Brazil alone. As in England, Bismarck's cautious and restrained policy cracked under the weight of popular enthusiasm. Empire-building became a growth industry. And as the Chancellor had foretold, a navy had to be built to defend the new colonies. Keels were laid down at Hamburg; rival keels were laid down on the Clyde. The naval race had begun. The stage was set for 1914. Nationalist antipathies were also deepened by the characteristc

seemed exceptionally sterile and remote. One learns with some amazement that no less a country than Germany, and no less a chancellor than Bismarck, continually urged the British to move inland and occupy what was then known as Damaraland. The Germans were concerned with the fate of the Rhenish missionaries, during the wars between the Hottentots and the Herero, and they kept suggesting that the British should tack on Damaraland to Cape Province in order to protect these people. The British demurred. The most they could be persuaded to do was to decree the occupation of a very limited area of 374 square miles, comprising the settlement at Walvis Bay and its immediate neighbourhood. Annexation, announced in 1874, was not formally ratified until 1878 by the Cape Parliament; and only in that year was a resident magistrate sent to Walvis Bay. Such was the pace of 'the grab for colonies' in the 1870s. Half a century later, when the British had entered the imperial meridian, a British delegate declared at the Versailles Peace Conference that 'South West Africa was lost to Britain through lack of decision and want of foresight'. Britain certainly missed a prize.

In 1874 Walvis Bay consisted of a few houses, including two trading-posts. Andrew A. Anderson, who published his *Twenty-Five Years in a Wagon* in 1888, estimated the European population in the whole of South West Africa at that time to be thirty. His description reveals that life there was stark and insecure. The Hottentots and Herero brought in valuable loads of pelts and ivory to the trading-posts, and in return received money, rifles, and whisky. But it was always on the cards that Jonker Afrikaner would murder these, as he had murdered other Europeans. And after a brief period, to increase their isolation, the British magistrate was withdrawn.

In 1881 the German trader Adolf Lüderitz arrived in South West. He established a trading-post 280 miles to the south of Walvis Bay, on the edge of a difficult harbourage to which he gave his own name. The following year he appealed to Germany for protection. Bismarck had declared ten years earlier that, in his view: 'Colonies would be a source of weakness, because they

a maritime power, and marched inland from their bases in order to acquire large and useless blocks of territory.

Originally, then, India, Canada, and later Australia were the major fixed points, the legacy of age-old rivalry with the French and Dutch. It was no part of the classic plan to establish colonies of enormous size. The aim was to secure naval bases which would guard the trade-routes to the east. Gibraltar, Malta, Cape Town, Durban, Alexandria—these were the links in the commercial chain. Cape Town was originally regarded as no more than a staging-point, not as the foundation-stone of a great British dominion in southern Africa. The proof of this can be seen in the fact that after the British had captured the Cape in 1795 they actually handed it back to the Dutch eight years later. When the circumstances of the Napoleonic wars induced them to capture it for a second time, they were only coaxed inland after a long interval and with immense reluctance and misgiving. It is interesting to note how strongly the staging-post idea still reverberates in the folk-memory of the British. Gibraltar, Malta, Hong Kong, Cyprus, Aden, Singapore: it is remarkable how reluctant the British have been to abandon these ports even when the strategic areas to which they are or were attached have long since disappeared. This illogical proceeding has cost the British, the most pragmatic of people, a great deal of spilled blood and wasted treasure. It must be an extremely stubborn sentiment that makes them cling to a barren rock at the tip of the Iberian Peninsula when they have parted without a pang with such huge stretches of the earth's surface as India, Pakistan, Ceylon, Malaya, Burma, Kenya, Nigeria, and Uganda.

Walvis Bay had been declared British in 1795, after the British had supplanted the Dutch (then the allies of the French) at the Cape. It was regarded as no more than an emergency and make-shift port-of-call between the Gold Coast and the Cape of Good Hope. The British seldom refused to snap up a viable harbour: but they deliberated for many years before assuming anything more than a very vague responsibility for Walvis Bay. The place was situated, after all, in a locality that

However, now that this epoch has drawn to a close, the British have been by no means as reluctant to relinquish their empire as their critics imagine. It was Lawrence of Arabia, of all people, who declared that: 'All the subject races of the Empire are not worth the blood of one dead English boy.'

The original British colonial policy, after the shock of being saddled with India and Canada had worn off, was to move slowly and pick up as little real-estate as possible. Colonies, as the American Rebellion had shown, could prove troublesome and costly. Of course, the British would have grabbed South West Africa quickly enough if they had known that it was crammed with diamonds. But this was the age before the complex commercial possibilities of kyanite, sillimanite, lepidolite and amblygonite were appreciated—or even the potential profit from crawfish tails. The civil servants in Whitehall evolved what they considered a more hard-headed plan, a plan that had been adopted by other small trading nations, such as Portugal and the Netherlands, before them. This was to establish a chain of ports and entrepôts in order to drain the wealth out of the hinterland, before shipping it back as speedily as possible to the mother country. If you took over the interior of the country itself, then sooner or later you would have to foot the bill for policing it, putting down revolts, settling internal disputes, and sending costly expeditions and flying-columns from one village to the next. This would cut down on profits. The simple and uncomplicated idea of the base-camp on the sea-shore had been embedded in the British mind from the earlier days of Calais, Dunkerque, Bordeaux, the Pale of Dublin and the Lines of Torres Vedras. Stay on the coast: it was fatal to get sucked into the interior. It ought to be remembered that the British had already gained and lost a considerable continental empire, under the Angevins, and had been soured by the struggle to retain it and the bitterness of losing it. What is called the British Empire was in reality the Second British Empire. And the British lost their Second Empire because the Victorians made the same mistake as the Angevins had done: they forgot the fact that they were primarily

enactments are made as applying to the 'Mandated Territory of South West Africa and the Port and Settlement of Walvis Bay'.

Contrary to accepted belief, the European imperial powers did not always acquire their empires indiscriminately or even enthusiastically. This was particularly true of Britain. There is a well-known saying to the effect that 'the British Empire was acquired in a fit of absent-mindedness'. In the high period of empire, Britain refused to annexe almost as much territory as she elected to control. It is hard to realize it now, but in those heady days it was common for territories to apply eagerly for membership in the British Empire—and be turned down. Even in the 'Scramble for Africa' of the 1880s and 1890s the British were by no means unselective. Their refusal to annexe South West Africa *in toto*, and to be satisfied with the enclave of Walvis Bay, is an example of this. Imperial schemers like John Lawrence, E. G. Wakefield and Cecil Rhodes encountered lifelong frustrations before they could persuade the British Government to incorporate large tracts of India, Australasia and Africa into the empire. These men were outward-looking, adventurous and romantic, and their visionary stratagems were diametrically opposed to the policies of Whitehall and a long line of Colonial Secretaries. By nature the British are cautious, insular and mercantile. True, they have sired great freebooters and men of action: but these people are sports, eccentrics, and have seldom been popular at home. In spite of Clive and Warren Hastings, we should remember that the Duke of Wellington complained, when he was Prime Minister, that a debate on India always emptied the House of Commons.

The British Empire came into existence because the strife between Britain, France and Spain in a European context happened to be extended to a larger stage overseas. Having gained control of Canada and India, the English did next to nothing with them for many decades: then suddenly, in the late nineteenth century, when the moment for it had already passed, the normally long-headed British became infected by the jingoism of men like Rhodes, Milner and Joe Chamberlain.

Where the Whales Make Love

celtolite, smaragdolite ... chthonium, memnonium, valerium.

It brings you back rapidly to the realm of reality when you learn that these enigmatic commodities are now valued annually at nearly 20 million pounds (48 million dollars). And if gem and industrial diamonds are included in the grand total, then the annual gross value of the minerals of South West Africa is something of the order of 60 million pounds (144 million dollars). So whatever they use beryllium for, the stuff is worth 50 pounds or 120 dollars a ton. There is money in beryllium. No wonder South West is infested with foot-loose prospectors scuttling around with shovels and geiger-counters....

With the exports of fish we are on almost equally lucrative ground. South West Africa's fishing industry is worth something in the region of 20 or 22 million pounds a year (about 50 million dollars), and the value is rising steadily. Most of this huge sum is earned from pilchards, by the fishing fleets of Lüderitz and Walvis Bay. The pilchards are caught between February and November, and in some seasons come swarming in enormous shoals right into the harbours. They are taken by ten-man boats by means of huge lampara nets, big enough to encircle an entire shoal. The catch is then sucked by means of a flume or pipe straight out of the boat's hold into a conveyor belt leading to one of the six canning-factories on the waterfront. Most of it is canned in tomato sauce, and the remainder is turned into fish-meal and fish-oil. A secondary and increasingly important industry is the rock-lobster or crawfish industry. The most profitable way of dealing with the crawfish (which is not, be it noted, the fresh-water crayfish, but a larger, clawless marine species of the lobster family) is to remove the head and deep-freeze the meaty tail; about a sixth of this catch is canned, and a very small proportion reduced to fish-oil.

By a quiddity of the type we have come to expect in this peculiar part of the world, South West's principal port does not belong to South West at all. It belongs to South Africa. Walvis Bay is technically a part of Cape Province. It is administered as part of South West Africa, but officially all

port through which South West can receive the bulk of her supplies. In spite of the fog and sand—you can experience both in the course of a single day—Walvis Bay is alive with activity. Ports always have a special atmosphere. Cardiff, Bristol, Newcastle, Amsterdam, Hamburg, Marseilles, Genoa, Galveston: the people in dock-land are not timid and inward-looking; they have their faces turned towards the oceans and the countries beyond. Wandering around Walvis Bay, among the maze of railway sidings, beneath the dozen giant cranes, my spirits lifted and I forgave the town for not being the decayed backwater of my imagination. There were two fifteen-thousand tonners tied up and being unloaded, and tugs were hauling and nudging another freighter along the thirty-foot channel towards the wharves. It looked a tricky manoeuvre: but my uncle, Captain MacCausland, who once brought a big tanker in here in an emergency, says it is an easy harbour for which you need pilotage only during the last half-mile. Beyond the big berths, at the north end of the bay, were clustered at least fifty fishing boats, just back from a large-scale foray for pilchards in the cold Benguela current outside the bar.

Into Walvis Bay flow the country's imports of timber, cement, bulk oils, and general cargo. The exports that are shipped out outnumber the imports by two tons to one. The largest single export is the mineral wealth with which South West abounds. The minerals are almost literally too numerous to mention: but I shall list a few of them simply for the pleasure of putting down their names, rich as the ores themselves, setting on one side for a moment the fact that for these rocks with pretty names men toil deep and dangerously in the earth.

Here we go then: lead, copper, zinc, manganese, tin, salt (these are the obvious ones); tantalite, columbite, vanadium, sillimanite, kyanite, lithium, germanium, caesium, cadmium, beryllium, wolfram. Enough? For good measure, let me throw in amblygonite, lepidolite, petalite. These names inspire an obscure excitement: they contain something of the hidden drama of the land they come from. The sound of them makes you want to discover and name some for yourself—olorite, indolite,

Where the Whales Make Love

Thus, drab and nondescript as it is, there is a touch of heroism about Walvis Bay. Those rows of ugly low bungalows, painted a strident red, yellow, or blue, are the houses of people under siege. A few hundred yards in front of them the army of the dunes inches forward, urged on by the desert wind; behind them waits the South Atlantic, the most bitingly cold of the oceans of the globe. The place is like a camp. There are few amenities, an almost complete absence of *douceur de vivre*. Existence is spartan. The shops are adequate but sell nothing frivolous, as if supplies had to be brought to the beleaguered garrison from enormous distances—as indeed they have. Water is always a critical problem, and has often been in short supply. Until thirty years ago every drop of it was brought in by tankers from Cape Town; now it is piped across the desert from wells at Rooibank, over twenty miles away. It is putrid and saline, and has to be dosed with chemicals before it is fit for consumption. Now and again the pump breaks down, or the pipeline becomes furred up. Then the trains stop running, industry comes to a standstill, and rationing is brought in.

All the cars and trucks in Walvis Bay are so caked with black muck you would think there was a prohibition against using water to wash them. The muck is thrown up by the roads, which at first glance appear to be made of solid tar or macadam. In actual fact they are ordinary dirt roads spread with material from salt pans and afterwards sprayed with a liquid binder. I am, alas, still infantile enough to be amused by the old banana-skin joke, and I was convulsed whenever the surface of the road became treacherous because of fog or sea-mist and the bicyclists went slithering sideways or came a spectacular cropper. I hasten to add that they were so used to it they simply brushed themselves down and remounted with nothing more than an amiable shake of the head, like wrestlers after a routine fall.

Sand and sea-mist. A devastating climate. Walvis Bay is no agreeable spot to make love, even for whales or mermaids. But it provides the only deep-water anchorage between Lobito Bay in Angola and Table Bay in South Africa, and is the only

the disappointment with which I awoke to a new day in Walvis Bay.

True, the sand was no longer 'lifting'. The wind had died away. The sky was a scoured and sparkling blue.

But where was my Hansa port? Where were the gables, the warehouses, the rusty anchors? Where was the picturesque little backwater, incapsulated in the twentieth century like a pearl in an oyster, or ambergris in a sperm whale? Where was the perfectly preserved historical showpiece, like Bath, or Nancy, or Venice?

Alas, Walvis Bay has been completely rebuilt from 1925 onwards. There is little that is quaint, beautiful, or romantic about it. It is one of the plainest and most utilitarian places on earth. All that remains of the old town about which Evan Evans or Ike or Zack used to reminisce is a line of rotting timbers at Pelican Point. These mark the site of the old jetty, and now serve as the House of Commons for a thousand screaming gulls.

'When God made Walvis Bay,' runs a saying in South West, 'he was so ashamed of it that He kept trying to cover it over with sand.' Man, in his impious way, strives to thwart the designs of the Almighty: but most of the time, and certainly in Walvis Bay, God appears to be holding his own. Wherever you turn your eyes the sand is marching towards you. The dunes are advancing down the end of every long straight street; there are drifts of it between the houses. When the sand is really flying it creates miniature sandstorms indoors, finding its way into your bath and into your bed, into the food and into your cans of beer. The sand dunes of the Namib Desert are said to be the highest in the world—higher than the sand dunes in the Sahara or the Gobi. I have read that the Namib is geologically the oldest desert in existence. They *walk*, those dunes: they move all the time: they are forever arranging themselves into new shapes and dispositions. The impression they give of being alive, ruthless and never-sleeping is enhanced by their habit of exploding at intervals with a hoarse *c-r-r-r-r-ump!* as they outreach themselves in their effort to swallow up the town, toppling under their own weight.

THREE
Where the Whales Make Love

ARTHUR WALEY, the famous Sinologist, never went to China; Powys Mathers, who translated *The Arabian Nights* and much Oriental poetry, never put a foot outside Europe.

They were wise to stay at home. They kept their visions intact. They avoided the error made by the great Egyptologist Adolf Erman, who decided when he was an old man that he must see before he died the country whose monuments and papyri he had studied for over half a century. He made the long journey from Berlin to Cairo. There the noise and the stink, the flies and the filth, appalled him. He took the first boat back to Germany.

A dreamer should think carefully before he decides to tamper with his dream. He should beware of measuring a pampered illusion against the hickory yardstick of reality. I can well remember the relief with which, on my own first visit to Egypt, I realized that for me a lifelong dream had not been damaged but intensified and enhanced. And I also remember

One of the few men who saw and described the love-play of these stupendous beings was Herman Melville. Awed, mesmerized, touched to the quick of his capacious intellect, he cried out:

'How, then, with me, writing of this Leviathan? Unconsciously my chirography expands into placard capitals. Give me a condor's quill! Give me Vesuvius' crater for an inkstand! Friends, hold my arms! For in the mere act of penning my thoughts of this Leviathan, they weary me, and make me faint with their outreaching comprehensiveness of sweep, as if to include the whole circle of the sciences, and all the generations of whales, and men, and mastodons, past, present, and to come, with all the revolving panoramas of empire on earth, and throughout the whole universe!'

To Melville was given the privilege of actually watching what he called 'Leviathan amours in the deep': and the sight which he shared with Starbuck and Queequeg of a family of whales cavorting below the *Pequod*'s boats prompted his chirography to expand even further into placard capitals:

'And thus ... did these inscrutable creatures ... freely and fearlessly indulge in all peaceful concernments; yea, serenely revelled in dalliance and delight. But even so, amid the tornadoed Atlantic of my being, do I myself still for ever centrally disport in mute calm; and while ponderous planets of unwaning woe revolve round me, deep down and deep inland there I still bathe me in eternal mildness of joy ...'

I sank into slumber, my mind soothed and haunted by the gently paddling grey hulks of the *Balaenidae* and *Ziphiidae*.

I was well-content to have reached this evocative place: even though I was sailing into sleep without a sea-shanty in my ears, and on an interior-sprung mattress instead of on a wooden bunk or the flock-and-feathers of an old four-poster ...

silence; silence from the road outside; silence at sea. Walvis Bay was evidently a very silent town. There was only the gritty hiss of the sand against the glass.

I lay with my hands beneath my head, staring up drowsily into the darkness....

... *Walfisch Bay* ... *Whale-Fish Bay*. ... This was the place to which the whales were said to come when they wanted to make love. ... Humpbacks, grey whales, cachalots ... curvetting and sporting in the icy depths, perhaps only a mile or two away from where I stretched out my limbs in my warm bed ...

The image of those great creatures, three times the size of an elephant, swam into my mind. How did they make love? Privately, two by two, in some secluded part of the ocean, or all sporting and splashing together, in their pods or gams? I had been lucky enough to see them twenty years earlier from the deck of a corvette: a moving and mysterious sight, those huge grey floating islands wallowing through the troughs in the middle of the empty waters, many hundreds of miles from the nearest landfall. And they were tender and warm-blooded like us: the males with penis and testes, retractable like a well-designed under-carriage; the females labouring to produce their calves, suckling them for a year on the milk from their enormous mammary glands, answering the high-pitched squeaks of their offspring with a deep creaking maternal grunt.

I had watched them from afar, yes—but who had ever witnessed, even at Walvis Bay, the supreme spectacle of the mating of the whales? The old-time whalers waited for their prey to come north from the Southern Ocean to their breeding ground in the Benguela Current, between the Walvis Ridge in the South Atlantic and the coast of South West Africa. They were interested in slaughter, not cetology; they were professional killers, not nature-watchers. When they sailed out of Walvis Bay, with their harpoons and grapnels, the copper cauldrons were already lined up on the beaches, waiting for the dead whales to be dragged ashore and flensed and the blubber boiled out of them.

thusiastic declaration that next morning I meant to set out early to go sight-seeing and make a thorough tour of the town. And indeed, I spent the rest of that evening in a mood of mellow anticipation of the treat that awaited me. I bathed and changed. I ate a first-rate dish of the crawfish thermidor which is a speciality of southern Africa—particularly South West Africa—and which is quite as good as the lobster thermidor I have eaten in good-class restaurants anywhere else in the world. And finally I spent an hour in the pleasant bar, drinking a couple of Cape brandies: the excellent Oude Meester, which may not be one of the world's great brandies, but which is extremely potable none the less.

While we were eating dinner a man came into the hotel dining-room, where up to that moment we had been sitting alone. He stood in the doorway, looking around; then, without giving any impression that he had noticed us, he went over to a table in the far corner and sat down facing the wall with his back to us. He was wearing a black polo-necked sweater and black slacks. I recognized him as the man with the battered Citroën. So did Klaas and Sarel; they scowled and said nothing. The man's sleeves were pulled back just below the elbows, and he sat relaxed on his chair as if he was tired. His fair hair was slicked back with water, but from his accent as it carried across the empty room while he was ordering his meal from the Cape Coloured waitress I judged that he was not German but Danish or Norwegian. He toyed with his fork while waiting for his food, paying no attention to his surroundings. I would have liked to have gone across to speak to him, but I judged that the moment was inappropriate. Also I was too weary myself, after a long day, to want to strike up a new acquaintance that night; the exploratory stage of any new relationship is always an exhausting, high-tension sort of business, entailing a great expenditure of energy. I decided to wait for a better opportunity.

When I turned off the light, the sand was still swishing against the window. There was a mild hum from the direction of the bar downstairs, a rattle of cutlery and crockery from the kitchen as the staff did the washing-up. Otherwise there was

refinery at the north end of the town the visibility was down to about forty yards, and even Klaas had been forced to slow down until we were dawdling along at fifty.

We made straight for the first hotel we came to. I had heard tales of the old Atlantic and Anchor: but we were glad to settle, after our long drive and the onset of the sand, for the Mermaid. We tied our handkerchiefs over our mouths and noses, grabbed our luggage, and ran across the car-park to the shelter of the hotel. Even then I paused for a second to turn and give a quick eager glance in what I took to be the direction of the ocean. Well, there would be plenty of time tomorrow to saunter along the quaint old streets, and sun myself on the sea-wall while I chatted with the wizened old salts. . . .

The Mermaid was newly built. As I hurried towards the door, carrying the two airline bags that contained my belongings, I got the impression of a modest white-painted concrete box with a flat parapet. The interior was bright and cheerful. It revived my spirits with the prospect of a good meal and a comfortable bed. There were no kerosene lamps, or roaring, drunken deck-hands in tarry jumpers: but no doubt, if I wanted to, I told myself as I signed the register, I could transfer to the more picturesque quarter of the town in the morning. . . .

The fact that we had arrived by land and not by sea had already been noted. One or two people were peering through the lace curtains of the foyer windows in an attempt to see the make of the car: and five minutes later, when I was in my bedroom, I saw someone cross to the Land Rover and bend down to decipher the number-plate with the aid of a flashlight. Additional curiosity was raised when I got out my pen and wrote down an English address in the hotel register. As I wrote, it sank in upon me how far my uncles had sailed from home to reach this place, and how far I had had to journey by plane and car to join hands with them across the years. . . .

They assured me at the reception-desk that tomorrow the east wind, the South West African *khamsīn* which brought the sand 'lifting' or 'running', as they called it, would certainly die down. They greeted with a twitch of an eyebrow my en-

My reverie was broken by a swerve of the Land Rover that almost threw me off the seat.

Klaas shouted out angrily in Afrikaans.

The Land Rover jolted to a stop. I collected my wits and looked round. A clash of gears and we were backing up. By the red glow of the brake lights I could see a car with its lights off, parked more or less in the middle of the road. We had just come round one of the very infrequent curves and had nearly run smack into it. It looked to me in the half-light like a beaten-up old Citroën.

Klaas was backing up because he had spotted the owner heading towards us. To judge by his indistinct form, and what I could see of his face, the man was about thirty; he was weighted down with equipment. Klaas began to bawl him out: an exercise for which the curt, tart, Afrikaans language is admirably suited. I wound down the window to enjoy the full flavour—and promptly wound it up again as a scurry of sand came skimming into my eyes off the desert.

Klaas is a big man with powerful lungs and an excellent flow of invective. It had less than no effect on the newcomer. Klaas was right, of course: what it does no harm to do in broad daylight in the main street of Karibib can cause a nasty accident on the wrong side of a bend in the middle of nowhere. The offender pulled open the back door of the dust-coated Citroën and began to sling his equipment carelessly in the back. I could now make out what it was: an easel, a camp-stool, a large flat box with a handle, a canvas that he took some pains to arrange on the seat. He never once glanced at Klaas.

Klaas, put out at his failure to provoke an argument, delivered a final verbal flourish and then drove off. I heard the back door of the Citroën slam like a contemptuous last word.

The sand-storm increased steadily as we covered the final stretch of road. The headlights revealed dunes rearing up on either side, some of them so high their summits were out of sight. The intermingling of the falling darkness and a thickening blanket of blowing sand produced a very odd and unsettling sensation. By the time we reached the storage tanks of the oil-

So it gave me the keenest pleasure imaginable, that first afternoon, to be on my way towards an obscure port in an inaccessible country to which my relatives had been before me. The Welsh are Confucian in the intensity of their ancestor-worship. For some reason, following their footsteps on the streets of Walvis Bay would be an act of more intimate identification with my dead uncles than doing so in Cardiff or Swansea docks. It might have been more appropriate to have stepped ashore there during the war-time years, when I was myself at sea: but life seldom permits us such tidy overlaps. And at least I would have the satisfaction of standing where my forefathers had stood, even if I had reached the place overland and in a more roundabout way. It was as if the intervening years had been abolished, and the little boy playing among the black boots under the dining-table had suddenly grown up and been invited to take a chair in the circle of old men exchanging their tall stories among the glasses of stout, the ships in bottles, the framed certificates, the seashells, the sepia photographs of jaunty men in pea-jackets and cheesecutter caps, the oleographs of East Indiamen, the piece of a shell from a German surface-raider that had hit the engine-room and failed to explode....

As the disc of the sun dipped beyond the rim of the desert, and Klaas snapped on his headlights, I speculated on what kind of town I would find awaiting me. After my stay at Windhoek, I imagined that I might possibly discover a small, gleaming, brand-new modern city, skilfully sited and designed: but I was more inclined to think that Walvis Bay would be a sleepy, forgotten, old-fashioned port, its character more or less unchanged since the days when my forbears had landed there. I expected to see something like a miniature version of one of the medieval Hansa towns: I had a cosy image of what I fancied Rostock must have been like, or Lübeck or Stettin: crooked gables jutting out over the water; stone bollards and mooring posts on moss-grown quays; corroded iron rings beside damp steps leading down into the sea; lop-sided warehouses, customs-houses with peeling coats of arms in corroded gilt; rusty anchors and rotting ropes....

me. I can remember crawling around on the carpet at their feet, among the well-polished black boots laced up at the front —they always wore black boots, planted solidly on the ground —while the deep Welsh voices dropped the names of far-distant ports like notes of music or bright snow-flakes all about me. *Callao, Valparaiso, Vancouver, Yokohama, Manila, Hobart, Bathurst, Freetown, Delagoa Bay, Djibouti.* All these places had been the scenes of desertions, floggings, drownings, sinkings, or of the cruel and violent tricks and hoaxes which the seamen of those days liked to play on each other, which as a child I used to find uproariously comic, and now find oddly touching and pathetic.

It was impossible to remember, as the Land Rover bumped across the hundredth vlei, exactly which of my relatives, all dead now, had stamped around the streets of Walvis Bay two and three generations ago. Was it my great-uncle Evan, the famous Captain Evan Evans, a little lump-shouldered man, a real hard-case skipper, who was so feared that men who wanted a berth were known to get down on their knees with the prayer, 'O God, please don't let me sail with Captain Evans'? Was it one of my other uncles with the Old Testament names, Captain Isaac White or Captain Zachariah White? Was it my step-grandfather, Captain Trott, the owner of *The Marguerite*, most celebrated of all the Bristol Channel cutters? Was it my great-grandfather, Captain Moses White, or my grandfather, Captain William White? My uncles always maintained that old William—massive of beard, noble of forehead—could have beaten *The Marguerite* hollow in his ship *The Maid of Sker*. He now lies buried in his sea-boots in the graveyard of St John's Church in the Centre of Cardiff, close to the wall of the public library where, on December 30, 1896, Captain Joseph Conrad came to write his name in the visitor's book. I remember how those buried sea-boots rankled with my uncle Evan Evans, the most close-fisted man who ever sailed. He had always coveted those sea-boots. He felt that old Moe had got himself buried in them to spite him. He petitioned the authorities to let him dig them up. Their refusal was a constant source of complaint.

I asked Sarel what this type of grass was called. He said it was called silver grass, or buffalo grass. Klaas leaned forward behind my head to tell me that in Afrikaans it was known as *Blinkhaar*—'Feathery Hair'. And indeed, I saw it was true that, when it was ruffled by the breeze, a slow wavering ripple curved through it, a ripple like a young woman shaking her head with a sigh. . . .

'I said to myself, "When I grow up, I shall go THERE . . ."'
For Conrad, the mysterious and compelling point on the map of Africa had been Leopoldville. For me, it was Walvis Bay.

Klaas had taken over the wheel for the last eighty or ninety miles. He drove fast. Driving fast and shooting things were his two pleasures in life. I sprawled on the back seat, staring at the landscape as it turned from veld to rock-bound desert, dreaming of what lay ahead of me on the coast.

Waalvisbaai . . . *Whale-Fish Bay*. . . . The name had a rough magic. It conjured up a picture of crews with matted whiskers rowing ashore from barques and brigantines to raise hell in bar-rooms lit by kerosene lamps . . . swearing, shouting, singing, laughing, shouldering their way to the mahogany counter to slam down their wages and plunge their mouths into tankards thick with foam . . . a reek of oilskins and heavy serge, saturated with salt, and sweat, and blubber. . . .

The name Walvis Bay had been familiar to me since childhood. It was one of a litany of ports whose names chimed across the dinner-tables of my uncles and great-uncles when I was a small boy in Cardiff. They were old men then, most of them, long retired from the sea: and this was about 1930, when I was only six. The chief pleasure left to them was to swap memories about their sailing days. In later years they had been Bristol Channel pilots, but for most of their careers they had been deep-ocean men, and had gained their mates' and masters' certificates under canvas before the turn of the century.

These hard old men had an immense and lasting glamour for

2 Windhoek: the Christuskirche. Palms and roundabouts with the Khomas Hochland beyond

1 The author at Fish River Canyon

The Land God Made in Anger

spruits (small streams) that had been engorged by the rains. The grass that sheathed the veld was butter-yellow, silken, knee-high. You could almost hear it growing after the sudden soaking. Sarel was told by the storekeeper that there had been no rain in Karibib for over twelve months. No wonder that girl had taken her shoes off.

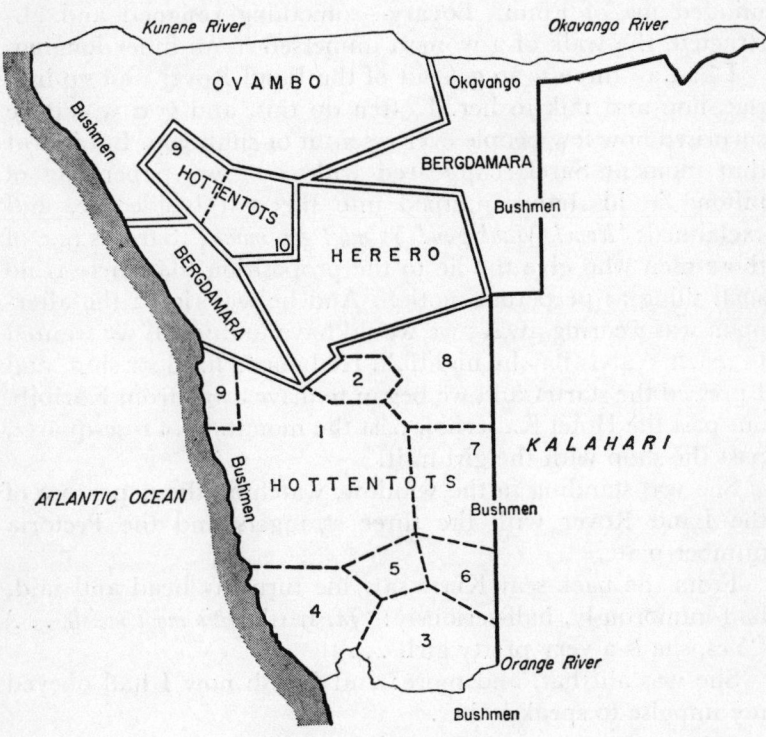

TRIBAL DISTRIBUTION: 1880
HOTTENTOT TRIBES

1. Witboois
2. Rehobothers or Baastards
3. Bondelswarts Hottentots
4. Aman Hottentots
5. Hei-Khaus and Tseib Hottentots
6. Veldskoen Hottentots
7. Fransmann Hottentots
8. Khauas Hottentots
9. Topnaars
10. Swartboois

She went through the open door of a shop far down the street. I slouched back farther in my seat and wondered what such a girl was doing in this isolated town. What did she feel about it? What did she dream about, hope for? Was she married? About to be married? Happily married? Unhappily married? Had she ever been to Cape Town—even Windhoek? It may have been something in that indolent walk that reminded me of Emma Bovary—something resigned and abstracted, the walk of a woman immersed in an inner longing.

I had an impulse to get out of the Land Rover and go into the shop and talk to her. I often do this, and you would be surprised how few people ever resent it or snub you. But just at that moment Sarel reappeared with a brown paper bag of biltong in his hand, jumped into the seat beside me, and exclaimed: '*Kom! Maak gou! Jy moet gou maak!*' Sarel is one of those men who give the lie to the proposition that there is no such thing as perpetual motion. And he was right: the afternoon was wearing away; we would have to hurry if we wanted to reach Walvis Bay by nightfall. He banged his door shut, and I pressed the starter and we began to drive away from Karibib, out past the Hotel Kaiserhof, past the mountain of rose-quartz, past the shop with the girl in it.

She was standing in the window, watching the departure of the Land Rover with the three strangers and the Pretoria number-plate.

From the back seat Klaas saw me turn my head and said, half-humorously, half-seriously: '*Ja, sy is'n baie mooi meisie . . .*' ('Yes, she is a very pretty girl. . . .')

She was all that, and more: and I wish now I had obeyed my impulse to speak to her.

A delicious soft damp breeze blew off the veld as we ran westwards towards the line of *kopjes*, or hills and the distant Atlantic. The sun had ripened into a rich Venetian red and seemed to hang motionless in the sky, like a wounded man fighting to stay on his feet.

We drove steadily, splashing through the innumerable

irresistible call for any of it to halt there. As I turned my head I saw her eyes drop automatically to the number-plate. Everyone in South West always looks at your number-plate: they wonder what branch of the diamond business you are in—whether you are a prospector, a diamond detective, or a dealer, illicit or otherwise. When she had registered that the Land Rover had a Pretoria number, she gave me and my companion a long and unhurried glance. All her movements were very deliberate.

She passed behind the Land Rover and emerged on the off-side as she walked down the main street (the only street) in front of us. She was a tall, well-built girl with a beautiful body that she carried proudly. She walked slowly, her shoulders square, her stance very upright and graceful. I had an immediate impression of a strong, frank, simple character. The sun made a helmet of her saffron-coloured hair. She wore a dress that was no more than a length of cheap cotton print, a dress that could have been cut out with a pair of scissors in ten minutes. It was a modest dress as became a young woman of Afrikaner or German stock, but it revealed the firm neck, well-rounded arms, and solid, shapely calves.

You hardly expect to encounter Juno in a place like Karibib, any more than Brecht's three gods expected to encounter Shen Te in Szechwan: so it was understandable if I stared a little. She took no notice and walked on down the street without turning round. She wore no shoes and walked through the puddles and sheets of water that lay in the dirt road after the storm. She was not sunburned, and had a smooth and creamy skin; her white feet trod majestically through the wet. A tall European girl, sauntering between the houses with bare feet, like a Bantu. Perhaps she had been brought up in this remote place to go barefoot; perhaps she merely wanted to save her shoes after the downpour. Her thighs and hips moved under the dress as she planted her feet firmly in the pools of water in the roadway. Her dress was an apricot colour, with a pattern of small white flowers with yellow centres; when I close my eyes I can see it distinctly.

streaming windshield I could see the hailstones beating a tattoo on the tin roofs of the houses. All the roofs in South West are made of tin or corrugated iron: even the roof of the Christuskirche in Windhoek, with its stained-glass window given by Kaiser Wilhelm, and its Bible presented by his Kaiserin. Tin roofs last forever, and you can paint them any colour you fancy.

On the other side of the road was a house painted a characteristically German dull lake colour, bearing the proud date 1908; a small tin Gothic church, painted another characteristic German colour, gooseturd green; a closed and shuttered tin-shack hotel, the Kaiserhof; and two shops with signs in Gothic letters.

Then the downpour stopped, as suddenly as if someone had turned off a tap. One of my two Afrikaner companions, a biltong-addict, got out and went into one of the shops; this area was celebrated for a very special biltong. A hundred yards away, in the gap between two houses, a line of battered trucks was halted beside a small mountain of rose-quartz, glistening pink and white in the wet. Half a dozen Bantu labourers wandered out of a hut with skimpy grey blankets round their shoulders, cast a troubled eye at the receding cumulus clouds, then lugubriously resumed their task of loading the rock into the trucks.

And then something happened which made a vivid impression on me. It was only a small incident: nothing of earth-shaking significance. Yet it lodged in my mind, and since that time I have remembered it and often think about it.

I was staring idly round, twisted sideways behind the wheel, my feet in my Mexican boots propped on the facia board, my bush-hat tipped over my eyes to shield them from the harsh watery sun. Just within my angle of vision, from the rear near-side of the Land Rover, a girl stepped out of one of the one-storey tin houses. There was no hall or foyer: she stepped straight out of the living-room into the street. When she caught sight of the Land Rover she stopped for a moment in surprise. There is no great rush of traffic through Karibib, and no

and his colleague Kleinschmidt to settle at Windhoek and start a mission there. He was a first-rate blacksmith and wheelwright and an expert gunsmith. For long intervals he would remain passive: then, goaded by a thirst for drink and a need for ammunition, and impelled perhaps by simple blood-lust, he would break out and go on the rampage. He turned Windhoek into an agreeable, even a beautiful settlement; but he stirred up so much hatred and lasting antagonism that twenty years after his death his people were scattered and Windhoek was desolate. When a young Swiss botanist visited it in 1885, on the eve of the German occupation, he found it inhabited only by jackals and guinea-fowl. The mission house was in ruins and the fig trees and Hahn's other European importations had run to seed. Hahn himself had written the epitaph of the Nama nation in some impressions he noted down thirteen years earlier:

'Jonker and his son Jan Jonker have driven their large tribe to disaster after gaining enormous booty and living in superabundance for twenty years. The women before wore silk dresses and costly kerchiefs and now they have hardly enough to cover themselves and assuage their hunger. The downfall of the Nama is their apathy and the delusion that they were born to rule, and the blacks (i.e. the Herero and the Bergdama) to serve them. They have learnt nothing from their past experiences and prefer hunger to hard work. Even today they have not come to a sober appraisal of the position.'

Then, an hour's ride beyond Okahandja, the rain came. It was a heavy downpour, drumming on the hollow-sounding soil, turning what was dry light biscuit to soggy dark brown gravy.

As we were driving into Karibib (population 1,321), the rain turned into hail. We stopped in the middle of the main street (why bother to pull over to the side?), and waited while the hailstones hissed and bounded off the roof and the hood.

All the time the sun never stopped shining. Through the

Jonker contemptuously called him, served his apprenticeship diligently. Within months of his tormentor's death, Maherero attacked and killed Jonker's heir, Christian. He went on to further triumphs. He instigated the second Massacre of Okahandja, which was a repeat of the first, only this time in reverse. He defeated Christian's successor, Jan Jonker Afrikaner, and dealt similarly with Hendrik Witbooi, second of the Orlam chiefs to be summoned to the chieftainship by the harassed Nama.

The Herero were riding high: and with luck they might have continued to carry everything before them if Samuel Maherero, Maherero's son and heir, had not fallen foul of the Germans. At first the Herero and the Germans, thanks to a treaty engineered at Okahandja by Doctor Goering, were blood-brothers. Then came the rising of 1904, culminating in the battle of the Waterberg and the years of the Herero diaspora. None the less, in the modest public park at Okahandja, you can see the graves of the three chiefs, Tjamuaha, Maherero and Samuel Maherero, who led the Herero nation in foul days and fair. 'Here lie three chieftains at rest,' runs their memorial; 'They ruled the country for the good of the Herero people, but now they are dead. They were chiefs indeed.' With them is buried Samuel's son, Friedrich Maherero, who died in 1962; and near by, not far from the Friedenskirche, is the grave of their arch-foe Jonker Afrikaner.

Jonker's name is pronounced with awe among his own people, and among the Bergdama and the Herero, to this day. He won respect as a tyrant in a country where competition in tyranny was keen. He was also a highly interesting character. His destructive phases alternated with periods of piety and positive achievement. As La Rochefoucauld pointed out: 'Some evil men would be less dangerous if there were no good in them at all.' The missionary Hahn recorded that Jonker's rule over his own Afrikaners was stern, and that drunkenness, unchastity and bigamy were outlawed. He built roads, established water supplies, and constructed a tin church where he held religious services, preaching the sermons himself. He permitted Hahn

resemble living skeletons, and on whose bodies are numberless scars of the rhinoceros-hide whip.' In 1861 the missionary Kleinschmidt wrote: 'The treatment which Herero prisoners receive from their Nama captors is fearful. They whip the poor wretches until the skin breaks at each blow, exposing raw flesh, and often the place of punishment is plastered with blood as if a sheep has been slaughtered there.' Olga Levinson, in her book *The Ageless Land*, recounts the dramatic circumstances of Jonker's last illness and death after a raid on Ovamboland from which he was returning with 20,000 stolen cattle.

'His old enemy Tjamuaha,' she relates, 'also lay dying on the other side of the river-bed at Okahandja. Victor and vanquished were dying, less than a hundred yards from each other. Tradition has it that it became a matter of honour to outlive the other. Every day messengers were sent from one chief to the other to find out how he was feeling. It was Tjamuaha, the one who had suffered so many defeats and humiliations in his life, who eventually triumphed over his oppressor. As Jonker felt his end approaching, he sent for his son, Christian, and Tjamuaha's successor, Maherero. He bade them live in peace, and to rule jointly over Herero and Nama land. He gave his right shoe to Christian and the left one to Maherero, signifying that they were to succeed him, but Christian came first. He then sent for the missionary Kleinschmidt, and in his presence—still unrepentent of his sins—died. He was buried near his hut under a camelthorn tree.'

It was noticed that when the two chiefs were dead a tempest suddenly blew up and knocked down the huts of the Nama. The Herero took this as a happy augury. 'There goes our father's spirit,' they said. 'A new day will dawn for us.'

The Herero were right. Maherero proved to be a great warlord. He had been one of the four sons of Tjamuaha who had been sent to be educated at Jonker's Kraal. Jonker had subjected him to countless cruelties and indignities, such as tying him to the wheel of a moving cart. But 'Tjamuaha's calf', as

enacted. Between 1840, and the arrival of the Germans at Windhoek in 1890, it was the scene of a succession of bloody events. These were the result of the half-century of warfare between the Herero and Hottentots which had begun in earnest in 1835. In that year the fearsome Jonker Afrikaner had been installed as military leader of the Hottentots, at a time when the latter, whom we shall call by their modern name of Nama, had been losing ground to the Herero. The Nama therefore appealed to Jonker, a man of great magnetism and resource, to lead them. They chose not only wisely but too well.

Jonker was head of the Afrikaners, who in turn were one of the three tribes of a branch of the Nama people known as the Oorlam. The Afrikaners were originally Dutch-Hottentot half-breeds in Cape Province, who had to flee across the Orange River in 1800 when Jonker's father, Jager Afrikaner, murdered his Dutch employer. They were familiar with the white man's firearms and methods of waging war: and immediately after assuming command Jonker led the Red People, or Kanub Khoin, as the Nama were called, to three crushing victories against the Herero. From then on he never looked back. In 1840 he planted himself on the Herero grazing ground at Aighams and changed its name to Windhoek. The Herero chief Tjamuaha entered into a craven partnership with him to plunder his own people, and even sent Jonker four of his sons as hostages. It was a foolish move. On August 23, 1850, Jonker attacked his Herero allies in force and committed what became known as the first Massacre of Okahandja. He drove away the splendid herds of Tjamuaha's brother-chief Kahitjene, killed a host of warriors, beat the captured children to death, and cut the hands and feet off the women in order to remove their copper ornaments.

Until his death in 1861 he was the undisputed king of South West, called by the Herero *Mukuru Oouje*, 'King of the World'. The Baltic missionary Carl Hugo Hahn, second representative of the Renish Mission to arrive in the country, wrote in 1859: 'The Red Nation's Herero slaves are treated horribly and often die of hunger. We saw some of these pitiable beings, who

crash on these sparsely tenanted highways: but they do. At intervals along the road you pass the hulks of burnt-out trucks and wrecked cars. Some of them have been there for thirty years. In the dry air of the desert they are as perfectly preserved as Egyptian mummies in the sands of the Sahara. Wandering herdsmen or Bushmen have stripped out the upholstery, the steering-wheel, the door-handles and the bumpers; otherwise the battered chassis remains where it is, and presumably will remain there until the end of time. I have seen a train that, together with its tender and trucks, fell into a ravine outside Port Nolloth half a century ago. It lies down there still, like a sunken ship on the floor of the ocean.

Sometimes, at night, the sudden sight of one of these wrecked cars gives you a nasty moment. You see the machine tilted at a crazy angle down a hillside, as if it had come to grief only a few minutes before: but when you stop your Land Rover and run across to it you quickly realize that whoever died behind that splintered windshield died there when you were still a boy at school. It is hard to account for such accidents. In a country where people drive 200 miles to visit a cinema, loading up afterwards with Windhoek Münchener, it is natural that now and again the monotony of the track should send them to sleep at the wheel. Or perhaps the sight of a pair of headlights approaching with an agonizing nightmare slowness induces a fatal hypnosis. On those roads you drive fast. You might not see a living soul, let alone another car, for an entire day, and you keep up your speed in order to counteract any unevenness in the surface. If you hit a bumpy patch at forty miles an hour, you are jolted and thrown about; at seventy, you skim over it like a bird.

After three hours you reach Okahandja—but there is no need to linger there, even though with 3,000 people it ranks as a large town. None the less it is an historic place, for it was at Okahandja that the principal Holy Fire of the Herero nation was kept alight, and it is still the place where the Herero stage their annual rally. It is a town where dark deeds were once

to be packed into a relatively small tribal area in the far north, leaving a quarter of a million people to occupy an area of three-quarters of a million square miles. The demographic picture is almost as empty as Siberia or Mongolia.

Before you reach harbour at Walvis Bay, you will have to drive more than 200 miles on dirt roads.

These dirt roads are in fact extremely good, as they must be if they are to give satisfactory service as the country's main arteries. They are up to a dozen yards wide, and aligned on the simple Roman principle that when building a road a straight line is the shortest distance between two points. They run absolutely direct for thirty, forty, fifty miles at a time. The surface is generally level and reasonably devoid of ruts, except when it gets cut up during the rainy season. Then the surface is turned into red porridge and torrents of water wash across the road through water-courses which are made fecund every two of three years, if then. The roads are shaped and shaved flat by means of huge mechanical scrapers, operated by men who spend their entire lives out in the bush, churning over their daily quota of road. At night they rig up a tent and sleep in the lee of their machines, while the Bantu servant who is their sole companion sleeps, such are the exigencies of apartheid, in a separate tent at a regulation distance.

Under normal conditions the roads can be irritatingly dusty, and as you pound along them you raise on all sides a tremendous cloud of dust like a destroyer hull-down making smoke. This plume of dust spiralling up behind you is dramatic. It lends the occasional vehicle that comes towards you or overtakes you an air of urgency and importance, and makes you feel you are in a car chase. Oddly enough, it is far more unnerving being approached or overtaken on one of those lonely roads than it is when you pass a hundred cars a minute in Piccadilly or on the Los Angeles Freeway. When you encounter another car only every four or five hours its appearance creates in you a sensation of crisis and mild alarm.

It seems inconceivable that anyone could possibly have a

Kalahari: on the west the Namib and the stinging Kaokoveld.

If you have flown into Windhoek from Johannesburg or Kimberley, you will have seen the Kalahari spread out league after burnt red league beneath you. The Kalahari is cruelly deceptive: it lacks the brazen barrenness of the Sahara. Its colour is lively and vigorous: from the air the vegetation that studs it thickly looks almost inviting, and strikes you as more monotonous than dangerous. It is not easy to realize, as you disembark at the spanking new airport at Windhoek, that you have arrived in such an unrelenting country. But if you have entered South West by road from the south—from Cape Town instead of Johannesburg—you would have been prepared for the drouth and dreariness of the whole region below Windhoek. From the fruiftul expanse of Cape Province, with its orchards and wheatfields, you strike into the stony nothingness of Namaqualand and Bushman Land. The contrast is raw, shocking. The pretty townships of Piketberg, Clanwilliam and Vanrhynsdorp, trim and prosperous, yield to the stark centres of the long-dead copper industry, Springbok, O'Okiep and Steinkopf. And once across the Orange River at Vioolsdrift the landscape becomes progressively harsher, as the dirt road carries you through the wastes of the Karasberg towards Windhoek, 500 miles away.

It now begins to dawn on you why Windhoek, set on the country's central plateau, is the only sizeable town in the territory. Windhoek is like one of von François's fortresses, hard-pressed on all sides by fierce and pitiless enemies. The bulk of the population has retired, as it were, into the shelter of the fortress, leaving only a small residue thinly spread across the countryside beyond. South West Africa is inhabited by only a little more than half a million people, European and African reckoned together. This amounts to less than two people a square mile. Compare this with 35 people a square mile in neighbouring South Africa, 50 in the United States, 79 in the Soviet Union, 158 in Spain, 217 in France, 561 in the United Kingdom. And even then the figure of two per square mile flatters the territory: for well over half the population happens

Off the Tar

South West covers an area of 318,261 square miles. You could make one bundle of England, Belgium, the Netherlands, Denmark, Norway, Austria, Portugal and Greece and fit it easily inside its borders. It is over two-thirds the size of the Republic of South Africa. You can now appreciate what kind of country you have started to drive across.

The territory is about 900 miles long and 350 miles wide. It is larger than Texas, the biggest state after Alaska in the United States—and Texas itself is larger than any country in Europe except Russia.

South West stretches from the banks of the Cunene and the Okavango Rivers in the north to the banks of the Orange River in the south—from the borders of Portuguese Angola to the borders of Bushman Land. Yet between the gigantic rivers that form its boundaries there are no other rivers to be found. The surface of the whole territory is streamless, and the water which jets from the artesian wells derives from subterranean rivers whose directions are uncertain. The 'rivers' so plentifully marked on those optimistic maps—even the so-called 'major' rivers of the Swakop, the Omaruru and the Nosob—are nothing but sterile slots in the sand, dried-up beds or *omurambas*, waiting for the capricious insemination of the rain.

The land pants eternally for moisture. It is not for nothing that the talk here is all of *lekker* water—sweet water—a monologue concerning dams and barrages, canals, pipelines and storage tanks. Even in the north, where there may be twenty inches of rainfall a year, there are many areas where a drought might drag on for years; and in the south, below the Tropic of Capricorn, there is never more than six inches of rainfall, and often none at all. The south is what the geographers call a 'rain-shadow desert', and is useless for any activity except raising sheep—the hardy karakul sheep that can thrive on the most miserable stunted scrub.

The only portion of the country that is satisfactory for agriculture and herding is the northern half—and, even then, only the narrow central strip of that. This fertile band is imprisoned, like the Nile, between two iron deserts. On the east sprawls the

you can drive north out of Windhoek for the first forty-five miles of your trip to Walvis Bay 'on the tar', as the South Africans say.

You are being spoiled, riding along like this in style. And your comfortable and painless introduction to the countryside provides, I think, a good opportunity to reflect a little more closely on the geography and population of the land you are setting out to look at.

The black ribbon of the wide straight road stretches out in front of you. In a smoothly unrolling dream you drive mile after mile across the veldt, yellow-green after the recent rains. Occasionally you see clumps of camelthorn, and the enormous plain is dotted with outcrops of scree and micaceous sandstone. There are cowslips and patches of a silvery thistle with a white flower. The six-foot high ant-heaps of the commandant-ants stand up like obelisks. From time to time an ostrich, scared by the Land Rover, lopes away into the bush with its comical floppy run. You pass flocks of goats, fifty to a hundred strong, guarded by an African boy—white, grey, black, brown, mustard-coloured—a Mendelian fantasia. Outside the entrance of a farm a number of Herero women are driving a herd of Hereford cattle—and it is startling to see a note of the lush, clipped English countryside in that unyielding landscape. A dozen miles farther on a humped Cape ox lumbers along beside the road, taking no notice of you, its head lowered in a huge beige dream. The African air is clean-rinsed, slightly metallic. Far above a black eagle or bateleur swings down on a current of air.

It is good to be leaving the town for the open country—even such an agreeable, well-ordered town as Windhoek. Windhoek and Cape Town are two of the very few towns in Africa which do not seem squalid and rubbishy in comparison with the majesty of their setting: but the greatness of Africa is not to be challenged by any of the works of man. The land lies illimitable, inviolate, indifferent to human pretensions, communing with itself.

Off the Tar

With your papers in your pocket, you are now ready to leave the shelter of Windhoek, the only one of the country's towns with over 5,000 inhabitants.

You have already decided that the next place you will visit is Walvis Bay, 266 miles to the west, on the South Atlantic Coast, a long day's journey away.

For this and your subsequent travels you will need a sturdy vehicle. Your best choice is a Land Rover with four-wheel drive. The vleis or river-beds can be treacherous; the roads are often more hypothetical than actual; and if you want to drive around in the desert you will be glad to bang in the red knob and engage the four-wheel drive that prevents you from sinking over your axles into the sand. Load up with canned food and camping equipment. Keep handy some biltong, the sun-dried raw meat that goes in Texas by the name of jerked beef, and boer rusks to gnaw between meals. Carry a couple of spare tyres; a tool-kit; a good thick rope with a hook at the end; a roll of matting or bale of chicken-wire to brace the rear wheels if you get stuck. Check your snake-bite outfit. Buy a box of cartridges for your .375 magnum express. Take more film for your camera than you think you will need. Above all, fill your polyethylene containers of water right up to the brim, see the tops are screwed on tightly, and bury them under your bedrolls and other gear to keep them away from the heat of the sun. Sling a couple of canvas water-bags from the front bumper: if you wet them on the outside, the air will keep them cool as you drive and prevent evaporation.

Water, water, and more water. The pioneers used to call this country Thirstland. Here the obsession with water is almost as intense as the obsession with diamonds. No Texan ever drills for oil as deep and anxiously as the South West farmer drills for water, or is as disappointed when the hole comes up a 'duster'. Until recently even Windhoek lacked supplies of surface water, and it still relies on its thirty-six boreholes.

In 1939 there were only five miles of macadamized road in the whole of South West. Today there are over 400 miles. So

splinters of a mirror that shattered a hundred million years ago —in their heart is the broken image of our earth as it existed at its birth. When you hold a gem stone in your hand, you are holding a fragment of the basic element of our planet, older than ammonites or trilobites, older than amber or ambergris, older than any of the primaeval objects which give one a queer atavistic sensation to stroke and touch. With their profound awe of nature, and their love of their own landscape, it is only to be expected that the South Africans should be irresistibly drawn by the idea of the diamond. A man who finds a blob of gold seldom hesitates to trade it in for cash: but a poor prospector will often prove extremely reluctant to part with one of his diamonds. Part of his reluctance stems from the fact that, if you want one, you have to sweat so hard for it. Diamonds are not often to be discovered in relatively pleasant places, like the beds of rivers; to find a diamond you have to go out deep into the desert. To a prospector, a diamond is a token of persistence and endurance, a badge of hardships overcome: and when he finally sells it, he is letting go a part of himself. Nothing can match the pride and anguish on a prospector's face when he unwraps his prize from its scrap of dirty rag and lays it on the table in front of the official diamond-buyer. So strong, I assure you, is the diamond-mania in South West that if you stop your car in a lonely place, or even bend down to pick something up from the floor of the desert, it is automatically assumed that you are scratching around for diamonds. And you probably are.

Wherever you travel in South West there is always the possibility of being delayed for questioning as an illicit diamond digger or dealer. It is therefore sensible to advise the authorities in Windhoek of your itinerary, to enable them to contact their diamond detectives and the regular police. And again, distances in South West are so enormous, and traffic so sparse, that it is best to keep people posted about your whereabouts in case you have a breakdown. The consequences of becoming lost or stranded can be dire.

less, just as you will receive little help if you have come to South West as a dyed-in-the-wool South Africa hater, so you will get even less if they think you might be an under-cover diamond prospector. It is hardly surprising that diamonds should be in the very forefront of the official mind. The diamondiferous deposits of the Forbidden Area yield a million-and-a-half carats of diamonds a year, worth 70 million rand (41 million pounds or 98 million dollars). By weight alone the yield amounts to over 400 pounds of gem stones. South West Africa is the largest producer of diamonds in the world. Diamonds are therefore destined to bulk large in the following pages: and in later chapters I shall be describing the Forbidden Area and the diamond-mining community of Oranjemund. Here I shall only remark that the people of South West, from the mandarins of the administration downwards, are all acutely diamond-conscious. Diamond-fever, or rather diamond-dementia, is a disease they share with the majority of South Africans. The diamond still has the hypnotic appeal for the South African that the nugget had for the American in gold-rush days. The clerk in his office in Beaufort West or Burgersdorp dreams of throwing up his job and trekking out into the desert in search of a pocketful of diamonds. The diamond does not signify merely riches: it exercises some sort of ancestral pull. It symbolizes the glorious freedom of the old trek days, the promise of the wilderness, the reward that comes to the man who dares to throw off the shackles of city life. Large numbers of South Africans actually take a fling at prospecting at one time or another. They try it as young men, or plan secretly for years and then suddenly take off in middle-age with a truck and a shovel. Failure does not sour or discourage them, any more than failure to find the philosopher's stone discouraged the alchemists.

Anyone who turns a diamond in his fingers knows that he is holding a mysterious, compelling substance. It is something that has come to us from the primaeval core of things. Its fiery beauty is as hard to account for as its origin in the volcanoes that turned night to day in the proterozoic period. They are

The Palace of Ink stands idle now, its functions usurped by the gleaming new administration building—a modern Palace of Typewriters—erected close by. Entering those air-conditioned corridors, you realize that the easy-paced world of the old empires has vanished for ever. The ordinary men and women of Windhoek may appear unconcerned by the squabbles about their future at the United Nations and the International Court: not so the members of the administration. They are shrewd, watchful and diligent. They have the air of men who are well aware that, with the League of Nations' mandate in continuous dispute, time is a precious commodity for the South Africans in South West: as precious as its diamonds, minerals, fisheries and karakul-pelts. They give the impression of sailors hauling in canvas as the glass goes down, or of soldiers making full use of the last few seconds before zero-hour.

They will greet you with the reserve that has become habitual among South African civil servants—not only in Windhoek, but in Pretoria, Johannesburg, Cape Town, and South African embassies abroad. They are afraid, often with good reason, that visitors come as spies, or as hostile critics making bogus professions of friendship in order to sneak within the gates. South Africans are by nature an open people, and on numerous occasions in the past they have been badly fooled. The experience has made them abnormally mistrustful, and their dealings with foreigners have taken on a foolish police-state character. They are reluctant to talk, reluctant to commit themselves, reluctant to assume individual responsibility for even small decisions. This is one of the minor by-products of the battle over apartheid, and another reason for trying to terminate that pernicious policy. It is an illustration of the way in which apartheid undermines the free-and-easy commerce between one man and another of which I shall speak in a later chapter.

However, once you can convince the men in the Main Administration Building that you come in good faith, the boisterous goodwill and traditional hospitality of the South African quickly cracks the crust of suspicion, and you will readily receive whatever permits and assistance you require. None the

TWO
Off the Tar

If you have been stimulated by the flavour of Windhoek, as I was, into exploring the rest of the country, you will have to pay an official visit to the Main Administrative Building. This is in the neighbourhood of the Christuskirche and the Alte Feste.

The new administration building is situated beside the old one, which was built at the turn of the century. The latter was the work of Willi Sander, architect of the Rhine castles, Windhoek's first town-planner. His building is extraordinarily graceful, and he was clearly a highly gifted practitioner. The senior citizens still call it by its old nickname of *Tintenpalast,* or Palace of Ink: and the vision of its long low white outline glimmering among the palms and bougainvillaea evokes an image of imperial rule in its sunset phase. From its wide windows the German governors once gazed down the hillside upon Windhoek, as Conrad's governors looked down on Macassar, Couperus's on Batavia, Kipling's on Calcutta, Maugham's on Kuala Solor.

The Land God Made in Anger

The sun would plunge behind the ramparts of the Khomas Hochland in an African glory of scarlet and cinnamon, mauve and lavender. Later, lying in bed, I would hear the boys with their sports-cars and motorcycles racing each other down the triple lanes of the Kaiserstrasse. This was a nightly performance, when the main streets of the town were turned into a dirt-track or drag-strip. If the racket became unusually raucous, I would get out of bed and go to the window to watch. It was an excellent free show. The police were unperturbed at the spectacle of the youngsters blowing off steam in this way. The Karmann Ghias and Hondas boomed along beneath the elegant concrete lamp-standards between the high white buildings. The bright light gleamed on the blonde hair of the girls crouched on the pillions or curled up in the passenger seats. The savage acceleration would jam them back against the cushions or make them twine their arms tighter round the waists of the boys in front and bury their heads on the boys' shoulders. Their mouths opened wide to show their fine white teeth.

This at least was different from *Heimat*. Young people did not behave in this uninhibited way in Stuttgart or Wiesbaden.

It reminded me, as I climbed back into bed, that I was in Africa, in a frontier town, in a land that was still a land of wildness and pioneers.

The Place of Fiery Waters

grow up, I shall go *there*. . . ." ' And when, finally, he reached his goal, he related in *Heart of Darkness* that: 'Going up that river was like travelling back to the earliest beginnings of the world, when vegetation rioted on the earth and the big trees were kings. An empty stream, a great silence, an impenetrable forest . . .'

'*The unsolved mystery of the continent.*' Would Gide and Greene, I wonder, returning to Africa today, be any more eager than they were thirty years ago to wander off beyond the bright lights of the perimeter fence? Would Conrad find the forest any more penetrable, or the great muddy river any less empty or silent?

In Windhoek, the traveller feels the same sense of necromancy that he felt at Kano, the same apprehension that he felt at Kinshasa. The African mystery is omnipresent. The deserts press round him as pitilessly as the jungle at Kinshasa. The same huge harsh fact of nature overwhelms the conflicts of the human inhabitants: and the conflicts are as age-old and unforgiving in South West as they are in the Congo.

Such were the reflections that would occupy me, as they would have occupied any traveller, when I used to make my way back to my hotel after my evening stroll. What had happened to the Relai, the Devinière and the Memling could happen to the Continental and the Thuringer Hof. What had happened in the Congo, Ghana, Nigeria, Guinea, Burundi, Tanzania could happen in South West. I used to pause at the foot of the beautiful statue of the kudu, with its gilded horns and mane, that stands at the bottom of Lüderitzstrasse, and watch the crowds sauntering home from the beergardens, from a concert in the Arts Theatre, or from the town's three cinemas (which in South Africa and South West go by the quaint name of *bioskops*). The people were prosperous and cheerful. They seemed no more concerned by the political tensions and the uncertain fate of the mandate than their relatives in West Berlin were disturbed by the closeness of the Red Army. They gave no overt sign that Windhoek was one of the world's most tender trouble-spots. Truly the human being is an adaptable and complacent creature.

second stop—at Kinshasa, say. There, in the Turkish-bath atmosphere of the Congo, you stand on the balcony of the transit-lounge and stare across the rain-drenched tarmac towards the distant lights of Brazzaville, on the opposite bank of the shrouded river. Who, these days, would not feel edgy in the Congo—anxious for the refuelling to end and the plane to take off again? *Brazzaville.* Does the famous Relai hotel still serve those delicious meals? If so, to whom does it serve them? Does the place even exist any more? And what about the Devinière in Kinshasa? Or the grand Hotel Regina, and the grander Memling? You could ask the negro *maître d'hôtel* whom you can see in the restaurant behind you, moving among the tables, speaking French to the guests and Lingala to the waiters who are hurrying round with platters of the fragrant lamb-and-curry dish called *moamb*. But somehow the thought of asking such questions fills you with embarrassment, sadness, trepidation. What has happened to them all—the thousands of Belgians, the millions of Congolese—in these last unspeakable years? An outrage of colonialism followed by an outrage of anti-colonialism; an outrage of white followed by an outrage of black. And less than fifteen years ago the travel agencies were inviting you to come to the Congo, 'the Switzerland of Africa'. The Switzerland of Africa! ...

No more strolls in de Bock Park or the Zoological Gardens; no more shopping at Pek's or the ivory market in front of the Regina; no more excursions to the Belvedere, Point Kalina, or the Cristal Mountains. ... Travellers have been making the hard journey to Kinshasa for more than a century to be moved and saddened by the Congo. Gide was here with his raw Protestant conscience; Greene with his raw Catholic one. In 1888 Conrad rode upstream in a paddleboat to take command of a Congo river-steamer, an ambition that had haunted him for twenty years and had driven him back to active life when he had already given up the sea. 'It was in 1868, when nine years old or thereabouts, that while looking at a map of Africa, and putting my finger on the blank space then representing the unsolved mystery of the continent, I said to myself, "When I

The Place of Fiery Waters

special areas in mid-course. I remember one who settled back with a sigh of relief to study South East Asia. He said it was pleasant to switch his attention to peoples who possessed wit and elegance, style and humour. True; they do. All the same, I wonder what he thought about the massacres that resulted in hundreds of thousands dead in Indonesia in 1965–66? ...

Africa is disconcerting because it possesses that air of enchantment and sorcery of which I spoke at the beginning of this chapter. On your way to central or southern Africa, the sense of mystery, of things being other than they seem, begins to stir as soon as you make your first landing on the African soil. At Kano, for example, you step out of the plane into the sudden, all-embracing heat of the African night, dense and opaque, as warm as the womb—for Africa is the world's mother, its cradle, the matrix of mankind. You stand beside a bed of marigolds, their copper petals gleaming like delicate plates of metal in the light from the lounge behind you, where the Ibo women in their flowing robes of coral and turquoise sit behind their baskets selling your fellow-passengers beads, fetishes, fly-whisks and magic bracelets of elephant hair. You suck at a bottle of Seven-Up, and feel the sweat soaking through your shirt as you watch the Nigerian ground-crew refuelling the plane. But the Boeing, like the fly-whisks and the coloured beads, seems to be taking on a different character, a new form and significance. The fuel-lines surrounding it are not fuel-lines but tangles of snakes. The Boeing itself is no longer a Boeing but some beautiful winged monster being brought its tribute of drink and sustenance: a silvery creature whose flanks, belly and fins are bedizened with ceremonial stripes. The dark-faced acolytes in white overalls manoeuvre the fork-lift trucks on their rubber-shod wheels in a ritual dance, illuminated by the pale ovals of light beneath the nacelles and tilted nose. Voices are deep, slow, and muffled. A pungent smell of dampened earth rises from the flowerbed beside you—and suddenly the heads of the marigolds bob as though a wind had touched them. But you can feel no breeze.

And the strangeness squeezes harder still when you make your

of twenty-five million years, from the times when the little proto-apes *Parapithecus* and *Propliopithecus* were scampering about in the neighbouring mountains to the racial antagonisms of the modern world, can all be clearly traced in South West. The layers of human development from barbarism to civilization, from Stone Age to Nuclear Age, can be laid bare in this remarkable country, as though it was a vast dissecting-table with the African sun for its overhead arc-lamp.

There were days, after I left Windhoek and journeyed up-country, when the harsh and ambiguous character of the landscape over-awed and oppressed me. A traveller, of course, is always a stranger. He is continually giving his wallet and passport a nervous tap. A man away from home is bound to be a little wary and apprehensive. He is not on the same wavelength as the people of the country he is visiting; he does not share their hopes and fears; he seldom stays long enough to fit his personal shape into the shape of the foreign culture. He is just a kind of hole in the air: a ghost with an appetite: a transient. The things he sees have no clear antecedents, he cannot judge their cause and effect, and therefore they are largely incomprehensible to him. And when he is a stranger in an exceedingly strange land like South West, he is bound to feel correspondingly uneasy.

To some extent Africa, though its history and reputation are fundamentally no more complicated and bloody than those of Europe, always makes me uncomfortable. I have known other people who shared this reaction. When I was at Cambridge, candidates in the anthropology school were required to choose a special area for detailed study: and friends of mine who chose Africa sometimes found that, in spite of their efforts to maintain an academic objectivity, they were haunted by a feeling of depression, a sense of something grim and sinister. They had bad dreams and came out in spots. Those terrifying masks of straw, ivory, and ebony; those ash-smeared, mud-streaked faces; those writhing limbs anointed with ochre, fat, and the blood of animals—little by little these things began to weigh on their minds. Several of the students changed over to other

The Place of Fiery Waters

has become the Fifth Province of the Republic of South Africa. If the subject peoples, led by the Herero, can seize power themselves, then good luck to them. There is nothing final and immutable about the maps in the atlas of 1968, any more than there was about the maps of 1668, 1768, or 1868, or about the maps (if any are printed) of 2068.

As a Welshman, a member of a nation that met its Waterberg at the hands of a greater power five centuries ago, I can feel an instinctive sympathy with the aspirations of Herero and Ovambo, Hottentots, and Bergdama. Yet, as a sensible man, I must always hope that, while the Good Old Rule goes grinding on its way, the cruelty and bloodshed which are attendant on it can somehow be minimized. If the map of South West Africa is to change its shape and colour, perhaps it can be induced to do so without the horrors that have recently accompanied the process elsewhere in Africa, from Algeria to the Malagasy Republic. Therefore I pray that the Herero and their allies should not allow themselves to be over-encouraged by speeches made in the gilt and plush of distant debating-chambers. After all, it is on the windy pavements of the Kaiserstrasse that the blood will be shed.

It is strange to walk through the residential district of Windhoek at night, wrapped in the warm velvet darkness, with the Southern Cross shining overhead, and hear someone practising a Bach *chaconne*, the sound of the violin mingling with the distant cries of jackals and wild dogs in the foothills of the surrounding Hochland. It is strange to walk past a house and see abstract paintings in the style of Wols or Hans Hartung on the walls of the brightly lit drawing-rooms. It reinforces the impression that imprints itself day by day more strongly on your mind that South West is a kind of compendium of human thought and experience. There is everything here from the rock-painting of the Bushmen to the most sophisticated expression of modern art; everything from the two-note whining of the Bushman *ramkie* to Schönberg and Karl Amadeus Hartmann.

South West is a living museum of human history. The annals

numbered by the Ovambo alone by seven to one. They are late arrivals in the territory they now claim as their homeland, and their right to it is far more tenuous than the Dutch and English claim to South Africa. But their bluff might work. They have courage, resilience, and a splendid self-conceit. Alone of the Africans in South West they have learned how to get off the reserve and become shrewd operators, sharp city-boys. All nations need leaders: and the leaders are the men who have faith in their mission to lead. The Herero have that faith.

Many of our principal politicians, in spite of half a century of global warfare and the imminent prospect of universal starvation, remain optimistic and chiliastic in their attitude to world problems. This unfocused attitude hinders a realistic approach to the problems in question: indeed, it raises more problems than it solves. The only countries which can face the future with any confidence are those which can produce resolute and clear-minded leaders, with an ability to concentrate on their own immediate difficulties. If there is to be another Congo or Nigeria in South West Africa, then we must hope that the Herero actually possess the qualities which they claim they do. Those are the qualities that Africa needs.

History, wrote William James, is a bath of blood. I would not be so gloomy as to observe with Pascal that 'All men naturally hate one another. At bottom there is nothing but hate.' On the other hand, as the larger percentage of the world's wealth is devoted to the purchase and manufacture of armaments, it would seem that, gloss it over though we might, the world's business is still conducted in accordance with what Wordsworth called the Good Old Rule:

> The Good Old Rule, the Simple Plan,
> That they should take who have the power,
> And they should keep who can.

Nowhere in the world is the Good Old Rule so transparently in operation at the moment than in southern Africa, particularly in South West Africa. The South African Government possesses the power in South West: and it means to keep it. South West

and that their menfolk had become sterile, as if the tribal experience at the Warterberg had had the same side-effects as Hiroshima. Then, slowly, they began to mend, and in the last half-century their numbers have almost doubled. While their white masters—German, English, South African—were reducing their manpower in two murderous wars of their own devising, the Herero were left alone in comparative tranquility. The establishment of the native reserves in 1922 also had the effect of providing them with shelter, however humble, from nature, from their overlords, and from each other. The general birth-rate in South West Africa in the last forty years has increased more rapidly than the birth-rate in any other African country.

It is a sad and curious fact that the Herero and their German overlords enjoyed a peculiarly close relationship. At the beginning of German rule the Herero regarded themselves, as they regard themselves now, as a black *Herrenvolk*. Their chiefs grew bristling moustaches with upturned points, in the style of Kaiser Wilhelm II. Today they still have a fondness for wearing tunics made of a fine khaki cloth cut in a quasi-military style. For a while, even after the débâcle, the Germans put them into uniform as policemen, and they were blissfully happy. The Lutheran religion had early attracted them, stressing as it does a love of discipline and hero-worship and a certain contempt for common humanity. Nor did the Waterberg altogether shake them loose from this martial brand of Christianity. Indeed, one of the reasons for the uprising had been their feeling of indignation and betrayal that the Rhenish missionaries had thought it worth their while to expound the sacred creed to such inferior people as the Bergdama, their *ovazarotua*, or 'black serfs'.

At the present time the Herero believe that if the Africans gain power in South West Africa they will exercise the right of an aristocratic caste to assume the leadership. Their pretensions are laughable: but it is impossible not to admire their cheek. In the past century they have been severely defeated by the Hottentots and the Germans. They are only the fourth largest of the nine African tribal groups in South West, and are out-

breaks that swept through South West at one time or another, and had to endure huge losses of cattle as a result of such visitations as the rinderpest epidemic of 1897. To have managed to hold together at all in a country where the grazing and water-supplies are so scanty and fiercely coveted is a signal feat, quite apart from coping with the onslaughts of the Hottentots.

For twenty years, beginning in 1885, the Herero enjoyed the protection and esteem of the Germans. Colonial powers have always made pets of their 'warrior' tribes: witness the special British regard for the Hausa, the Masai, the Ghurkhas, or the Punjabis. The Germans made sincere efforts to educate the Herero and help them to combat their diseases, both human and animal. Then came the mad month of January, 1904, when the Herero suddenly attacked German garrisons and mission-stations and massacred their inhabitants. Eight months later almost the whole Herero nation was entrapped at the mountain called the Waterberg, a hundred and thirty miles north of Windhoek. In the ensuing battle the Herero warriors died practically to a man, while the survivors fled north and east in two broken columns with the old folk and the women and children. One column went towards Angola and Ovamboland, the other towards Bechuanaland (now Botswana) and the Kalahari. Few Herero who began either of those long marches finished them. And by the time the German commander, General von Trotha, ended his hangings and shootings, even though their scale was derisory in comparison with, say, the total the British executed after the Indian Mutiny, the Herero nation was broken. To this day a large part of the Herero people still live in Botswana and have no intention of returning to South West.

It seemed unlikely that the Herero would ever recover. The remnant that survived von Trotha's *Vernichtungsbefehl*, or Extermination Order, were ravaged by tuberculosis and venereal disease, the incidence of which remains abnormally high among them even at the present time. For many years after the defeat their numbers remained static. It was said that their women had lost the desire and ability to produce children,

The Place of Fiery Waters

with her smooth copper cheeks judiciously touched up with brown boot-polish, is an impressive experience.

The Herero man is just as fussy about his dress as his wife. Not for him Messrs Leibowitz's second-hand stock. Herero men are peacocks, and they like to wear good suits and smart shoes. Their schoolmasters and storekeepers in particular are extremely well turned-out: and you will see Herero men wearing collars and ties even in the remotest reserves or on the most isolated farm-steads. They are a people who keep up their standards. Splendid horsemen, when they ride home at the end of the month to visit their parents they sport riding-breeches and leather leggings. They spend lavishly on their appearance and buy well, although in almost every other walk of life they tend to be thrifty, even puritanical. They accumulate larger savings than their brother Africans, and drink, smoke, and gamble less. They are provident people, capable of looking ahead: therefore it is interesting to learn that they are prone to disconcerting outbursts of hysteria and have a high suicide rate. They are fanatical about their cattle, and it is difficult to persuade them, even for financial or social reasons, to part with a single animal. When they leave their reserves to go to work in Windhoek, or in one or other of the four or five smaller towns, they regard it as beneath their dignity to be agricultural labourers. They have a great pride. You can see it in their lithe, lazy stride as they walk down Kaiserstrasse. On the reserves they will turn no soil, till no gardens: but their dwellings, whether they are the traditional wattle-and-daub huts or more permanent structures, are usually more spick-and-span than those of the Bergdama or other groups. Their fellow-Africans regard them as arrogant and aloof.

To have clung to their pride and self-respect after the trials of the past century and a half is a remarkable achievement. They fought two major wars with their great enemies the Hottentots during the nineteenth century. The wars were bitter and protracted, and even though they emerged the eventual winners, the long-drawn-out hostilities had a weakening effect. They were further depleted by the smallpox and other out-

still an opportunity for a man, even an African, to breathe a more vigorous and bracing air.

The Herero are an altogether different proposition. There are only 36,000 of them in South West's total population of 555,000: but they act as the African spear-head, the pace-makers. Herero men and women are both inordinately handsome and striking. They are tall and slender, with magnificent coffee-coloured skin and features that are not negroid but sharply defined. There is something ascetic about their faces, with the thin-boned nose, wide narrow lips, strong jaw-lines and bold, quick eyes.

One's first sight of Herero women as they saunter down Kaiserstrasse is startling. They have the proud gait of empresses, and are arrayed like Queens of Sheba. The skirts of their Victorian dresses sweep the ground and are made from ten to twelve yards of cotton print of the most vivid design and colour —scarlet, blue, emerald, orange, purple. The dresses are lined with three to four yards of cheaper but no less colourful material, while their elaborate petticoats are made from a cloth they call 'checks', though they dislike silk and wear no stockings or other underclothes. Over the skirts they wear bodices of the same cotton material, long-sleeved woollen cardigans, and deep-fringed shawls in some brilliantly contrasting colour. Their fine heads on their slim necks are adorned with head-scarves, usually matching the dresses. The scarf is known as the *otjikaiva*, sometimes referred to by Europeans as the 'Minerva cap'. They receive the *otjikaiva* at puberty, when they are permitted to grow their hair to its natural length, and it adds greatly to their appearance of height and stateliness. Their highly unusual mode of dress is derived from that of the first white women who entered the territory, the wives of the Rhenish missionaries who began their work in South West Africa in the 1840s and 1850s. It seems doubtful, however, whether the good German ladies would have worn garments quite so gorgeous, even for Sunday-best. To see a Herero beauty in her full glory, with her delicate glass ear-rings, her ostrich-shell necklaces, her ornamented *otjikaiva*, her elaborate rings and bangles, and

The Place of Fiery Waters

can hasten back to their beehive huts and their cattle kraals. I shall have more to say later about this genial Bantu tribe, which numbers almost half the population of South West Africa, but which is virtually unknown to the outside world.

As for the Bergdama, or Berg Damara, they are the second largest ethnic group in the country after the Ovambo. They are also the most unfortunate. A race of mysterious and much-debated origin, they probably entered the country some decades before the Hottentots and the Bantu: and their relations with the Bushmen, who had owned and occupied the territory since the dawn of time, appear to have been reasonably friendly. But with the coming of the Herero and the Hottentots the Bergdama suffered an abominable fate. First the Hottentots, then a second wave of Bantu represented by the Herero, defeated and made servants of them. The Hottentots and Herero habitually referred to them by such names as 'baboons' and 'black bondsmen', and for generations they served as the helots of these more powerful tribes. It was their very meekness that enabled them to survive in numerically superior numbers to their African oppressors, and in their eyes von François and Dr Goering came to South West Africa as saviours and liberators. To this day, however, the Hottentots and the Herero still despise them; their long captivity has robbed them of their distinctive customs; and they often strike the modern observer as being nothing more than poor relations of the two more powerful groups, attempting to copy the manners and appearance of their former oppressors. Be that as it may, it is nevertheless fair to point out that none of the Africans on the streets of Windhoek, not even the Bergdama, possess the terrible, disjointed, boneless look of the Africans you see on the streets of Johannesburg—men like grey ghosts, in tattered rags, sprawled in doorways, men who seem paper-thin, husked, gutted, listless, hopeless—detribalized, demoralized, dehumanized. In many respects South West has had a more brutal history than South Africa: but it still retains some of the freedom you find on a frontier. South West is enormous, largely unsettled and unexplored. The régime does not bear down quite so heavily here. There is

veld', one of the first men to find diamonds in Namaqualand, to Jack Levinson, one of the first to find them on the Skeleton Coast. The Jews of South West must have had a rough time of it to survive the harassments of the pre-war years: the Quota Act of 1930, and the Aliens Act of 1936, which the South African government put through in the teeth of opposition by Jan Smuts and Jan Hofmeyr. They must have had an even rougher time to survive the violence and Jewbaiting that were a feature of life in South West during the Hitler era. But survive they did. Today there is a synagogue among Windhoek's fifteen places of worship, and the Jews make an outstanding contribution to the prosperity of the city. Therefore it was a pity to discover that it was a firm called Leibowitz Brothers Limited which was the principal purveyor of 'Second-hand military overcoats for African labourers'—those appalling reach-me-downs that make a gang of African workmen look like the inmates of Dachau or Auschwitz.

The Mercedes and the Porsches carry the Windhoek businessmen down the Kaiserstrasse to their appointments—and less than a hundred miles away the Bushmen are tracking down their own particular prey by means of bow and arrow. The windows of the shops contain meticulous pyramids of European articles—but most of the people who pause to inspect them are Africans. This is part of the contrast, the contradiction of Windhoek.

There are nearly 22,000 Africans employed in what is officially called the Rural District of Windhoek. The two largest groups are the Ovambo and the Bergdama—though it is the third group, the Herero, who are the most likely to catch your eye. The Ovambo are exceptionally virile and impressive in physique; strapping men, broad in the shoulder, and over six foot tall. Unfortunately, they tend to be clad in Messrs Leibowitz's left-overs, which takes away a good deal of their impressiveness. Their homeland is in the far north of South West, and they tend to wander about like distracted giants, dreaming of the time when their work-contracts have expired and they

identical design. Again, in Windhoek, as in any town in Germany, there is not only a uniformity in the external appearance of the shops, post-offices, libraries and museums, but a uniformity in the way they arrange their windows and mount their displays. This uniformity derives from the sense of fitness and superiority of the German outlook. The German middle-class has always been convinced that things are done better at home. And one must admit that, in many ways, they are. It is a real pleasure to browse around the well-stocked bookshops of Windhoek and Swakopmund and find that the latest books and journals in all languages are on sale as a matter of course, and that there is a noticeable absence of the philistinism and the intellectual emptiness that have always been a feature of most exiled minorities.

If there is a certain uniformity in the appearance of the buildings, the modern German style is at least an acceptable one. If you see similar articles in the chemists' or photographers' shops in Windhoek that you would see in Worms or Wuppertal, the goods themselves are of the same excellent quality. When you have been driving about in the wastes of Namaqualand or in the deserts of the Kalahari or the Namib, it is marvellous to come upon this brisk, shining town with its impeccable hotels and rows of prosperous shops with good solid German names over the entrances: *Kandler, Wecke und Voigts, Koch und Schultheiss, Metje und Ziegler*. Furthermore, in view of the recent history of Germany and South West, it is intriguing to see that at night the biggest and brightest neon sign, soaring over the rooftops, dwarfing all the others, is the name 'Cohen'. Cohen's are the largest vehicle-dealers in South West. They were established early in the century by one of those tough Jews who have played a leading part in the commercial history of southern Africa. The Jews not only supplied the great entrepreneurs of the calibre of the Oppenheimers, the Barnatos, the Beits, the Dunkelsbuhlers, the Joels: they also supplied a host of those obscure, adventurous spirits who did the hard work in the field. Many men of this type figure in the romantic annals of South West, from Sol Rabinowitz, 'King Solomon of the Richters-

The Land God Made in Anger

The Muzak dispenses waltzes by Strauss, Kotlar, Cibulka, Hellmesberger: but the finishing Teutonic touch is the blonde *Mädel* with the braided hair behind the desk. And when you leave the hotel and walk down the main street of Windhoek, the Kaisertrasse (formerly the Kaiser-Wilhelmstrasse), you will quickly discover that the receptionist has several hundred sisters and cousins just as blonde and pretty as she is. The girls of Windhoek are famous throughout southern Africa: men fly up from South Africa to spend their vacation here, with the aim of finding themselves a beautiful and capable German wife. And as there are five women to every man in Windhoek, their chances are good.

Kaiserstrasse, Goeringstrasse, Leutweinstrasse, Grabenstrasse, Bulowstrasse, Kasinostrasse—the street names are all German. The town is bursting at the seams with Germans. There are 75,000 Europeans in South West, over 20,000 of whom live in Windhoek: and of the 25,000 Germans in the country the bulk seem to be concentrated in the capital. Despite the efforts of the Administration to maintain the Afrikaner preponderance, the German proportion is unlikely to diminish. An analysis of the immigration figures for 1951–60 reveals that, of a total of 4,327 immigrants from abroad, 3,371 came from West Germany, while only 184 came from the Netherlands and a mere 71 from Britain. The Germans like South West. It suits them. They feel at home there.

The buildings that line Kaisertrasse are constructed, like the hotels, in the modern German taste. That is to say, they have the well-made appearance of the post-war buildings in West Germany. It is not easy to fault such a neat and functional architecture, although one might take legitimate exception to its anonymity. In a modern main-street in Germany it is impossible to tell whether you are in the north of the country or the south, in Bonn, Bochum or West Berlin; there is little individuality, little sense of regionalism. The same, of course, is true of Britain, where six or seven firms of multiple tailors and chains of supermarkets have been allowed to tear down the Victorian and Edwardian shopfronts in order to erect stores of

of whom 23,500 are Europeans, it is more of a German town than ever. As in Germany itself, the Germans in South West have demonstrated the knack of thriving in defeat. The local *Wirtschaftswunder*, that since 1945 has transformed South West, has been founded on English, American, and South African money: but the impetus has been largely German.

German is one of the three official languages of the territory. It is the only European language which most of the urbanized Africans speak, but it is very curious to be spoken to in German by a Bergdama servant. Why this should be so is difficult to explain. There is no surprise when a waiter at Leopoldville (now Kinshasa) airport addresses you in French, or a waiter at Kano airport addresses you in English. But German ... in South West Africa. ... It produces a definite shiver. It can only be compared with the shock of flying into Patagonia and discovering that many of its inhabitants speak a singularly pure and beautiful Welsh. To wander about Windhoek and listen to its African citizens speaking German is a tribute to the stubborn tenacity of the German nation. After all, the character of Hanoi is no longer French, and the character of New Delhi is no longer English: but after half a century Windhoek can still be compared to a thriving town in Swabia or Bavaria.

In the Thüringer Hof or the Continental Hotel, you will hear the precise tones of the receptionist calling over the loudspeaker: '*Achtung! Herr Hassler, bitte! Achtung! Fraülein Rottluf, bitte!*' As an afterthought, she may repeat the announcement in Afrikaans or English. The entire hotel gives the impression of having been snatched up from a German hillside and spirited away to the Khomas Hochland. There is the same elegant furniture in pale-toned wood, the same highly polished floors, the same acres of spotless glass. Like hotels in Germany, the hotels in Windhoek have the appearance of having been opened only yesterday. Everything is well-kept and functions with the efficiency which is the hallmark of the German hotelier. The German hotels in South West, though modest in size, are more up-to-date and competently run than anything I encountered in Cape Town, Johannesburg or Pretoria.

neighbours and maintained a continuous reign of terror, fortified in his cruelties by the white man's rifles and the white man's brandy, for which he would raid missionary stations and trading depots on the coast.

The Germans therefore made a shrewd move when they picked on Windhoek, with its clear air and warm springs. But hardly had they set to work to build the Alte Feste before they were involved in the first of a series of strenuous campaigns. In 1893 Major von Leutwein, who had taken over from von François, embarked on operations against the Witbooi, one of the most aggressive and best-armed branches of the Hottentot nation. And after the Witbooi had been successfully dealt with, there came an even more serious rising by the Herero. The Herero War of 1904 was extremely savage. When it began the Herero nation numbered 60,000; when the rising ended it had been reduced to 20,000. The Germans lost between 2,000 and 3,000 troopers. The fighting was conducted without quarter on both sides. The Germans shot their prisoners; the Herero flayed theirs alive, or pegged them naked over thorn-bushes. The campaign has been ennobled in a manner it hardly deserves by an excellent and compassionate novel, Gustav Frenssen's *Peter Moor's Journey to South West Africa*, published in 1907, a kind of German counterpart to *The Red Badge of Courage*. It is also celebrated by a statue of outstanding beauty which shares a hillside in Windhoek with the Christuskirche and the Alte Feste. The figure, created in 1911 by Adolf Kürle of Berlin, is known as *Der Reiter von Südwest*: and it is a moving experience to sit at sunset on one of the boulders of the plinth, beneath the figure of the lean, alert horse, and turn one's head in the same direction as the leathery trooper to watch the sun drop behind the rim of the mountains.

When von François arrived at Windhoek—the German form of its name was Windhuk—there were only 600 Europeans in South West Africa. By 1915, when South Africa took over the territory, the European population still numbered only 2,000; and by 1939 it had risen to no more than 7,500. But today, when the total population of Windhoek has boomed to 47,000,

The Place of Fiery Waters

The Germans annexed South West, then called Damaraland, in 1884. The newly appointed Reichs Commissioner, Dr Goering, the father of the Reichsmarschall, decided that the capital should be at Otjimbingwe, midway between Windhoek and the coast. Next, in 1888, Goering withdrew the civil administration to Swakopmund, the new German port, and ordered von François to push on to Windhoek and to establish a military headquarters there. Von François set off for Windhoek with a total force of twenty-one soldiers. He marched from Swakopmund to Otjimbingwe, built another Foreign Legion fort called the Wilhelms Feste at Tsaobis, and finally reached Windhoek in the autumn of the following year. The ox-carts which carried his men and supplies can still be seen parked in a forlorn row behind the Alte Feste. They are Boer trek-wagons of the usual magnificent construction, solidly made of stinkwood, with stout canvas hoods, huge wheels, and the tremendous disselbooms to which eight span of oxen could be yoked. Once they used to rock and creak their way across the empty plains like caravels across an empty sea. Now they rest in port.

There were sound geographical and strategical reasons for adopting Windhoek as the white man's capital. It was superbly situated in the middle of the Khomas Hochland, the mildest, best-watered, most fertile area of the entire country. It stood in a marvellous natural amphitheatre of blue-white mountains, at an elevation of over 5,500 feet: yet it was poised on a hill whose escarpment gave views of the whole surrounding plain. The Khomas Hochland was not only the richest and healthiest spot in South West: it was also at the exact geographical centre. It was the obvious place from which to govern an unruly country. Moreover its adoption as a capital was symbolic of the conquest of the indigenous peoples. It had been the seat of the legendary Jonker Afrikaner, who had settled there in 1840. One of the Hottentot invaders from the Cape, he changed its name from Aighams, 'The Place of Fiery Waters', to Windhoek, after the name of his ancestral home in Cape Province; and until his death in 1861 he ruled South West with a rapacity and brutality which are still remembered today. He enslaved his

The Land God Made in Anger

This is not a part of the world which has ever known a long peace. Life here has always been rendered vivid by a constant sense of crisis and menace. There are ten distinct ethnic groups in the country, most of whom have fought one another in the not-too-distant past, and who eye each other with a barely concealed antagonism. The Europeans, the second largest group, are divided into three separate blocs. Afrikaners, Germans and British have no great historical compulsion to be unduly fond of each other, and act in partnership only because they realize that if they fail to hang together they will hang separately. Nevertheless it can hardly be dull, even if it is nerve-racking, to be a citizen of a country where it is a daily necessity to remember not to drop your guard and to keep your back against a handy wall. Living in a country which has dispensed with the polite fiction that men love, respect and trust one another must sharpen up the senses in a wonderful manner. In South West there is a tingling sensation of being always on the stretch. The hint of danger makes the air keener and brighter; the mind functions more incisively. There is no room for complacency or standing still: the mood is one of urgency. Paradoxically, it may be this very harshness and lack of sentiment that is responsible for the feeling of change, the sense that great things are being attempted or are about to be attempted.

The Alte Feste was not built simply for the purpose of ornament, decorative though it is. The German Imperial *Schutztruppe* were emphatically not toy soldiers. Outside the gateway of the fort still stands a sturdy six-pounder cannon with the date 1879 and the Hohenzollern eagle engraved on its black barrel, together with that grim motto that the old European artillerists liked to put on their hardware: *Ultima ratio regis*: '*His Majesty's final argument*'. The foundations of the fortress, the first European building in Windhoek, were laid in 1890 by a very capable officer, Kurt von François, a member of one of those Huguenot families which left France and entered Prussian service after the massacre of St Bartholomew. A General von François was one of Von Moltke's commanders during the Franco-Prussian War. A terrible revenge.

The Place of Fiery Waters

rooming up in Africa: it is not like Nairobi, Salisbury, or Johannesburg. Windhoek has personality—the kind of odd yet distinctive personality that belongs to the territory at large.

The cluster of castles was built by a German architect called Willi Sander, who came out to Südwestafrika in the 1890s. He built Sanderburg for himself; the other two were bought by a German baron who lived in one of them and installed his mistress in the other. The baron was a man of rare courtesy and discretion. I was told that every afternoon before visiting his mistress he sent his butler across with his calling-card.

The Windhoek skyline is dominated by other venerable buildings of *echt-deutsch* appearance. On the central eminence, presiding over the wide sweep of the town, is the Christuskirche, the German Lutheran church, completed in 1910: and beside it, perched on the edge of the hill with a broad view over the escarpment, is the Alte Feste, or Old Fort.

If it is a shock to stumble on Rhenish castles in a town in southern Africa, it is almost as great a shock to stumble on a Foreign Legion fortress. The Alte Feste is one of the string of fortifications with which the Germans studded the country. Most of them are ruins now, each standing like the castle of the sleeping princess among thickets of hook-thorn and umbrella-thorn in some desert oasis. Others, like the Alte Feste, have been preserved or renovated: and to step through their gateways is to step back into the boyhood world of Beau Geste and his brothers. Here are barrack-rooms, mess-halls, magazines and storerooms, laid out in the manner of a modest-budget movie. Along those narrow alleyways men once ran towards the rifle-slits in the walls, struggling with the straps of their equipment, dazed by the sudden blare of the bugle, the rattle of the kettledrum, the shouted orders, the yells of the attackers.

The Alte Feste is a reminder that only a generation ago Windhoek was a town on the colonial frontier. Today the territory still retains the edgy atmosphere of a frontier province. Its boundaries are fluid; there is a feeling of wariness. People move about their business in a condition of subdued siege, uncertain what the next turn of the wheel of fortune will bring.

The Land God Made in Anger

Deutsch-Südwestafrika had been surrendered by the Imperial German Army to General Botha and the troops of the South African Army in July 1915. For nearly half a century, since December, 1920, when the Mandated Territory of South West Africa had been handed over by the League of Nations to the care of the South African Government, the country had been administered not from Berlin but from Cape Town. Yet the former colonists had not merely managed to stay put: they had actually flourished and increased their strength. They had made the city of Windhoek even more German in character than it was in the days of the old German Empire.

As I stood on the hill below the three castles, craning my head back to gaze at Schloss Schwerinburg, I might have been in Europe, in the Hunsrück, or the Westerwald. I could have been standing in one of a hundred well-kept German towns. Though in what German town do you see African women walking the streets wearing brilliantly coloured Victorian dresses, complete with bustles and leg-o'-mutton sleeves? In what German town do you see masses of magenta bougainvillaea? Or hyphaene palms in full flower? Or silvery *kameeldorings* with their five-inch seed-pods and yellow blossoms? And where in the watery north do you bask in sunlight so finely spun, or breathe an air so much like wine?

South West Africa is a country of extraordinary contrasts. More than any other country I have visited, it is a land of the fantastic and the unexpected. It is endlessly absorbing and exciting. Africa, of course, is the continent of the great surprises: it constantly shows you fresh aspects of people, objects, and situations that you had believed were ordinary and familiar. In Africa everything takes on a touch of mystery, of witchcraft. But nowhere in Africa do you encounter such bewildering metamorphoses and juxtapositions as you do in South West.

Rhine castles—and bougainvillaea.... Nothing in this vast, under-populated, virtually unknown territory turns out to be quite what you expected. That is its appeal, its special character. Even Windhoek, its one and only genuine city, is not the kind of featureless and haphazard modern capital now mush-

ONE
The Place of Fiery Waters

THERE is nothing surprising in the spectacle of three Rhenish castles, even when they stand close to one another. But it is certainly astonishing to see three Rhenish castles rising above a town in southern Africa, 6,000 miles from the Rhine and well below the Tropic of Capricorn.

Yet there they are: small, eccentric, with drainpipes running down from the battlements, and big square sash windows in their thick stone walls. But they are Rhenish castles none the less, complete with round turrets and crenellated keeps. And called by resounding Teutonic names: Schwerinburg, Heinitzburg, Sanderburg.

When I first set eyes on them I stopped in my tracks and stood staring with amazement. Of all the bizarre sights I had seen in this remarkable country they were among the most bizarre.

I had not been prepared when I first arrived in South West Africa for the intensely German character of its capital.

Prologue

There are billions of stones in the Kaokoveld. The Kaokoveld is all stones. Nevertheless I search about diligently, rejecting one stone after the other until I discover a curiously shaped pebble that for some reason satisfies me and strikes me as suitable.

Slowly and with great care I drop it on the *ombindi*. Then I move on again towards the scratched and mud-streaked Land-Rover.

I shall be glad of that mug of black coffee.

Prologue

right and comes rushing down the river-bed towards me. I take a hasty step backwards as it swishes past, spattering me with brown spray, rattling between the rocks, drowning the thorny little *duwweltjes*, or *morgensters*, that have somehow survived for eight parched years in the clefts of the baked boulders.

I stare down for a long time at that liver-coloured water with its fringe of tawny foam. Eight years. The rains we wallowed through up-country last night were the first moisture this part of South West has known for eight years.

Standing beside a lusher stream in Ireland, a poet once asked: 'What's water but the generated soul?' And as I stare at the flood at my feet, I feel I am watching the dark soul of Africa pouring past me.

A sense of sadness comes over me. Soon I will be leaving South West. I have learned much there. I have grown to love it.

There is a shout behind me. For a moment I remain where I am, reluctant to leave the spectacle of the river in spate. Then, abruptly and unaccountably, as I have seen in other vleis during the course of these past few days, the mahogany waters begin to bate and dwindle. In less than a minute the turbulent bulk of the water has gone, like a rogue elephant, leaving behind it the muddied and half-uprooted *morgensters*.

Another shout. I turn and start to stroll back through the gritty desert sunshine towards the Land Rover beneath the dusty *swartkameel*. I shall miss South West.

Beside the dirt-track, a dozen yards from the lonely tree, there is a large heap of stones. I have come across several of these heaps in various parts of the Kaokoveld during my days in that emptiest, harshest, and noblest of places. They signify that this spot was once sacred. A chieftain or a hero had died here, or a wise man had paused on his pilgrimage. Here someone had received a wound, a vision, or a blessing.

On this heap, which the Tjimba and Himba call an *ombindi*, the traveller is required to cast a stone or a twig. This *ombindi* is a large one, signifying that in this desolate and uninhabited region it must be several hundred years old. It has stood there from the Days of the Ancestors.

Prologue

BEHIND me the Land Rover is parked in the thin patch of shade provided by a battered camel-thorn. My two companions are squatting on their heels beside the spirit-lamp, brewing up the kettle for the coffee. Now and again they exchange a brief word or two in their native Afrikaans, and when the coffee is ready one of them will shout across to me in his queer, squeezed English. They will hand me a mug of the scalding rust-coloured liquid, as thick as *samp*, or kaffir beer. Klaas will spoon seven or eight spoonfuls of sugar into his mug, and Sarel will put in a couple of good pinches of salt.

My muscles are sore after the eight hour drive across the desert. To stretch my legs I have wandered over to the bank of the empty vlei which we have just crossed, the last of thirty or forty. It looks like the bed of a river which has given up the ghost a thousand years ago.

A sudden hissing and scraping sound makes me lift my head. A broad sheet of water is sweeping around the bend on my

We carry with us the wonders we seek without us: there is all Africa and her prodigies in us.

SIR THOMAS BROWNE

ILLUSTRATIONS

1. The author at Fish River Canyon	*facing page* 64
2. Windhoek: the Christuskirche. Palms and roundabouts with the Khomas Hochland beyond	65
3. The Orange River at Vioolsdrift	96
4. Walvis Bay: the end of a dream	97
5. Swakopmund: south-western baroque Swakopmund: African shanties or pondoks	128
6. Dunes at Swakopmund	129
7. Namib Desert above Lüderitz A kokerboom in the Schwarzrand	160
8. The Brandberg	161
9. Lüderitz Bay	192
10. Aus: a town in a river bed	193
11. Boundary of the *Sperrgebiet* A diamond prospector's claim in the Namib	224
12. The Windhoek kudu	225
13. Etosha Pan: birds on the salt flats	256
14. Fort Namutoni	257
15. Oranjemund: trenching by hand Oranjemund: sweeping the bedrock. Behind the diggers is the gravel terrace, and beyond the terrace the sand overburden	276
16. Fish River Canyon	277

MAPS

South West Africa	*frontispiece*
Tribal Distribution: 1880	*page* 64
The Proposed Homelands of the African Peoples Under the Odendaal Scheme	170
Tribal Incursions into South West Africa in Historic Times	200

CONTENTS

Foreword	*page* 9
Acknowledgements	13
Prologue	21
1. The Place of Fiery Waters	25
2. Off the Tar	47
3. Where the Whales Make Love	73
4. Pondok and Baroque	88
5. Kokerboom and Kaokoveld	97
6. Forbidden Area	118
7. Diggers and Donkeys	141
8. In the Land of Fat Cattle	164
9. The Wa-benz and Others	189
10. Wild Honey	221
11. Muskets and Assegais	235
12. Close Goods	259
13. A View Across the Canyon	288
Epilogue	299
Index	301

ACKNOWLEDGEMENTS

I OWE many individual debts to people both inside and outside the country. In particular, I must thank Mr David Farrell for skilfully translating my colour transparencies into black-and-white prints. And I must pay a very special tribute to Mrs Cynthia Smith Vartan, of the New York staff of my American publishers. Perceptive, she first suggested that I should write the book; patient, she waited for it. As always, I must thank her for her assistance, advice, and encouragement.

J. M. W.

Minsterworth Court, Gloucester, England
The University of Texas at El Paso, Texas

Foreword

the world. He had sailed for South Africa from Australia aboard the *Torrens*, writing home that: 'The first mate is a Pole called Conrad, and is a capital chap, though queer to look at: he is a man of travel and experience in many parts of the world, and has a fund of yarns I can draw on freely. He has been right up the Congo and all the way round Malacca and Borneo and other out-of-the-way parts, to say nothing of a little smuggling in the days of his youth.'

Galsworthy then travelled from Cape Town to the coppermines of Namaqualand, on the borders of South West Africa. His Forsyte-like family had investments there. At O'Okiep he found the supply of reading-matter in the miners' hall scanty, and characteristically set about shipping out an entire library once he had returned to London. He never went back to Namaqualand, but the memory of it lingered for thirty years. In his satirical *Reverie of a Sportsman* he recalled 'The springbok, that swarm in from the Karoo at certain seasons, among which I had that happy week once in Namaqualand . . .'

South West Africa is not a land a man could easily forget. Sometimes, as I am on the brink of sleep, majestic images of the Namib, the Kaokoveld, and the Kalahari unroll before me, vast, remote, noble, like the landscape of another planet or a country to be glimpsed in dreams. Then I know that the words of Sir Thomas Browne that I quote in my epigraph are true: that the wonders without us can become the wonders within us and that the prodigies of Africa are now a part of me.

Foreword

Gladstone and by Milner. Gladstone, who introduced the now universal canting style into British politics, provoked the Boers, by means of his notorious Midlothian campaign, into the rising of 1881, which led to the slaughter of British troops at Majuba. Lord Milner, the man who flogged the coolies, decided when he was High Commissioner of South Africa and Governor of the Transvaal that a war with the Boers squared with his policies. As Lord Loreburn, then the Lord Chancellor and later the founder of the Court of Criminal Appeal, wrote privately to Winston Churchill in 1906: 'There are many of us who believe after close study that Milner has not only been rash but also deceitful and that the more the thing is investigated the more it will appear that he has engineered the war by forcing the hands of foolish ministers. He has received honours and incense while ruining South Africa.' It is not, therefore, for a *Rooinek*—British 'redneck'—like me to indulge in one of the ritual castigations of the Afrikaner that are obligatory at the present time. Instead, I have sought to adopt the less spectacular but saner approach of Miss Sarah Gertrude Millin, in her *The People of South Africa*. 'Since we are not alone on our planet,' she wrote, 'and, so small as we are, cannot control our own destinies, the problem that chiefly concerns us is how, being here together, we may live and grow with the least unhappiness and enmity.'

This has not been altogether the easiest assignment for a first travel book. South West Africa—which the United Nations has now bidden us to call the Republic of Namibia—is devoid of the palaces, cathedrals and great art-galleries that lend lustre to more sophisticated works in the genre. Nevertheless it has a character and appeal of its own and, as the reader will perceive, it is likely to have a profound effect on the personality of anyone who wanders at large there. Its advantage as a subject is that few other European or American writers have visited it and described it at length. From a literary point of view it is virgin territory: and territory of that kind is becoming scarce. I hope I have managed to convey to the reader something of its fresh and novel quality.

Galsworthy almost got there, in 1892, during a trip round

Foreword

his narrative. How a man reacts to South West Africa or any other country depends on the kind of person he is. It also depends on the mood he is in when he makes his journey: even the age at which he makes it. A traveller sees a country with different eyes at different periods of his life. This is what keeps the world perpetually new and interesting. It is not only countries that change: people change with them. After all, our lives themselves are nothing but complicated journeys, explorations, discoveries and rediscoveries.

A religious writer would have devoted more space to the history of the religious missions; a political writer would have discussed at greater length the international status of the country and its forms of government; a technologically-minded writer would have gone into exhaustive detail about the ramifications of mining and marketing. I have tried to satisfy as many of these special interests as possible, without bringing to the book any overriding bias. I have attempted to cultivate the long perspective, and to describe this ancient land with Gauguin's Kantian triple question in mind: 'Where do we come from? Who are we? Where are we going?'

We live in uneasy and enquiring times. Our political leaders —or rather, those people who choose to play at the game of politics while pretending to lead us—are coming at last to sense that the world listens to their pronouncements with an increasing mixture of boredom and alarm. If the reader is seeking instant remedies for the political troubles that plague South West Africa and her neighbours, there is little use in him reading this book. I am only too conscious that my opinions will be wholly acceptable neither to the South Africans nor to their opponents. Why should they be? I agree with the view of Mr Graham Greene, whose *Journey without Maps* remains one of the best and most biting of African travel books, that a writer's duty is to be a stubborn little bit of grit in the social machinery. I am not by nature *bien pensant* and I do not like received opinions. Certainly I have criticized the South Africans: but my strictures have been tempered by the memory of the crimes committed against them, not so very long ago, by

FOREWORD

THE following pages contain a great many facts and figures about the remarkable country with which I am dealing. I want to offer the reader as much information about South West Africa as possible.

On the other hand, as I shall indicate later, the history of South West Africa is a compendium of the world's evolution, from earliest to latest times. So this is not designed to be a narrow, localized, dry-as-dust account, a mere compilation of statistics. It is an attempt to put South West Africa into the context of the African continent—and on occasion, because of its colonial background, into the even wider context of Europe and the world in general.

Moreover, in addition to the factual armature, the book is fleshed out with speculations and excursions of a personal nature. It is sub-titled *Reflections on a Journey*. A traveller is not a mere machine for collecting data, but a living, breathing creature, with opinions and prejudices that are bound to colour

To

BORIS DE CHROUSTCHOFF

Fortunate senex ergo tua rura manebunt
Et tibi magna satis

FIRST PUBLISHED IN GREAT BRITAIN 1969

*This book is copyright under the Berne Convention.
Apart from any fair dealing for the purpose of private study,
research, criticism or review, as permitted under the Copyright Act,
1956, no portion may be reproduced by any process without written
permission. Enquiries should be addressed to the publishers.*

*Rand McNally & Company edition published in the
United States of America and possessions in 1969.*

Library of Congress Catalog Card Number : 68–25127

DT
703
W5

The Land God Made In Anger

REFLECTIONS ON A JOURNEY THROUGH
SOUTH WEST AFRICA

BY
JON MANCHIP WHITE

RAND McNALLY & COMPANY
Chicago . New York . San Francisco

WITHDRAWN

By the same author

ANCIENT EGYPT
EVERYDAY LIFE IN ANCIENT EGYPT
ANTHROPOLOGY

MARSHAL OF FRANCE
   (The Life and Times of Maurice de Saxe)
DIEGO VELAZQUEZ :
   Painter and Courtier

THE ROUT OF SAN ROMANO

MASK OF DUST
BUILD US A DAM
THE GIRL FROM INDIANA
NO HOME BUT HEAVEN
THE MERCENARIES
HOUR OF THE RAT
THE ROSE IN THE BRANDY GLASS
NIGHTCLIMBER

The Land God Made in Anger

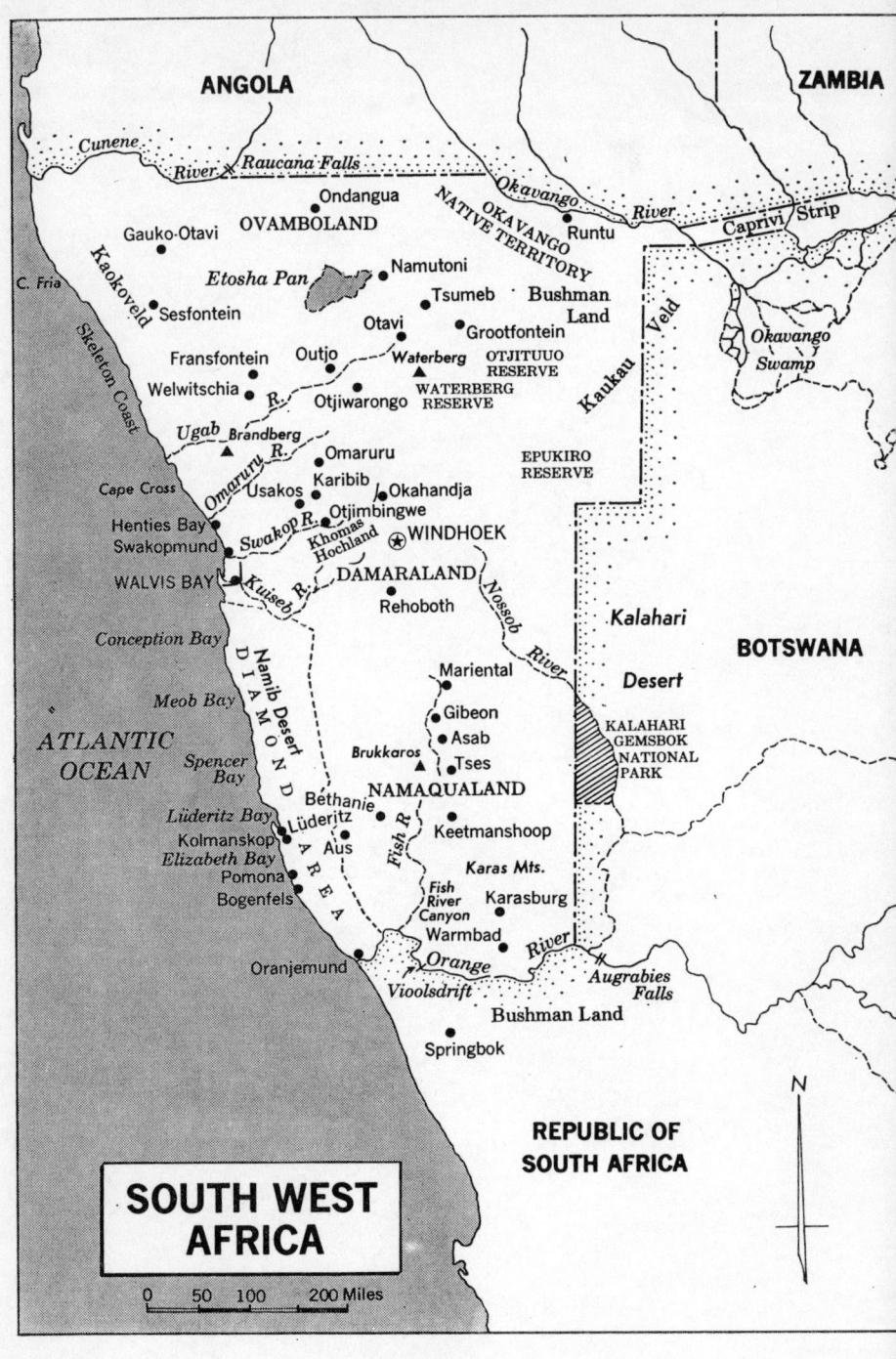